SOCIAL COHESION COUNTER-TERRORISM

A policy contradiction?

Charles Husband and Yunis Alam

First published in Great Britain in 2011 by

The Policy Press
University of Bristol
Fourth Floor
Beacon House
Queen's Road
Bristol BS8 1QU
UK

t: +44 (0)117 331 4054
f: +44 (0)117 331 4093
tpp-info@bristol.ac.uk
www.policypress.co.uk

North American office:
The Policy Press
c/o International Specialized Books Services
920 NE 58th Avenue, Suite 300, Portland, OR 97213-3786, USA
t: +1 503 287 3093
f: +1 503 280 8832
info@isbs.com

© University of Bradford 2011

British Library Cataloguing in Publication Data
A catalogue record for this book is available from the British Library.

Library of Congress Cataloging-in-Publication Data
A catalog record for this book has been requested.

ISBN 978 1 84742 801 1 paperback

This book was supported with funding from the Joseph Rowntree Foundation and
the Association of West Yorkshire Authorities. However, the statements and opinions
contained within this publication are solely those of the authors and not of the
Joseph Rowntree Foundation or the Association of West Yorkshire Authorities,
nor those of the University of Bristol or The Policy Press. The Joseph Rowntree
Foundation, the Association of West Yorkshire Authorities, the University of Bristol
and The Policy Press disclaim responsibility for any injury to persons or property
resulting from any material published in this publication.

The Policy Press works to counter discrimination on grounds of gender, race,
disability, age and sexuality.

Cover design by The Policy Press
Printed and bound in Great Britain by
Marston Book Services Ltd, Oxfordshire
The Policy Press uses environmentally responsible print partners.

To Barbara and Razia

Contents

Acknowledgements

Producing a research based book such as this always requires the unique contribution of so many people, without whom it would never have reached completion.

As the dedication above shows we are always deeply indebted to our wives who are our permanently present co-authors.

The project owes much to Jo Miller and Tony Reeves whose support and encouragement enabled the project to get off the ground, and to the five authorities of the Association of West Yorkshire Authorities (AWYA) and the Joseph Rowntree Foundation who co-funded it. Fundamentally the project could not have been started without the agreement of the chief executives of AWYA who gave us permission to interview the staff who are at the heart of this project. The steering group who were set up to facilitate and monitor the project were immensely supportive, and the Social Cohesion Board of AWYA to whom we reported provided an essential dialogue throughout our work, and were central in defining the terms of our reporting. The staff who made themselves available to be interviewed were the living heart of this project, and it was their openness and their experience that has provided the core substance of this project.

We have been very fortunate in having had the support of a team: Alison Shaw, Dawn Rushen and Laura Greaves in particular have helped bring this publication to fruition. From the Joseph Rowntree Foundation we have been most fortunate in the unstinting support and essential advice we have received from Anne Harrop and Emma Stone, who have sustained us throughout our work.

We are grateful to Heidi Mescher for the fruitful discussions on integrated threat theory, and to innumerable colleagues and friends who have allowed us to 'bend their ears'. In particular we are deeply indebted to Professor John Flint and Dr Tufyal Choudhury for the insightful and careful comments on our text.

However, irrespective of all this support the final product is our responsibility; and in particular we wish to make quite explicit, that notwithstanding the support of the AWYA and the Joseph Rowntree Foundation, the analysis presented here represents the views of the authors alone, and not those of anyone cited above.

ONE

Introduction

Living together with a capacity for mutual respect, space for self-expression and a credible sense of personal and collective security has been a modest ambition of societies as they have sought to manage human co-existence. In recent decades in Britain and elsewhere this aspiration has taken on a particular meaning as a centuries-old pattern of cross-border, and inter-continental, migration has taken on a new form. Through processes that we have come to familiarly call 'globalisation', the flow of resources, and human beings, across national borders has become extensive and routine. The myth of a homogenous people that has lain behind traditional ideologies of 'the nation' has been increasingly exposed by the reality that we are all multi-ethnic societies. This demographic reality produced a political response from the 1960s onwards in many European countries, and elsewhere, that saw the emergence of a growing openness to diversity. The politics of multiculturalism took many different forms as it developed in specific countries (Kymlicka, 2001; Modood et al, 2006), but for a number of decades it seemed that recognition of diversity had become the normative political stance in liberal democracies. So much so that in 2001, Kymlicka spoke optimistically of the ascendancy of multiculturalism and a widespread acceptance of the claims of minorities for recognition and rights (Kymlicka, 2001: 33). Writing in 2010, that claim seems now to have been grossly optimistic. As we shall see below, there has been a European-wide retreat from multiculturalism and a reassertion of narrowly conceived nationalisms. But the reality remains that European countries are demographically multi-ethnic, and Britain in particular has well-established minority ethnic communities of people who are third or fourth generation British, and who are British citizens. Thus, the current political vogue for belittling multiculturalism sits uncomfortably with the ongoing relevance of these foundational aspirations for a viable co-existence among citizens who are distinguished by multiple forms of diversity.

In the contemporary British context this question of how to maintain civility among fellow citizens has been an active and multi-headed issue that has stretched across a number of governmental agendas. We have seen the 'problematic' status and behaviour of sections of the majority white working class being addressed through concerns with youth disaffection, urban violence and the failure of many to enter the labour market. The recent narratives around the concept of 'Broken Britain' have in essence revisited earlier discussions about an alienated 'underclass' that had, in some perplexing way, dropped out of the generic social contract. At the same time, related concerns about youth delinquency and urban disorder were reflected in the government's Respect agenda, a policy that aspired to promote appropriate civic virtues. It would be fair to say that the broad issue of social cohesion has been a recurrent theme in the policy agenda of the Labour government over the past 13 years. Within this policy environment the specific circumstance of Britain's Muslim population has emerged as a 'political challenge'. As we shall see below, the international polemics surrounding the 'clash of civilisations' debate (Huntington, 1996), and the growth of an international Islamic identity politics, has placed the issue of faith, and of Islam specifically, at the centre of current liberal democratic politics across the world. In the British context, a series of specific events, to be discussed below, has positioned the British Muslim population within a highly sensitised political debate. *Their* difference from the majority culture has become acutely problematised. *Their* loyalty to Britain, and *their* ability and willingness to demonstrate a capacity to share common values and behaviour with the majority has been questioned. In the context of Britain's concern with social cohesion, the British Muslim population has been defined as an acute problem requiring a specific remedy. This concern became all the more acute following the 'riots' in northern towns in 2001 where the issues of urban decay and violence acquired a distinctive new focus: the problem of 'self-segregated' Muslim communities.

The linkage between Islam and violence had of course been graphically established with the outrage of 9/11 and the polemics of the 'War on Terror' that followed. In the British context this acquired a new and much more immediate relevance with the bombings in London of 7/7/2005. Britain now had the reality of 'home-grown' bombers, and Britain's Muslim communities acquired a new, and potent, basis for being placed outside the national norm. The question of how these Muslim communities might be brought more into acceptable participation in British life was now complemented by a parallel agenda: namely, their subjection to appropriate measures which respond to their status as a security threat. There is of course an apparent tension between the inherent logics of these two constructions of the Muslim population as specifically problematic, and it is the purpose of this book to explore this tension as the two related policies of Community Cohesion and counter-terrorism (Prevent) emerge to address them.

Both Community Cohesion and counter-terrorism policies have a generic remit which provides for them to address the majority white population, all minority communities and Muslim communities. But, as will become apparent below, in reality they were both developed within a focus on the British Muslim communities, with a disproportionate impact on them. It is for this reason that the argument developed below has a focus on this reality.

A core motivation for pursuing the research to be discussed here, therefore, was the expectation that there were reasonable grounds for anticipating that the implementation of Community Cohesion policies in tandem with those of Prevent would present some difficulties at the local authority level. The rationale behind this supposition is that both are targeted at the Muslim communities in Britain and yet they have very different underlying agendas. Community Cohesion as it developed following the civil disturbances in the North of England in 2001 was quite specifically attached to concerns with the disaffection evident in Muslim communities. In the main, rather than presenting an assault on the well documented discrimination and disadvantage that reproduced the marginalisation of large parts of this population, the language of Community Cohesion instead focused on inculcating shared values and a common understanding of the obligations and rights of citizenship.

Put bluntly, the agenda of Community Cohesion was to say to Muslim communities that while government was concerned to recognise the citizen status of the Muslim population, it was felt necessary to point out that many members of this population appeared to have a limited grasp of what was involved in possessing British citizenship. Indeed, their propensity for 'self-segregation' and living in parallel cultures was indicative of their failure to fully embrace their obligations as British citizens. This collective failure to embrace their 'Britishness' was itself then seen as creating a social and cultural space facilitating the drift into 'radicalisation' of young members of these communities. Thus the ambition of Community Cohesion was to promote 'active citizenship', and in a somewhat crude way, to promote an assimilationist definition of citizenship based on an acceptance of a body of shared beliefs and values that constitute the basis of a shared national identity. The fact that these core beliefs and values proved to be rather elusive and contrived did not detract from the assertive nature of this political project, as defined by Tony Blair and David Blunkett. For members of the British Muslim population the message of Community Cohesion appeared to be: *We want you to be more actively engaged as citizens, but we want you to be more like us.* Community Cohesion, therefore, questioned the national commitment of Muslim Britons, but offered them a route to recognition as full citizens at the price of accepting an assimilationist programme of cultural re-education.

The Prevent agenda, on the other hand, with its roots in 9/11 and the London bombings of 7/7/2005, addressed the Muslim population of Britain from a quite different perspective. It started from a recognition that Britain's 'home-grown bombers' had come from within these communities and concluded that it was highly probable that such future terrorists were being nurtured and recruited in the same locations. From the government's perspective it was therefore both logical and reasonable that their counter-terrorist activities would include a specific focus on these Muslim communities. Given the prior agenda of Community Cohesion, and its concerns with 'self-segregation' and 'parallel lives', the Muslim populations were already perceived as being only partially integrated into British society and its values, and consequently the construction of these same communities as being potentially the locus for the production of future terrorists was framed by this sense of their pre-existing marginality. The Muslim 'enemy within' were already perceived as having established their detachment from the cultural norm, and they had demonstrated their capacity to provide young people who would launch terrorist attacks into the heart of British national life. In the urgency that was attached to the development of Britain's counter-terrorism policies the sense of immanent threat drove a robust programme of policy development in which surveillance of the Muslim communities became a key priority. From the perspective of the Muslim communities situated within the local authorities that participated in this study, the British government was signalling a very specific message: *You must know that we cannot fully trust you and that we must, in the name of national security, subject your communities to intensive and intrusive surveillance.*

Community Cohesion appears to offer an invitation to greater participation in civil society by Muslim communities, at the cost of biting the assimilationist bullet, while the counter-terrorism strategies of Prevent unambiguously assert that they must share a common burden of being targeted as legitimate objects of suspicion through the assertion that terrorist activity is being nurtured within their communities. This study has its focus on the experience of five local authorities in seeking to implement these policies. The aim is not to assess how successful they have been in implementing them, but rather to explore what it has been like to seek to implement both of these policies in tandem. This reveals something of the nature of these policies *in practice*, for in the next two chapters we review their development *as policy*. The data contributes to our understanding of how the framing of British Muslim communities within particular policy initiatives affects these communities. Furthermore, it reveals something of the relation between local government, local communities and the central state. In sum, the data offers a distinctive insight into the relation between the British state and Britain's Muslim communities.

In the next section, as we outline the methodology for this project, we hope the reader will also gain a more in-depth understanding of the ethos and focus of this research.

Background and development

In 2006/07 the authors of this book published the outcome of a Joseph Rowntree Foundation-funded project that had looked in a qualitative way at the experiences of young men of Pakistani heritage, and of Muslim faith, who were living in Bradford. One output was an edited account of the ethnographic data itself which sought to give direct voice to these young men (Alam, 2006). Another output took this material in a more abbreviated form and related it to the current political and policy context (Alam and Husband, 2006). This research had meaning for many people working in the local state in West Yorkshire, who valued the insights that it provided. From this background came an invitation to revisit this approach, but with a remit to carry it out over the five metropolitan authorities of the Association of West Yorkshire Authorities (AWYA) (Bradford, Calderdale, Kirklees, Leeds and Wakefield). Yunis Alam's remit was to carry out a qualitative survey of the experiences and views of a wide range of individuals defined by age, ethnicity and gender across the five authorities while Charles Husband's remit was to address a specific aspect of the current policy environment by focusing on the implementation of two policies that had a great significance in the area: namely, Community Cohesion and counter-terrorism (Prevent). This book is a report from the latter project.

The previous project had looked at the experience of young men for whom their Muslim identity was a very significant factor in shaping their interaction with the world. In this project it is also apparent that Islam was relevant to the focus of the study. Following the 'riots' of 2001 in Bradford, Burnley and Oldham, the London bombings of 2005 and subsequent terrorist offences within Britain, Islamic communities within Britain had become the focus of heated political debate and *de facto* a specific policy concern. The demography of four of the five local authorities participating in this study meant that they were inevitably situated within this political framework in which the perceived 'self-segregation' of Muslim communities and their pursuit of 'parallel lives' was an issue that they could not help but address. For some of the authorities this was given added salience by the fact that members of their local Muslim communities were successfully prosecuted for terrorist offences. Local public servants were subject to national pressure at the same time as local Muslim communities were feeling exposed and stigmatised by the national discourse on Islam, British identity and security. Two policies constituted particularly robust vehicles for driving this awkward relationship between the British state and local Muslim communities: Community Cohesion and Prevent, within the counter-terrorism strategy of CONTEST. In focusing on these two policies, this project provided a very sensitive test of the relationship between the concerns of the central state, the responsibilities of the local state and the communities that they serve.

Each of these local authorities has a particular history that has involved the incorporation of previous townships which had their own administration. The West Yorkshire demographies include dense urban inner-city neighbourhoods, affluent suburbs and dispersed rural communities that frequently include localised instances of rural poverty. The detail of this diversity is not addressed specifically but it becomes apparent through some of the analysis just how aware local staff and councillors were of this diversity within their area and of its implications for practice. Of these authorities, Leeds could comfortably be described as the largest, with a population in the 2001 Census of 715,402 (all figures below are based on the 2001 Census: www.statistics.gov.uk). In the last few decades Leeds has emerged as a northern centre of financial and legal activity and the city centre has acquired a reputation of affluence and high end consumerism. Leeds has a long established Jewish community (8,267), a small Sikh community (7,586) and a more numerically substantial Muslim community of 21,394.

Bradford, meanwhile, a mere 30 minutes away by train, was in the 19th century a highly successful and affluent city. But with the decline of the textile industry Bradford has struggled in recent decades with the collapse of its economic base. Although it has small Sikh (4,748) and Hindu populations (4,457), the South Asian labour recruited in the 1960s to service the textile mills now constitutes the basis of a significant Muslim population (75,188). At 16 per cent of the total population (467,665), this Muslim presence has contributed to the current ease with which Bradford is used in the British media as a simplistic iconographic representation of Islam in Britain, being used in news, film and television drama as the quintessential expression of the problematic presence of Islam in Britain.

Calderdale and Kirklees are also locales that were previously highly dependent on the manufacturing industry, and have experienced the difficulties that followed the demise of these industries. Calderdale, with a population of 192,405, is the smaller of the two and has a substantial Muslim population (10,198) and small Buddhist, Sikh and Hindu populations (350, 222 and 378 respectively). Kirklees, with a population of 388,567, also has a substantial Muslim population of 39,312, with small Sikh, Hindu and Buddhist communities (2,726, 1,222 and 397 respectively).

However, Wakefield, with a population of 315,172, has a quite different ethnic profile from the other cities in as much as it has small minority ethnic populations: 3,589 Muslims, 617 Hindus, 302 Buddhists and 266 Sikhs. One feature in common to all authorities, other than Leeds, is that they have small Jewish communities (Bradford, 356; Calderdale, 147; Kirklees, 171; Wakefield, 111).

Since the 2001 Census these numbers will have changed significantly, but the overall profile in proportionate terms will have remained relatively similar. There have of course been new immigrant populations added to this profile, with East European migrants from the new accession states making a significant impact along with changing refugee populations, adding nuance and numbers to the ethnic profile of each authority. However, for the purpose of this analysis, it is sufficient to say that the Muslim presence within the local authorities that constitute AWYA is significant, and they therefore provide a sound locale for a study with this focus. It has to be said, however, that the different ethnic profile of Wakefield did make the salience of the Muslim issue much less pressing there than was apparent across the other four authorities. Each of these authorities has their own unique experience of managing ethnic diversity, and diversity in general, and a different research project could have fruitfully revealed the importance of the cumulative impact of local circumstances, and political responses to them, in shaping the institutional context in which these two policies came to be implemented.

Method

Social research is undertaken as a means through which, in conjunction with human participants, data can be generated. Data, in usual research contexts, can be described 'of two main types: quantitative data in the form of numbers, and qualitative data not in the form of numbers'

(Punch, 1998: 3). Clear and coherent as this statement is, there are countless variations in terms of methods which result in diverse data formats with varied utility, forms of interpretation and analysis. Before outlining the specific elements of the actual research methodologies employed for this project, it is useful to explore background issues that fed into our research design.

A useful way of situating any research endeavour is by establishing the type of data sought. It is through knowing, for example, whether 'numbers or not numbers' are needed that decisions can be made about which tools are most suitable for the task in hand. Research methods, therefore, have to be acutely tied in with the nature of required data, or data type. Research methods, however, are not to be confused with methodology: while a method is a means through which data can be generated (a questionnaire, for example), methodology is a series of connections which ensure, as far as possible, that both ends of the research process connect or are otherwise symbiotic:

> *Methodology* entails a perspective or framework. Thinking methodologically involves describing and analysing the methods used, evaluating their value, detailing the dilemmas their usage causes and exploring the relationship between the methods that we use and how we use them, and the production and presentation of our data – our 'findings'. Thinking methodologically is theorising about how we find things out; it is about the relationship between the process and the product of research. (Letherby, 2003: 5)

Thinking methodologically from the outset provides a means to work backward from the intended outcomes. For researchers interested in measuring social and sociological phenomena operating across large scales (often through the generation of numerical or statistical values), it makes logical and practical sense to use instruments which are easily replicable and, broadly speaking, yield data of a quantitative nature that offer statistical or numerical validity. For those seeking perception, definition, meaning, nuance and subjective insight, those research methods that can produce qualitative data become more relevant and suitable.

Of course, the term 'qualitative' research is in itself broad and occasionally contested. For example, 'Tesch (1990) lists 26 distinct kinds of social research which can fall under the term "qualitative", and, no doubt, as time goes by, the list could be extended' (Denscombe, 2003: 267). For our purposes, we have interpreted qualitative approaches to mean those which generate data that are situational, borne of one or more interpersonal interactions as well as, perhaps significantly, being self-evidently rich, textured and giving in-depth literal and at times figurative meaning. In order to tap into how individuals see themselves and the world around them, whether as a local government post holder or a local councillor, a qualitative approach offered the appropriate tools in order to meet the aims of the project.

The essential purpose of qualitative data is to generate *insight* into situations/behaviour that is not heavily over-determined by the prior assumptions of the researcher. Qualitative interviewing allows the interviewees to respond in their own terms to a range of questions which do not invite simple yes or no answers. Questions are placed in the context of a conversation where the interviewee can reject the basis of the question being asked, and can introduce new issues or ideas. In the context of this study where the ambition is to *understand* the local authority personnel's *experience* of implementing these two policies, rather than *measuring* their success in implementing them, a qualitative approach offers the most rewarding and appropriate form of data.

A further benefit of this approach is that over the span of a qualitative interview the respondent can develop a coherent position and show the linkages between the elements in their comments, and indeed develop contradictory positions not routinely allowed for in quantitative techniques. This adds significantly in enabling the researcher to understand the meanings attached to particular statements precisely because they do not stand alone as isolated utterances. At the same time, the approach gives the researcher a greater level of confidence in interpreting the data that emerges throughout the interview.

The sample

It is in the nature of qualitative data that the analysis cannot be presented in terms of statements such as '60% of the respondents agreed that…'. This is so because in the first case the sample sizes involved in qualitative research do not make such statements legitimate. In this study the sample size is indeed small: 12 senior staff, 9 councillors and 21 operational staff; 14 of these interviewees were Muslim. However, it is the close organisational coherence of this sample that gives it its relevance. The people interviewed constitute an elite sample of exactly those people (including senior managers) who had responsibility for managing these two policies, complemented by a sample of those who implement them at the community level.

A project Steering Group defined by the five participating authorities identified the senior staff in each of their authorities who had managerial responsibilities for Prevent or Community Cohesion, or both. Thus, while this sample was small, it was also inclusive. It allowed the researcher who carried out all the interviews to have access to those people with in-depth knowledge of the experience of implementing these policies at the local level. These were exactly the individuals who were engaged in translating legislation and guidance from central government into policy and practice in their own authority; they shaped local practice and were responsible for policy implementation. Thus, in each of the five authorities the senior staff directly responsible for managing these policies were interviewed as were the councillors in each of the authorities with responsibility for oversight of these policies. To complement this, a small sample of fieldworkers responsible for the implementation of these policies at local community level were interviewed.

Gaining access to this cohort required some necessary negotiation and involved setting some ground rules agreed by all the parties. In order to ensure that the interviews provided honest and open responses there was a need to be able to guarantee the anonymity of the respondents, particularly as there were so few senior managers that the possibility of their being individually identified through the data was potentially high. Specific ground rules were developed for the project, laid out in the initial research agreement and clarified through dialogue with a Cohesion Board that spanned the five authorities.

Similarly the Steering Group identified the councillors who had responsibility for the oversight of these policies within each of the local authorities. Thus the project was able to have privileged access to the very people who could talk most intimately about the relationship between the receipt of central government policy and its conversion into local practice. To complement this sample, the Steering Group also identified a small sample of staff in each authority who were actively engaged in implementing these policies. This sample deliberately included Muslim staff, a feature common to the other two samples.

There is then in this sample the possibility of identifying themes that are present across the responses of all three components constituting this sample, and those that reflect the particular perspective and experiences of specific players within the sample. The analysis will be able to draw out the ways in which organisationally the location of these different players in the determination and delivery of practice shapes their experience and their input. Where voices across the three cohorts echo similar themes we will have reason to see this as indicating an issue that has some consensual support. Other insights will reflect the unique functions and perspectives of those occupying a particular location in the authority.

Terms of engagement

In order to ensure that the confidentiality of the respondents could be respected it was agreed that the data from the five authorities would be merged in order to provide a regional data base. This was given some legitimacy by the fact that these authorities did in fact have a strong regional structure of sharing experience and collaboration. A corollary of this strategy was the agreement that there would be no comparisons made between the performances of the different authorities. Clearly these constraints had some effects on the way in which the data can be reported. The necessity of ensuring confidentiality means that the use of quotations had to be judiciously sensitive, as, for example, indications of the locale could reveal a probable source. Similarly some wonderful concrete examples that illustrate a particular point have been omitted because their very particularity would make them identifiable.[1] If the purpose of this research had been to assess the effectiveness of local authority practice then the absence of a comparative framework would have been more serious. But, as it transpires, the echoing of *experiences* across the five authorities provides a source of credibility to the analysis that is developed here.

It will come as no surprise that there were anxieties expressed in various quarters about the implications of facilitating this research, and it is all the more commendable therefore that the interviews were characterised by a remarkable degree of candour, as will be apparent in the quotations presented later. All the interviews with senior staff and councillors were carried out one to one, and after the first five minutes the degree of openness was remarkable. Only one interviewee was judged to be offering self-censored, 'managed' responses, in a parallel reflexive way, during the interview, and that interview has therefore been treated with some caution. A number of individuals on completing the interview expressed their satisfaction in having been able to talk through issues, and found the process cathartic and rewarding. The quotations presented in the text are not traceable back to their source, and where necessary have been edited to ensure that no potentially revealing reference is included.

Interpretation

We might consider what sort of data emerging from the interviews would contribute to the development of an interpretation of the interviews. As a starting point, we can sketch statements in a *hierarchy of concreteness*.

There are statements that an interviewee may make which are free-standing statements of an opinion. That is, they could be taken out of the transcript and inserted into the analysis and they would need virtually no contextualisation or interpretation for the reader to understand exactly what is meant. It is exactly this sort of statement that will be used here to illustrate a point in the argument. They make the argument real and concrete to the reader.

There are statements that an interviewee may make which indicate absolute agreement or disagreement with a statement that has just been made by the interviewer. They might say 'You are absolutely right' or just 'Yes, I agree'. For the interviewer these statements are crucial to building confidence in having a sound understanding of the position being taken on an issue being discussed. But simple statements of agreement may come after a relatively convoluted few sentences of discussion. It is therefore not easy to give credit to the dialogue without copying out a long sequence of sentences. While this is not an attractive option for a readable report, it is a very important form of data.

There are also, of course, things that the interviewees do not say. They do not reject the basis of a question asked. They do not provide an alternative perspective to one that has emerged through the dialogue, or been put to them. You cannot quote silences, but they add to the picture that emerges from the transcript of an hour-long interview.

Then there is the cumulative position on issues that emerge over the context of the whole interview. As the respondent refers back to previous things that they have said, or adds statements that complement earlier statements, a sense of solidity, coherence and perspective is evoked.

Finally, there are the non-verbal cues that lead you to 'believe' that the respondent is openly engaged in the interview, that they are being honest. In some interviews you get a very clear sense of reservation and self-censorship in the behaviour of an interviewee at the beginning of the interview. Frequently this vanishes rapidly. Occasionally it never does. This influences your willingness to give credibility to the data you have generated in a specific interview.

In this study we have been amazed at the level of openness and disclosure that has been characteristic of the great majority of the interviews. People have been forthright and open, remarkably so! This project is deeply indebted to their generosity.

The findings presented below are not *proof* of the realities that are sketched here. For what it is worth, we as researchers are confident in the arguments that we present and have endeavoured to be careful in indicating findings that we feel are 'robust' and solidly supported by the data (often because the issue emerges across the three samples). Similarly, we have identified some arguments as more speculative. Interim findings were presented in draft form to the Steering Group and to the Management Group and chief executives, where they generated a meaningful and constructive debate. For the Management Group and chief executives, the independence of the research team having been guaranteed, there was a concern that they should not be held responsible for the political framing of the analysis which remains entirely that of the authors, a point willingly acknowledged above. Additionally, at a late stage of the project any outstanding matters regarding issues of confidentiality were resolved and agreed with the chief executives on behalf of all the participants. A further meeting with two of the chief executives, and an individual interview with one of them, were particularly helpful in clarifying the capacity of the senior management to inform central government policy and thinking.

The aim of this research has very clearly been to tap into the local experience of trying to make sense of two central government policies that *prima facie* might be expected to be problematic when run in tandem. The aim of the project, however, was not to evaluate the success of these five authorities in implementing these policies but to understand their experience of implementing them. In a perfect world this research would have been complemented by a parallel study carried out within the communities represented within these five authorities. This would have fleshed out a missing element in this story, namely, the local citizen's relationship with the same policy discourse. A significant theme that emerges through this data is the question of intergroup competition and hostility, particularly that between white working-class communities and the local Muslim communities. Insights into this situation are presented through the data as the interviewees *report* the nature of these relationships with some confidence and local familiarity. Although the community research element of the project has indeed yielded some, albeit limited, reference to these areas, direct and thematically focused interviews with members of these communities would have added significantly to our understanding of this and other issues.

In the next two chapters the reader is provided with an account of the emergence of these two policies in order that the data offered in Chapter Four may be understood in its political and organisational context. The frankness of our interviewees has provided a rich and illuminating body of data that has significant implications for the ways in which future policies may be expected to operate within the context of a period of social stresses that will follow from the major cutbacks in state expenditure that are now being developed.

Structure of the book

In the following chapters the intention is to first present the reader with an account of each of the two policies, in order that they can be placed in the wider context of British ethnic relations and social policy. In Chapter Two the background to the emergence of Community Cohesion is discussed, including aspects of the development of British 'race relations' policy, since, as will become apparent, the two policies to be tracked here are intricately interwoven with the wider issue of ethnic diversity in Britain. By placing Community Cohesion policy within the context of wider Labour Party policy this chapter also points out something of the discourses that run through the narrative of Community Cohesion. This leads to an invitation to be reflexive and critical in relation to the definition and use of Community Cohesion as a concept and policy, given its framing within very specific political constraints.

Chapter Three follows a similar trajectory in outlining the development of the British counter-terrorism policies post the London bombings of 2005. By placing the development of Prevent within the wider issue of the securitisation of everyday life, and of the history of managing threat in Britain, this chapter shows that Prevent has been developed and implemented within a very specific political context, part of which has been shaped by the assault on a commitment to fundamental human rights following the impact of the 'War on Terror'. Both Chapters Two and Three show how the British Muslim population has been specifically targeted within these two policies. The context and analysis provided in these background chapters provides necessary insights into the framing of these two policies that will be essential to understanding the data to be presented in Chapter Five.

However, prior to presenting that data, Chapter Four takes a strategic pause in order to explore the nature of Islamophobia. Since the existence and experience of the Muslim communities in Britain is central to the unfolding story being told through the data presented here, it is important that we bring to our discussion of the data an informed understanding of the ways in which Islam has been conceived and perceived in Britain. Particularly in the world post 9/11, the Muslim world and the Islamic faith have been placed into a new and contested space; in Britain there has been a growth of hostility to Muslim communities and individuals. At the same time, in multi-ethnic local authorities conflicts emerge between neighbouring communities, and resentments build between identity groups who have never met, on the basis of perceived conflicts of interest. Through examining both the history of Islamophobic sentiments and social scientific insights into intergroup behaviour, in Chapter Four we provide a more robust basis for understanding the issues emerging through the data and thereby put the reader in a better position to contemplate responses to current challenges.

The final two chapters in this book are intimately tied to the data generated through this research. Chapter Five presents the data without interpretation. It lays out for the reader an account of the themes that have been revealed through the analysis of the data following the approach outlined in Chapter One. This data is presented in relatively independent sections so that readers can make their own links and develop their own comprehension of the information being provided there. In Chapter Six, however, we present our own analysis of this data and develop our view of its implications. AWYA rightly wish to remain dissociated from this analysis but in concluding this introductory chapter it is important to again recognise the indebtedness of this research to the chief executives and others who facilitated its realisation through allowing access to examine a potentially contentious issue. Additionally, as we have noted, the strength of this data lies in precisely the intimate association the interviewees in this research have with the translation of central government policy into local practice. It is their frank and explicit engagement with the questions raised in this research that has given us confidence in the data presented here.

Notes

[1] This is perhaps particularly regrettable in denying the reader access to some distressingly comic anecdotes of visits of Whitehall persons to the 'North'.

TWO

Community Cohesion:
its development and limitations

Introduction

This chapter provides an introduction to the development of the Community Cohesion policy in Britain. Since this policy is so intricately implicated with other political agendas the story developed below adopts an eclectically broad approach so that Community Cohesion can be understood within its wider context. As will become apparent, Community Cohesion as a policy is quite specifically linked with the experience of Muslim communities in Britain and to their relation with wider society. The impetus for the development of Community Cohesion came from a number of civil disturbances in northern English towns in 2001. These disturbances were linked to Muslim populations in these towns and the political response to the events centred very much on prevailing majority views about the fit of these communities with mainstream society in Britain. Therefore, the ways in which the Muslim communities came to be defined, and the ways in which the Community Cohesion agenda developed, has to be understood within the wider context of the history of British ethnic relations. This chapter therefore begins by placing the development of Community Cohesion within the context of British ethnic relations. This will of necessity be a brief and truncated account that will serve to make visible some of the threads that will be apparent in the unfolding story of the relationship between Community Cohesion and the Prevent agendas.

Among the issues discussed is the early history of 'race riots' and the response to them, as the response to the 1981 riots and the subsequent Scarman Report have a significant role in framing the response to the more recent events. Similarly the Rushdie Affair is discussed as a critical defining moment in the development of non-Muslim/Muslim relations in Britain. This revealed a great deal about the European/ liberal response to an assertion of Muslim, faith-based, concerns. These events did a great deal to stimulate the transitions in self-identity among British Muslim communities while also feeding into the development of Islamophobia, a development discussed more fully in Chapter Four. The growth of a distinctive Islamic sensibility within the South Asian communities in Britain, and the majority population's response to that, has been central to the identity politics that permeate through the discourse of Community Cohesion.

Throughout the postwar decades Britain has developed a substantial policy and administrative infrastructure to address ethnic diversity and discrimination, while at the same time cumulatively building a quite draconian border policy. As the argument develops over the subsequent chapters, it will become apparent that this 'race relations' agenda cannot be kept hermetically sealed from considerations of cohesion. Indeed the two are intimately interwoven as the minority ethnic status of the Muslim population is intricately involved in the majority response to their faith-based identity claims. Thus the Macpherson report into the murder of Stephen Lawrence is significant in both revealing something of the nature of British racism and in providing an insight into the state response to revelations of the endemic nature of discrimination.

Not only is the broader context of 'ethnic relations' policy relevant to our understanding of the development and implementation of Community Cohesion, but so too are other elements of government policy. For this reason a section in this chapter examines Community Cohesion within the context of wider Labour Party policy. This discussion reveals how alternative narratives may be present within the discursive construction of policies. These narratives are critical in 'selling' the policies to the wider public through providing a legitimacy for the specific actions that arise from the broad policy statements. In this case we will see that quite particular explanatory models feed into the framing of Community Cohesion, and have implications for its evolution in practice. Additionally, before looking more concretely at the emergence of Community Cohesion as a policy, we will pause to note the centrality of the notion of 'social capital' as a concept in shaping the understanding of the nature of Community Cohesion. This is another necessary element in maintaining a critical concern with understanding the conceptual and political history that has been relevant to the British definition of Community Cohesion.

The penultimate section in this chapter looks in some detail at the construction of Community Cohesion in the British context, in a process that links back to much that has gone before in this chapter. It becomes apparent that this policy was shaped within a specific political context in which there were already very strong, and politically dominant, views about the dislocation of Muslim communities from the mainstream of British life. These views, when placed within the wider context of Labour Party policy and British ethnic relations, resulted in shaping the distinctive political package that is Community Cohesion. The significance of this for our later analysis, and perhaps particularly for the discussion in the concluding chapter, is addressed in the final section which notes the ideological nature of Community Cohesion as policy and discourse.

Community Cohesion: putting its initial emergence into the historical context of British ethnic relations

In moving to examine the application of Community Cohesion policies in the UK it is necessary, and revealing, to make an initial exploration of the origins of the concept in UK policy discourse and practice. A good place to start is with the account offered by Professor Ted Cantle in his 2008 text, *Community cohesion: A new framework for race and diversity.* Following the civil disturbances in northern towns in 2001, Cantle was appointed by the UK Home Secretary to chair the Community Cohesion Independent Review Team, which produced the report *Community cohesion: A report of the Independent Review Team* (2001). Subsequently and ubiquitously known as *The Cantle Report*, the document defined the basis of emerging government policy, the author subsequently remaining a central player in the development of policy.

In Chapter Two of his 2008 text, Cantle provides his own account of the emergence of Community Cohesion in the British context. Importantly he immediately identifies the significant shift from a more widely used concept of '*social* cohesion' to the specific emergent UK usage of '*community* cohesion'. He records that while previously social cohesion and community cohesion had sometimes been used as equivalents in their meaning, the term 'community cohesion' 'was effectively created in response to the riots in northern towns of England in 2001' (Cantle, 2008: 50). It is therefore noteworthy that, in his words:

> ... 'social cohesion' has tended to be used more broadly and aligned particularly with general socioeconomic factors, whereas 'community cohesion' has emerged as a more specific term to describe the societal features which are based on identifiable communities defined by faith or ethnicity, rather than social class. (Cantle, 2008: 50)

The significance of this is made more explicit some pages on when working definitions of the two terms are offered:

Despite the lack of any clear and generally accepted definitions for each of these terms, there is now an emerging consensus which will hopefully support a basic division between 'social cohesion' and 'community cohesion' along the following lines:

Social Cohesion reflects divisions based on social class and economic position and is complemented by social capital theories relating to the 'bonding' between people and the presence of mutual trust. It is seen to be undermined by the social exclusion experienced by individuals or groups, again defined by their social class and economic position.

Community Cohesion reflects divisions based upon identifiable communities, generally on the basis of faith or ethnic distinctions, which may reflect socio-economic differences. It is also complemented by the social capital theory of 'bridging' between communities. It is undermined by the disadvantage, discrimination and disaffection experienced by the identifiable community as a whole and by the lack of trust and understanding resulting from segregation and social separateness. (Cantle, 2008: 54-5)

In coming to frame the analysis developed below, this background to the evolution of the dominance of the concept of '*community* cohesion' deserves some attention. First, we can recognise that this policy emerged very rapidly in response to the social disturbances in the North of England in 2001. There was a specific trigger to the formation of this policy-making machinery and a specific focus for their outcome: that is, from the outset the analysis was *racialised* (Omi and Winant, 1986) in its focus on ethnicity and cultural difference, and the locus of this difference was definitively seen to lie with the characteristics of certain minority ethnic communities. Of particular significance in this process was the centrality of faith, specifically Islam, in the construction of 'difference'. Thus it is important to recognise the extent of the national political and media coverage that these events created (Hussain and Bagguley, 2005; Bagguley and Hussain, 2008), and to note the intense national debate that was generated, focusing on inner-city Muslim communities, specifically the 'problematic' nature of their culture and demography.

While consultation strategies and reports were commissioned and delivered after the original trigger points, for example, *Strength in diversity* (Home Office, 2004) and *Improving opportunity, strengthening society* (Home Office, 2005), the then Home Secretary, David Blunkett, repeatedly responded to the disturbances by first taking a strong law and order line and then by placing the idea and significance of (weak) citizenship into the discourse itself:

> The UK has had a relatively weak sense of what political citizenship should entail. Our values of individual freedom, the protection of liberty and respect for difference, have not been accompanied by a strong, shared understanding of the civic realm. This has to change. (Blunkett, quoted in McGhee, 2008: 83)

Blunkett, perhaps more than any other politician at the time, fully accepted Cantle's thesis and what is more, his comments fed into the shaping of the debate. Thus, the new two-pronged citizenship mantra – community cohesion and civic attachment – spoke not only of unruly northerners who, problematically, happened to be Muslim, but to the indigenous British and, of course, especially to new communities. How this new way of doing 'race' and community relations manifested itself depended on who was the focus of concern. It should be borne in mind that various, and in some cases disparate, facts of British life were beginning to change, and the means by which 'bad' behaviour could be controlled, modified or eradicated were certainly an area of policy interest as well as political rhetoric (see the Special Issue of *Cultural Studies*, 2007, vol 21, no 6; Hughes, 2009). The growth in targets and monitoring continued as an expressive form of invasive central government policy. It served as an explicit demonstration of 'strong' government while not necessarily aiding those working in law enforcement, healthcare or education. Meanwhile, government calls for the expansion of police and holding powers, along with increasing levels of surveillance and the restriction of movement for some individuals, continues as a routine element in party political populist rhetoric.

Although the development of community cohesion policies drew on prior developments and policy review (the Ouseley Report, 2001, for example), it did not take place in the context of a dispassionate periodic review of community relations policy, but rather within the centre of the maelstrom of post 'riot' outrage. Nor was this outrage framed within an historical vacuum but rather it was experienced as the most recent event in a historical trajectory of 'race riots' associated with the 20th-century development of an immigrant and then multi-ethnic population in Britain's inner cities. The framing of events is widely recognised as critical in shaping the discourse within a national public sphere (Scheufele and Tewksbury, 2007), with consequent effects on the development of public opinion and emergent social policy. Thus an available and historically grounded framing agenda, with its own strong emotive resonance, aided the interpretation of these current events and, indeed, proved significant in shaping subsequent reactions.

Britain has a long and varied history of riot and civil unrest, ranging from a series of political riots during the reign of Charles II known as the 'Bawdy House Riots' (Harris, 1990: 82), to the more recent riots in Belfast in 2009 (McDonald, 2009). Rioting and civil unrest, then, are not new phenomena to the UK and neither are civil disturbances with a specific 'racial' provocation or agenda. As Solomos (2003) notes, following the Bristol riots of April 1980, the Brixton riots of April 1981 and the nationwide disturbances of July the same year, the conflation of 'race' with civil disturbance became a key and potent element within local and national debates. In his words:

> Whatever the symbolic importance of the Bristol riots and the Deptford march, there is no doubt that the period between April and July 1981 was the crucial phase in the racialisation of discourses on violent protest. (Solomos, 2003: 144)

The shock and outrage at the scale of these events caused a moral panic that in some ways anticipated the scale of the response that was to follow the events of 2001.

While there is a long history of concern linking the arrival and presence of immigrants with the potential for civil unrest and hostility (Foot, 1965; Walvin, 1971), within modern British political discourse a linkage between migrant communities and civil disturbance was initially[1] created in 1958, with the 'race' riots of Nottingham and Notting Hill, London. In Notting Hill, large groups of white youths attacked West Indians over several days. While some in the press and judiciary condemned the violence of the 'criminal minority', the events focused the lens of imagination further still, with fears that immigration, and by extension, black and minority ethnic groups, would be directly responsible for yet more rupturing of future social relations, a banner that was subsequently perhaps best and most effectively carried by Enoch Powell.

The 1960s and 1970s was a period where immigration became a major issue in party political populist rhetoric and in the public sphere (Hartmann and Husband, 1974; Miles and Phizacklea, 1984). The increasing competition between political parties to be seen to be presenting the most robust opposition to immigration by then not only

---

resulted in increasingly draconian border controls, but contributed to a rapid escalation of immigration from populations who feared that entry to Britain would be sealed off. It should be noted that throughout this period the rise of the neo-fascist National Front had a significant impact on the saliency of 'race' and immigration in Britain (Billig, 1978). At the same time there was a highly visible academic debate about 'race' and intelligence which fed into this populist construction of a heated debate about 'race', ethnicity, immigration and identity (Richardson and Spears, 1972; Kamin, 1977). The 1960s and 1970s were a critical period in the formulation of British 'race relations', where historical sentiments of racial superiority, rooted in the imagery of the empire and colonialism, came into fraught contact with the demographic reality of postwar immigration, itself driven by a need for labour power.

A specific symptom of the state and populist racism of the time was the escalation of tensions between the police and the creation of a 'race'/violence/law and order agenda which anticipated much of the dynamics of current situations (see, for example, CCCS, 1982; Gordon, 1983). By the 1980s, this linkage had been embedded and at that time, a quite specific and overarching agenda addressing the rule of law and policing helped frame minority ethnic relations.

The 1981 'riots' and the Scarman Report

The early 1980s saw a number of riots in Britain (see Kettle and Hodges, 1982; Joshua et al, 1983; Benyon and Solomos, 1987; Bagguley and Hussein, 2008: Chapter 1), and in the aftermath of the Bristol riots, Lord Scarman was invited to provide a report into their causes and to outline policy recommendations. The subsequent *Scarman Report*, published in late 1981, provided a measured account of the events and was careful to resist simple, essentialising and mono-causal explanations. As Solomos (2003: 161) notes, Scarman's model acknowledged:

> The problems faced when policing and maintaining order in deprived, multiracial, inner city localities.

> The social, economic and related problems faced by all residents of such areas.

> The social and economic disadvantages suffered particularly by black residents, especially young blacks. (Scarman, 1981: paras 2.1-2.38)

Scarman's linkage of civil unrest with social deprivation went a long way to challenge some of the simplistic analysis in the media. His recommendations on improving police training were to some extent, although subject to significant police resistance, taken up by the government. However, one element of Scarman's analysis was to prove highly attractive as an acceptable account of the perceived propensity of young African Caribbean men to riot. In accounting for the potential for young black men to enter into crime, he noted:

> Without close parental support, with no job to go to, and with few recreational facilities available, the young black person makes his life on the streets and in the seedy commercially run clubs of Brixton. There he meets criminals, who appear to have no difficulty in obtaining the benefits of a materialist society. (Scarman, 1981: para 2.23)

This linkage of the perceived failings of African Caribbean culture, with its tendency toward violence and criminality, was to prove highly attractive to a range of social commentators. The idea of the supposed pathology of the West Indian family, (un)headed with an absentee father, along with a loose family structure, became a convenient scapegoat which directed attention away from police culture and the range of social disadvantages which Scarman had so clearly identified as critical (Lawrence, 1982). As we shall see below, the deployment of explanatory models which find the basis for social exclusion in the flawed culture and character of the excluded has an obvious political payoff, as the debates around the 'underclass' and its pathologies have demonstrated in relation to class exclusion (see, for example, MacDonald, 1997).

Perhaps what would prove most significant in later years was Scarman's rejection of the charges that the Metropolitan Police was racist:

> The direction and policies of the Metropolitan Police are not racist. I totally and unequivocally reject the attack made upon the integrity and impartiality of the senior direction of the force. The criticisms lie elsewhere − in errors of judgment, in a lack of imagination and flexibility, but not in deliberate bias or prejudice. (Scarman, 1981, para 4.62)

As for the idea of *institutional* racism, this again was admitted as a possibility, but not pursued with any force:

If by that is meant that it is a society which knowingly, as a matter of policy, discriminates against black people, I reject the allegation. If, however, the suggestion being made is that practices may be adopted by public bodies as well as private individuals which are unwittingly discriminatory against black people then this is an allegation which deserves serious consideration, and where proved, swift remedy. (Scarman, 1981: para 2.22)

Ultimately, Scarman's report seemed to come to a conclusion which rejected systemic failures or shortcomings and instead, pushed for the credibility of a 'rotten apples' thesis, where the racism held by a minority of police officers tarnished the whole organisation. As touched on above, Scarman's recommendations ranged from increasing the recruitment of black officers, 'race' awareness training as well as, again, an idea that would be echoed in future years, the development or nurturing of a black middle class, a middle class with the right kind of social capital which would play a significant part in the reshaping and promotion of a more agreeable black ethnic life and culture. This shifting of responsibility from structural weaknesses to those suffering the consequences of these weaknesses is a stratagem that has built in attractiveness and has repeated itself in later years.

Post-Scarman and 'the enemy within'

Solomos provides a telling summary of the Thatcher government's response to the *Scarman Report*, noting that while the then Home Secretary accepted many of its recommendations, particularly in relation to policing, racial discrimination and other issues, he nevertheless emphasised that the government's immediate priority was to restore order on the streets. Thus:

> ... when the Home Secretary talked of the need for the government to tackle racial disadvantage he saw this as a longer-term project. On the other hand he was much more specific about the reform of the police and the development of new tactics to manage urban disorder. (Solomos, 2003: 64)

In turn, Cantle's more recent conclusion comes as no surprise:

> ... the poor social conditions in urban areas recognised by Scarman were not addressed in any meaningful way and

the overall economic position did not improve. (Cantle, 2008: 47)

We might usefully remember that this policy debate was taking place within the rigours of Thatcher's neoliberal, market-oriented and market-driven regime where levels of unemployment were escalating and a brutish individualism defined much of the policy discourse of the time. It was difficult for this regime to respond fulsomely to the social agendas of the *Scarman Report* which invited state intervention to remedy social disadvantage, an invitation to employ the policies of the 'nanny state' that were so abhorrent to Thatcher and her mentors (Evans and Cerny, 2003: 21-2). Indeed, in a way that was to anticipate more recent events, the Thatcher government was engaged in strenuous attempts to avoid any linkage being made between their policies (and their consequences) and the outbreak of violence and civil disorder (Solomos, 2003: 164). Rather, it was more congenial to focus on the specific agenda of police–community relations and issues of law and order than to address in a meaningful way the macro-socio-structural issues that Scarman had also identified. This preference became even more marked after the disturbances of 1985 in Handsworth, Birmingham, where even the potential willingness to accept a multicausal explanation of riot was essentially replaced by a more robust social pathology model within which the potent political language of the deviant outsider was widely employed. As Solomos argues (2003: 165), the government in 1985 explicitly rejected any prospect of a Scarman-type enquiry since they had already concluded that the basis of the civil disturbances lay in criminality. Douglas Hurd gave a flavour of the discourse accepted and projected by the spheres of mass media and government alike:

> Poor housing and other social ills provide no kind of reason for riot, arson and killing. One interviewer asked me whether the riot was a cry for help by the rioters. The sound which law abiding people heard at Handsworth was not a cry for help but a cry for loot. (*The Daily Telegraph*, 14 September 1985)

Again it is fruitful to locate this specific response to inner-city disturbances within the wider context of the time. A revisiting of Hillyard and Percy-Smith's (1988) *The coercive state: The decline of democracy in Britain* and Ewing and Gearty's (1990) *Freedom under Thatcher: Civil liberties in modern Britain* provide a salutary reminder of the intense struggle over rights and civil liberties at the time. This was the period of 'the enemy within' which involved, among other things, a concerted assault on the trades unions, best exemplified by the bitter confrontations (political and physical) which defined the Miners' Strike. Although the Miners' Strike of 1984-85 saw public unrest of a different order, it nevertheless fed into the same Thatcherite polemic of 'law and order under threat' to be dealt with, at least in part, through a range of intelligence measures, legal or otherwise (Milne, 2004). The same law and order rhetoric was used to legitimate a series of assaults on civil liberties through legislative and procedural changes, and to a promotion of police powers with, for example, the new public offences created under the Public Order Act 1986 (see Ewing and Gearty, 1990: Chapter 4). Thus the construction of a governmental and public account of the roots of riot in the 1980s was taking place within a very specific authoritarian neoliberal regime (Jessop et al, 1988). It is one of the ironies of Thatcherism that its ideological commitment to a minimal state and to market forces contributed to levels of social unrest that produced a governmental construction of an ever more intrusive regulation of civil society and the labour market. Inner-city 'race riots' were thus placed within this frame as an intolerable assault on law and order by elements of 'the enemy within'.

Given our concerns with the significance of the broad ideological framing that gives legitimacy to government policies, we should not fail to recognise the moral and imaginative shift that was central to the success of Thatcherism. As Jessop et al (1988) note, for example, *popular capitalism* marked a major shift in British values and practice:

> ... the very notion of popular capitalism implies that individuals (or, at most, families) participate in the new order through their atomized consumption of benefits and values. This is why the Conservative Party can claim to speak for the whole people while simultaneously eroding those remaining representative structures with any real power. In the broad range of institutions of civil society (churches, schools, media, etc), Thatcherism has attempted to restructure them around its preferred agenda of the pursuit of possessive individualism and the attachment to an increasingly authoritarian definition of the national interest in moral and political affairs. (Jessop et al, 1988: 177-8)

As Jessop et al argue, popular Thatcherism marked a break from traditional one-nation Toryism. The *noblesse oblige* of the old Tory king makers and the postwar commitment to the welfare state as a guarantee of some minimal protection for the vulnerable and disadvantaged had been mocked as the perfidious characteristics of the '*wets*' who had been ejected from the Thatcher government. What was created in its place was a politics that was prepared to entertain, through rhetoric and policy, a conception of a two-nation Britain with a bi-polar population: the enfranchised and the disenfranchised, those who could be won over and those who had to be contained, responsible citizens and the enemy within, the productive and the parasitic. It was a politics which accepted and guaranteed a widening of differentials between 'worthy citizens' and the marginalised residue, a politics characterised by the short-term consumerist self-interest and moral hypocrisy described by Galbraith (1992) as 'the culture of contentment', a culture shared and nurtured by the two thirds of the population whose relative prosperity coexisted with the exclusion of a disenfranchised segment of the working class. The creation of a political consensus in which significant elements of society were seen as 'other' and profoundly incorrigible in their difference came to be essential in legitimating the inherent inequity in Thatcherite policies.

The particular fragment of the unruly citizens who had been involved in the civil disturbances of 1985 carried an additional feature which amplified their problematic nature: they were non-white and of immigrant background. At this juncture, therefore, we must also record the extent to which Thatcherism was marked by a harsh anti-immigrant polemic and policies. This was a period when 'race relations' was sustained as a persistent salient aspect of public debate in the media and in politics (Seidel, 1986; Gilroy, 1987). It was also a period when the 'New racism' (see Chapter Four, this volume) was being vigorously promoted in public debate as a preferable complement to the vulgarity of old fashioned scientific racism. The new racism found the basis of inalienable differences between the majority and immigrant communities to be founded in the non-negotiability of culture. Thus this cultural underpinning for discourses of racist exclusion fed into a focus on minority culture, the same underpinning that pre-figured the contemporary framing of Muslim communities in Britain.

The events in Handsworth of 1985 were caught in what news theory would recognise as an example of the *deviancy amplification spiral* outlined by Cohen (1972), in which events fed on themselves in confirming a crisis for the state and civil society. African Caribbean men, already stigmatised by their origins in a 'failing culture', were seen through the 'enemy within' lenses of immigration and criminality locating them as an alien, dissident and threatening presence in British cities.

White liberals may have danced to reggae music and bourgeois young city workers may have enjoyed their flirtation with ganja, but African Caribbean inner-city youth had become constructed as a specific manifestation of the problems of immigration and difference.

While this populist criminalisation of the riots figured very prominently in the public discourse of the time, there were still voices pointing to the social malaise of the inner cities, and indeed, throughout the late 1980s and early 1990s, a series of government initiatives were aimed at tackling inner-city problems. However, as Solomos notes, 'there was a major discrepancy between these promises of action and the allocation of resources to them' (Solomos, 2003, 167; see also Benyon and Solomos, 1987). A rigorous development of an increasingly repressive state apparatus through the 1980s and into the 1990s was accompanied by a range of piecemeal initiatives aimed at promoting inner-city regeneration. Post Scarman there was a belief that significant strides had been taken to improve police–minority community relations, a belief, as we shall see, that would be blown apart by the murder of Stephen Lawrence.

The 'Rushdie Affair' and the emergence of a Muslim political identity

There remained throughout the late 1980s and early 1990s tensions between the police and youth, both minority ethnic and white working-class youth (see Campbell, 1993). In 1992 there were confrontations between the police and young people in Blackburn, Burnley and Coventry. Then, in 1995 a major disturbance in Bradford guaranteed national visibility, but the fact that this was the first major civil unrest involving mostly Asian youth gave it a new and quite specific edge (Burlet and Reid, 1998; Bradford Commission, 1996). This was not, however, the first time that Bradford's Asian community had achieved national visibility. In 1989, Bradford had a central role in the media response to the burning of *The satanic verses* (by Salman Rushdie) in the centre of Bradford. The book burning produced potent television coverage and contributed significantly to the rapid escalation of the public outrage and heated debate that became the 'Rushdie Affair' (Akhtar, 1989; Appignanesi and Maitland, 1989; Ruthven, 1991). This was not a civil disturbance in any meaningful sense of the term, but it established the visibility of the Asian community in Bradford as substantial in its number, and as a provocation to the normative operation of 'British' values. The furore created by the Rushdie Affair is perhaps difficult to recall in its intensity and massive dominance in the public sphere two decades later, but it is certain that it caused a quantum shift in the ways in which ethnic relations in Britain became framed for any future debate. Among other things, it helped fracture the united language of 'blackness' and forced a political distinction between the experiences and priorities of African Caribbeans and South Asians in Britain where the latter felt, with some justification, that the British form of multiculturalism framed around 'Black struggle' had marginalised the centrality of faith, specifically Islam, in the life of many of Britain's settled South Asian communities.

The Rushdie Affair was a watershed in the emergence of an independent Muslim political identity in Britain (Modood, 1990; Ruthven, 1991; Samad, 1992). The assumed natural alliance of the liberal British left with a defence of minority rights received a sharp revelatory testing as significant voices on the white left sided unequivocally with Rushdie and the principle of freedom of speech, notwithstanding the reasonable offence articulated from within Muslim communities (Akhtar, 1989). A nuanced understanding of the Muslim sense of offence seemed to be obscured in the rush to defend a non-negotiable commitment to freedom of speech, and it has to be said, Salman Rushdie's life. While the Rushdie Affair fuelled a new intensity of majority ethnic concern about fundamentalism among members of British Muslim communities, it simultaneously politicised British Muslims into a recognition that they did stand alone and needed to mobilise in ways that had not previously been typical of them (Modood, 1990, 1998). It also simultaneously created a concerned dialogue *within* the British Muslim population about how they should situate the diversity of interpretation, tradition and practice of Islam within the context of British and European political values and systems. The unravelling of these two processes had significant consequences for the restructuring of local politics within British cities (Back and Solomos, 1992; Solomos and Back, 1995). At the national and local level in Britain, issues of religious identity could no longer be assumed to be quietly subsumed in debates about multiculturalism defined in terms of rights and anti-racist initiatives. At the level of city mobilisation, Muslim communal and religious organisations began to take on a new political role in the local political scene, while the national government struggled to develop new structures through which a dialogue with Muslim communities could originate and be sustained.

The ambiguous and nervous dynamics which permeate the relationship between the UK government and the wide range of organisational entities which emerge from within Muslim communities more than ever constitutes a significant expression of the struggle over political power in contemporary Britain. The government needs, as an element of its exercise of governance, to have effective access to the experience and opinions extant within British Muslim communities. Additionally within the politics of Community Cohesion the government also needs *to be seen* to have effective dialogue with Muslim communities. This has resulted in the unedifying process of the government seeking to have a key role in defining the *legitimate* voices of the Muslim populations of Britain. As Spalek and Lambert (2008: 261) have argued:

> It appears that government projects aimed at fostering dialogue and community participation tend to be underpinned by broader questions and debates around what sorts of Muslim identities should be encouraged in the UK, a form of identity building, and what kinds of Muslim identities should be actively discouraged and/or suppressed.

A page later they conclude that:

> Legitimate Muslims are perceived to be those who engage with governments on the terms set by those governments. Those Muslims who refuse such an engagement (irrespective of their motivations or reasons) are likely to be perceived as 'radical' and hence a potential terrorist threat. This creates an untenable situation for many Muslims. (Spalek and Lambert, 2008: 262)

Issues of autonomy, voice and access continue to be central to the political struggles with which Muslim communities must currently contend (Modood, 2005; Spalek and Imtoul, 2007; Maussen, 2007; Lambert, 2008; for a wider analysis of the issue of state management of Islamic representation, see European Parliament, 2007; Maussen, 2007).

Muslim difference and British identity and values

The Rushdie Affair, like the issue of the veil that was to gain momentum in the following decades, was hotly debated in Britain. Here, 'European values' – particularly the freedom of speech and expression, including the 'right to offend' – were perceived as being put in jeopardy by the emergence of the new 'enemy within' European states: Islam. The availability of a shared Orientalist European tradition in making absolutely self-evident the *reasonable* anguish and outrage felt by good liberal members of the majority society faced by the threat of 'Islamic fundamentalism' should not be underestimated. Media coverage of the international response to the *fatwa* against Rushdie was a central part of the UK's experience of this phenomenon (Karim, 2000; Poole 2002; Poole and Richardson, 2005). A new heightened concern with defining and protecting *our* national identity became a companion process to the growth of Islamophobia in the next decade (Runnymede Trust, 1997; and see Chapter Four, this volume). Solomos cites John Patten, the then Home Secretary, making a statement in 1989 which reflects something of the mood[2] of the time:

> [If Muslims] are to make the most of their lives and opportunities as British citizens then they must have a clear understanding of the British democratic processes, of its laws, the system of Government and the history that lies behind them, and indeed of their own rights and responsibilities (*The Times*, 5 July 1989, cited in Solomos, 2003: 214)

The heightened significance of Islam continued into the 1990s, with new issues and perceived cultural characteristics being added to the debate to form, in some cases, a stereotypical, prevailing and monolithic notion of (British) Muslim identity. The problems of forced and transnational marriage, Muslim schools, involvement in the illegal drugs trade, the prevalence of educational under-achievement among certain Muslim communities, as well as the issue of loyalty to Britain, particularly during the first Gulf War in 1992 (Saeed, 2007), all served to reinforce the perception of Muslim communities and Islamic values as being at odds with 'British' values and practices. The linking of 'problematic Muslims' to critiques of multiculturalism as a policy has in fact been a distinct trope in public debates since 9/11 (see Modood, 2006, for a comment on this process). This powerful negative double helix formed by tying negative assertions around multiculturalism into a tight linkage with the supposed negative characteristics of Muslims has proved to be a potent discursive ploy. What this rhetoric studiously neglects to acknowledge, however, is the reality of the successful creative translation of the former immigrant populations into becoming a settled, confident citizenry who negotiate their religion, ethnicity and Britishness in unique ways (Alam, 2006; Alam and Husband, 2006). Nor does it recognise the role of white working-class communities in proactively accommodating to increased diversity. Additionally, as Finney and Simpson (2009) indicate, members of Muslim communities have increasingly achieved class mobility within British society, creating new areas of interethnic demography within British cities. What remains regularly obscured or downplayed within discussions of Muslim identity politics in the West is the fact that despite Islamophobia and other discriminations, the British Muslim populations have developed new syncretic identities precisely attributable to Western notions of freedom. The British infrastructure of anti-discrimination legislation and practice built through political struggle over the last five decades has enabled such expressions of identity to emerge. Britain, we need to remind ourselves, is *de facto* multi-ethnic and multireligious.

By the 1990s, the new Muslim 'other' had supplanted Britain's previous favoured threat to society, the young African Caribbean male. Of course, the young, male African Caribbean of working class background was still present, but the perceived risk and danger presented by the new 'enemy within' was far more salient for reasons explored above, and because of the wider international context and resonance of 'assertive Islam'. This was a context that was radically sharpened by the events of 9/11.

While the profile of Muslims, and the construction of a quite specific Islamic threat, was a major feature of the 1980s and 1990s, it must be remembered that the wider generic politics of British 'race relations' was simultaneously being continuously sustained (Solomos, 2003). The two parallel strands of British policy since the 1960s continued as a cumulative ratcheting up of restrictive border control policies, with the attendant xenophobic politics of anti-immigration and asylum seeking on the one hand, and the extension of anti-discriminatory legislation and practice, with its supportive language of rights and equality, on the other. This twin process of contradictory policies has been described as 'doing good by stealth whilst flirting with racism' (Husband, 2003: 191). Certainly the replacement of a Conservative regime by a Labour government did little, if anything, to change the anti-immigrant and anti-asylum seeker policies of the British state. Nor did it see an end to the party political acquiescence to the xenophobic and Islamophobic sentiments within the British electorate (Back et al, 2002a; Fekete, 2009). However, tragic events in 1993 provided evidence that older racisms were still very real, and propelled a new phase in the definition of the state's response to racism while giving a new centrality to policy concern with institutional racism.

The murder of Stephen Lawrence and the Macpherson Report

On the evening of 23 April 1993, a group of white youths attacked a young black South London teenager while he waited at a bus stop. The attack, lasting less than a minute, left Stephen Lawrence with fatal stab wounds. This murder was no doubt the result of a racist attack, but the subsequent police investigation to all intents and purposes ignored any racial motivation held by the perpetrators, a perspective that was to provide a basis for the subsequent inquiry into the mismanagement of the investigation (Macpherson, 1999). For example, Stephen's friend Dwayne Brooks who managed to escape the attack was treated as a suspect, not a witness. Furthermore, surveillance of the actual suspects began *two* days after the murder because the area surveillance team was already scheduled to stake out a young black man alleged to have committed a relatively petty crime. What could be inferred from the latter is that for the investigating team the *actual* murder of a black teenager seemed to be less of a priority than the *alleged* crime of a black man. At the same time, the assumption that Dwayne, by virtue of nothing more than his presence at the scene and the colour of his skin, was the potential murderer indicates racial bias and prejudicial stereotyping in action. This form of 'differential' policing, the targeting of non-whites, is not new and nor has it been isolated to parts of London. Indeed, the disproportionate use and impact of 'stop and search' policies, among others, on black people has been well documented (Cohen and Bains, 1988; Skellington and Morris, 1992; Pilkington, 2003; Bowling and Phillips, 2007) and continues, in the light of the Terrorism Act 2000 (specifically Sections 44-47), to be an area of policing that raises concerns about discrimination, human rights and justice.

Although five men were arrested some two weeks after Stephen's murder, they were not charged with the crime. Again, the report found significant issues of concern regarding the manner of the investigation and the beliefs that underpinned some of the decisions taken. Perhaps most notably, Doreen Lawrence, Stephen's mother, speaking six years later at a news conference at the Home Office, stated that the police had investigated the killing like 'white masters during slavery' (Orr, 1999). By this time, The *Official Inquiry into the Murder of Stephen Lawrence*, more commonly known as *The Macpherson Report*, was completed. Among its findings, it concluded that the police had failed to carry out its duties due to a range of factors including institutionalised racism, professional incompetence and a lack of leadership on the part of senior officers. (Bridges, 1999; Lea, 2000).

For the Lawrences, and perhaps for many of Britain's minority ethnic groups, institutional racism was a 'normal' and very real aspect of daily life. Indeed, even those Black Britons with relatively greater power and status than 'ordinary' citizens have been far from exempt:

> It [police powers to stop and search] became particularly controversial at the turn of the millennium when prominent people of African Caribbean origin including the late Bernie Grant MP, Lord Taylor of Warwick, Lord Herman Ouseley and the Most Revd and Rt Hon Dr John Sentamu Archbishop of York disclosed their personal experiences of being unjustifiably stopped and searched. (Bowling and Phillips, 2007: 936)

What the Stephen Lawrence investigation revealed to the wider world was that Britain, still riding on a crest of New Labour optimism, needed more than tolerance and the veneer which coated comfortable multicultural performance. Saris, samosas and chai, the fun and familiarity of 'ethnic' carnivals along with the presence of high-profile black public figures, entertainers and sportspeople was all good and well, but when it came right down to it, 'race' still mattered and it mattered across the board, not just in deprived inner-city areas with relatively concentrated black and minority ethnic populations, and not merely for the organised and increasingly mainstreamed far right. What the Lawrence case and subsequent inquiry evidenced was that Britain remained fractured along lines of both 'race' and class. It also demonstrated that the state has a capacity to engage with its own failings and to attempt to provide a systematic response. In this it illustrates the importance of the argument made by Wacquant (2008) in his comparative analysis of US and French urban ethnic relations, namely, that any understanding of specific urban ethnic relations must be framed within an analysis of the specific national and local socio-political circumstances, and the historical values that inform them.

The inquiry into the murder of Stephen Lawrence and the subsequent report originated from a New Labour government attempting to demonstrate its 'good' or at least 'better' 'race relations' credentials than its Conservative predecessors. Specifically, the inquiry was one of Jack Straw's first acts as Home Secretary, himself having spoken previously in the House of Commons on the Stephen Lawrence case, as well as being critical of Conservative asylum and immigration legislation, namely the Asylum and Immigration Acts of 1993 and 1996.

Macpherson offered 70 recommendations, nearly half of which were explicitly concerned with the reporting and investigation of racist incidents (Pilkington, 2003: 256). His discussion of institutional racism was a key element, not only in relation to the specific case but also related to broader 'stop and search' anomalies, attributable in part to racist stereotyping. What Macpherson also did was to offer up a working definition of the term 'institutional racism' itself, as:

> The collective failure of an organisation to provide an appropriate and professional service to people because of their colour, culture, or ethnic origin. It can be seen or detected in processes, attitudes and behaviour which amount to discrimination through unwitting prejudice, ignorance, thoughtlessness and racist stereotyping which disadvantage minority ethnic people. (Macpherson, 1999: para 6.34)

Scarman's findings and recommendations were based on the downplaying of structural and systemic weaknesses within, for example, policy infrastructure and legislation. Consequently, the recommendations themselves remained isolated from broader policy or legal instruments which would serve to decrease levels of deprivation and discrimination; the protections afforded by the Race Relations Act 1976 were deemed competent and wide ranging enough. However, Macpherson recommended that this particular piece of legislation be amended in order to achieve the required reach over public authorities and services, previously exempt. The Race Relations Amendment Act (2000) put the onus on all public bodies and services, especially the police, to implement strategies that would ensure non-racist[3] operation, including recruitment, training and monitoring.

The emphasis on the pervasive power of institutional racism was highly significant for the development of wide-ranging policy initiatives. Not least, it produced a rejection of the simplicities which come from defining racism as 'prejudice plus power', with its inherent focus on disturbed individuals. Institutional racism spelt out quite transparently that even 'nice, *tolerant*, people' can discriminate. And it removed the focus of attention from the intentions of individuals, replacing it with a focus on the consequences of their routine actions. This constituted a major shift in the framing of policy and practice. One of the major consequences of the Macpherson Report, and the subsequent changes in organisational practice, was that by the time Community Cohesion had emerged as a central focus of local authority activity, local authorities across Britain already had in place well-established organisational structures, policy frameworks and routinised practice for the implementation of anti-discriminatory equality policies. In turn, then, this cohort of practice and expertise fed into the local states' response to the government's Community Cohesion strategy.

Echoing Wacquant's (2008) argument above, we must keep an eye open to recognising the unique mechanisms in British legislation and policy that allow for diversity to be addressed and for discrimination to be identified and challenged. This is not a perfect situation, but it would be a significant error not to recognise the possibilities allowed within British social policy that would be much more problematic in other European countries (ECCAR, 2010). The accumulation over several decades of anti-discriminatory legislation, and the embedding in state and other organisations of institutional mechanisms for challenging discrimination and addressing the challenges of ethnic diversity, should not be ignored. This brief review has sought to provide a schematic outline of salient aspects of British ethnic relations since the 1960s, which have a continuing relevance for our understanding of the events and actions revealed through the events and data presented in the chapters that follow.

Social cohesion in the context of wider Labour Party policy

In the English context social cohesion as a conceptual basis for state policy emerged from the pre-existing academic debate. As Flint and Robinson (2008) note, Kearns and Forrest's (2000) construction of social cohesion was constituted from five interactive elements:

- common values and civic culture
- social order and social control
- social solidarity and reductions in wealth disparities
- social networks and social capital
- place attachment and identity.

These elements were directly referenced in the influential Cantle Report (as a definition of community cohesion) and were subsequently incorporated in the formulation of Community Cohesion outlined first in the Local Government Association et al's official guidance document entitled *Guidance on community cohesion* (LGA et al, 2002) and then later the report of the Commission on Integration and Cohesion (2007) entitled *Our shared future*.

The discourse of social cohesion/community cohesion has been characterised by conceptual ambiguity, a communitarian ideological sub-stratum and by a transnational flow of ideas framed by key academic and policy people (Field, 2003; Cheong et al, 2007). It is thus worth noting, as we move to a brief outline of the English trajectory of Community Cohesion as policy, that Flint and Robinson (2008) identify a significant transition in the framing of these five core elements (as extracted from Kearns and Forrest's [2000] earlier academic analysis) into these two critical policy documents. As Flint and Robinson state:

> Note, in particular, the emphasis within the two official definitions on equality of opportunity rather than on Kearn's and Forrest's assertion regarding the importance of reducing wealth disparities, a subtle variation indicative of the reticence of the community cohesion agenda to acknowledge and address structural inequalities rooted in economic processes. (Flint and Robinson, 2008: 4–5)

This underlines the importance of seeing the development of Community Cohesion, as policy in the English context, as necessarily interwoven into other core values and policies of the Labour Party's ideological repertoire. In this immediate case we can acknowledge that the Blair government's explicit commitment to, and discursive exploitation of, the rhetoric of the 'Opportunity Society' has constituted a significant force in shaping the emergence of the broader Community Cohesion policy. In this context, Community Cohesion's concern with common values and intergroup behaviour has facilitated an apparently reasonable neglect of the fundamental role of class and 'race' inequalities in shaping ethnic relations.

RED, SID and MUD: competing underlying discourses

In a telling and detailed account of the development of New Labour's policy and philosophy surrounding social exclusion and citizenship, Levitas (2005) maps the shifting relation of three competing explanatory models and their role in shaping Labour Party and government policy on social cohesion. The first of these is *RED*. Here, social exclusion is intertwined with poverty and has its academic and intellectual roots in critical social policy and has a *redistributionist* agenda. In comparison with RED, however, MUD is linked with a *moral underclass discourse* which focuses on the moral and behavioural delinquency of the excluded themselves. Offering further comparison, SID operates within a *social integrationist discourse* whereby (paid) work is the central means of delivering inclusion (Levitas, 2005: Chapter 1).

These three models have differing political roots and have emerged in late 20th-century British policy debates through concrete policy foci that have been rendered potent, and often raw, in the demographic and economic transitions that have been characteristic of postwar Britain and were again given renewed but particular power through the new right politics of Thatcherism (Jessop et al, 1988). During the 1990s, and now, these three models were analytically separable, but were also capable of being co-opted into pragmatic specific discursive alliances within the *real politik* of political struggle, both within and between, the major political parties. The development of New Labour, and its break with the redistributive core sentiments of the 'Old Left' through the emergent politics of the Third Way (Giddens, 1998), produced a new environment within which these models competed. In a chapter entitled 'From social justice to social cohesion' (Levitas, 2005: Chapter 2), Levitas notes New Labour's shift toward SID in which the interdependence of social cohesion and economic growth are understood as being constituted through the centrality of paid employment as a means of social integration and social control. Consequently, unemployment is the key factor in determining social exclusion (Levitas, 2005: 47-8). As becomes apparent in Levitas's later analysis, a focus on employment within the Third Way's commitment to neoliberal economics and variants on communitarian constructions of civility leaves ample opportunity for the tactical exploitation of MUD discourses of moral incapacity as explanations used to account for those who fail to thrive in New Labour's 'Opportunity Society'.

Importantly, this development of a policy around social exclusion took place within a wider framework of continuity with earlier policies, namely those relating to 'race' and migration. As Schuster and Solomos (2004) argue in their review of New Labour's policies on 'race' and migration:

> While there may have been shifts in these policies, for example from multiculturalism to social cohesion and towards the promotion of selected migration and a hardening of attitudes toward asylum seekers, these shifts remain consistent with a belief shared throughout the post war period, and across the political spectrum, that social cohesion and harmony depends on limiting and controlling the migration of certain groups into Britain. (Schuster and Solomos, 2004: 267)

In postwar Britain the themes of 'race' and immigration have remained central and contentious in the country's political culture, with a successive ratchet-like process of increasingly punitive regulation of immigration being paralleled by attempts to introduce progressive anti-discriminatory legislation (Solomos, 2003; Husband, 2005a). The long imperial history of Britain and its relatively recent engagement with accommodating the independence of its ex-colonies has left Britain with a historically specific sensitivity to 'race' and ethnicity. Thus, the centrality of immigration and the 'difference' of British Muslim citizens in the developing politics of social cohesion and the prevention of violent extremism necessarily imports a whole area of ideological and political baggage into the debate and ensuing operational policy (see Chapter Three, this volume). The ongoing salience of 'race' in the British imaginary has, among other things, contributed to the resistance within sections of the majority white population to acknowledging the transition of most of Britain's Muslims from being once migrant to now resident, British-born citizens. They may speak with British regional accents, they may have established positions within the labour market and civil society, they may indeed formally be British citizens but they remain 'not one of us'. Their 'race' continues to be sufficient basis for their exclusion from British identity, to the extent that third generation Muslim Britons are still routinely included in the category 'immigrants'. Thus faith as a salient determinant of identity has emerged in recent years within this already powerfully racialised construction of difference.

The rhetoric of the 'Opportunity Society' within New Labour's political agenda provided a flexible discourse for a wide raft of government policies, ranging from education to health and from employment to immigration, where the individual became the salient target of policy. Echoing the earlier possessive individualism of Thatcherism, redistributive politics addressing collective marginalisation became buried beneath neoliberal concerns with individual agency and individual responsibility. Thus, when the senior Labour Minister John Prescott was interviewed on the occasion of the Labour Party's centenary and was asked whether Labour had abandoned its traditional commitment to redistribution, he replied that the Party was in favour of 'the redistribution of *opportunity*' (quoted in Levitas, 2005: 227, emphasis added). Similarly, in Blair's speech to the Labour Party Conference in 2004, he suggested that the aspiration is 'not a society where all succeed equally – that is utopia: but an *opportunity* society where all have an equal chance to succeed' (Levitas, 2005: 227, emphasis added).

Not surprisingly, an attempt to meld neoliberal economic policy with communitarian concerns with a shared common system of values opens up a fertile domain for identifying individual reasons for failure to thrive economically, and hence to achieve social inclusion. Within this discourse a chronic absence of the right sort of moral virtue and social capital among specific 'communities' is recurrently invoked to explain the persistence of exclusion. This focus on the character of communities had the virtue of applying equally well to the white 'underclass', black and minority ethnic communities and to Islamic communities. Its ubiquitous applicability added to its apparent legitimacy. In the Blairite commitment to the 'Opportunity Society', Levitas notes that 'the MUD focus on behavioural manipulation of those stepping out of line remains crucial to the Blairite agenda' (Levitas, 2005: 227). This opens the way for 'punitive conditionality' (Halpern et al, 2004), the employment of a strategy of fines and the withdrawal of state support as means of promoting self-efficacy and participation in the labour market.

For New Labour it is individual, and therefore quite specific, factors that have become the focus of policy. For example, any communitarian-informed attempts to promote 'local autonomy' in devolved policy development for an 'active citizenry' become perversely problematic when the community in question wants to develop Muslim faith schools, or other expressions of local identities that challenge the implicit 'shared values' (Back et al, 2002a, 2002b). There is a tension in Britain between the formal status of Christianity and the *de facto* secular model of the welfare state and of citizenship, which has rendered the engagement with Islam deeply problematic. As we shall discuss, it is partly about the historical construction, and current anxious defence, of British (English) identity and partly about the routine practices operating within state and civil institutions which are shaping the specific forms of resistance to the expressions of Islamic identity within Britain. The communitarian ethos underpinning the drive for active citizenship sits uncomfortably with a strong *normative* vision of the community identity that is to be nurtured through activity. Active citizenship seems to be conceived of as an individual and political virtue, sufficient unto itself. When, however, Muslim individuals mobilise around a collective identity in pursuit of a shared community agenda it seems likely that they will be vulnerable to being accused of employing the wrong sort of social capital in pursuit of sustaining 'parallel lives' and cultures.

Social capital: the elixir of social cohesion

The propensity to drift into, or exploit, MUD rhetoric when discussing marginalised communities in Britain's cities within the Community Cohesion agenda is exacerbated by the central location of the language of *social capital* in constructing the concept of Community Cohesion. As Field (2003) extensively illustrates in his book-length overview, the concept of social capital has a substantial history within the social sciences, and in recent years became politically visible in the writings of Robert Putnam, particularly through the impact of his book *Bowling alone* (Putnam, 2000). Taken up by the Clinton administration, his theoretical work came to enjoy a wide cache in policy milieus in the US and in Europe (see Field, 2003; Jacobs and Tillie, 2004).

Arising from Putnam's work, social capital has typically been seen as having two dominant forms in terms of their impact on social cohesion. One is *bonding social capital* which relates to those social networks and relationships which operate within relatively homogeneous groups and which help to sustain shared identity and civility within the group. These are exactly those relationships which were celebrated when present in the traditional working class, and whose loss was lamented in the postwar suburbanisation and embourgoisement of these communities (see, for example, Young and Willmott, 1957, 1960). *Bridging social capital*, on the other hand, is seen as a product of those relationships and networks that transcend differences of ethnicity, religion or socioeconomic status and hence build civility across group identities. These two forms of social capital can be seen to be written into the core definition of Community Cohesion outlined by Cantle above, and by the Cabinet Office (Aldridge et al, 2002). Within the contemporary discourse of Community Cohesion, bridging capital is seen as the 'good stuff' to be facilitated and the core of the new community development work. However, the erstwhile virtues of bonding capital are routinely seen as the lamentable characteristics of the dispossessed working classes and the minority communities still mired in 'identity politics'. This of course takes place within a wider policy context where resilient ethnic and cultural diversity is framed by a consensual assertion of the failure of multiculturalism (Back et al, 2002b; McGhee, 2003; Joppke, 2004). As Cheong et al (2007) helpfully point out, it is within this context that 'diversity and difference [are] posed in opposition to unity and solidarity' (2007: 27).

McGhee (2003), in his critical examination of the core texts of Community Cohesion's evolution,[4] points out the explicit emphasis on the negative effects of bonding social capital and the need to promote bridging social capital in this foundational literature. Speaking directly about the Cantle Report he concludes, thus:

> What this amounts to can be described as a fully fledged Putmanesque [sic] problematization of excessive bonding social capital in a context of insufficient bridging social capital. (McGhee, 2003: 385)

The centrality given to social capital in the definition of Community Cohesion and in the practical proposals for its implementation outlined in the guidance documents sits comfortably with the Blair government's dalliance with communitarian philosophy. Its emphasis on the engagement of individual responsibility, in the context of it being embedded in a social environment with shared common core values, is consistent with a retreat from a concern with the socio-structural determination of inequalities. Its strong 'moral' agenda again reflects the continuity between New Labour and the moral certitudes of high Thatcherism that framed her response to the multiple 'enemies within'. As Arneil (2007) points out, Tony Blair actively drew on Putnam in championing his commitment to social capital and civic renewal, within which 'active citizenship' and 'national cohesion' were core issues. She goes on to indicate how 'Social capital provides the language of civic renewal to buttress New Labour's critique of the welfare state while justifying its reform in softer packaging' (Arneil, 2007: 42). Within Blairism social capital provides an individualised focus on personal social behaviour and responsibility, and a comfortable fit with an eclectic flirtation with communitarian philosophy. At the same time, social capital provides a perspective within which the structural reproduction of exclusions is obscured by a focus on the personal and the interpersonal dynamics of sociability (see also McClenaghan, 2000; Muntaner et al, 2000; Kalra and Kapoor, 2008).

Regrettably, for those who find themselves engaged in implementing policies framed by the Community Cohesion agenda, not only is the definition of Community Cohesion ambiguous and, as we have seen above, racialised, the conceptual engine of so much British Community Cohesion policy – social capital – is itself an unstable and potentially contradictory construct. As a number of reviews have pointed out, the founding authors of this literature do not themselves share a common perspective. This, of course, has consequent implications for its translation into coherent policy (see also Field, 2003; Cheong et al, 2007; Edwards et al, 2007). Thus, for example, Savage et al (2007), in juxtaposing Bourdieu's approach with that of Putnam's, conclude that:

> A satisfactory approach requires that social capital be
> placed within a more developed sociological perspective,
> in which we see it as tied up with processes of boundary
> maintenance which define social categories. Effectively, this
> means placing the study of social capital within an emphasis
> on social stratification – of race, class, gender, and so forth
> – as fundamental features of the social fabric. (2007: 73-4)

While this may find some echoes in the descriptive body of *Our
shared future* (Commission on Integration and Cohesion, 2007), it is
effectively lost in the shift to guidance and implementation so that it
is quite reasonable to accept Cheong et al's (2007) modest conclusion
that: 'The politics and practices of racism and discrimination are often
underplayed in initiatives promoting bonding and bridging social
capital' (2007: 33). Leading on from this and through drawing on the
points made earlier, overall, it is equally reasonable to suggest that
the extensive and often contradictory literature on social capital has
for political purposes been reduced to a seemingly taken for granted
wisdom. It is this taken for granted, new conventional wisdom and
logic that enables simplistic assertions about complex social forces to
have a credibility the research literature would not warrant.

The benefits of locating government policy on social cohesion (and
Preventing Violent Extremism: PVE) within the wider framework of
the major political agendas of New Labour is beneficial in many ways,
not least because it provides insights into the likely efficacy of the
government's policies themselves. New Labour's attempt to operate
with a fusion of neoliberalism and social democracy, where the social
democratic element is systematically subordinated to neoliberal ends,
necessarily results in a 'double shuffle' of governing in the interests of
capital while employing spin and strategic modicums of redistribution
to keep its supporters on board (Hall, 2003). For Levitas (2005), the
prognosis and resulting conclusion is pessimistic:

> The flexibility of the concept of social exclusion is, in this
> context, part of the point. Conceptual ambiguity, however,
> is less easy to disguise when it translates into policy. Thus,
> the ambiguities and contradictions in the strategy to tackle
> exclusion can be seen as the outcome of the contradictory
> nature of the New Labour project itself. If this analysis is
> right, the prospects for greater equality are bleak. So too,
> then, are the prospects for inclusion. For to tackle social
> exclusion without making serious inroads into inequality

is to fight the battle with both hands tied behind our backs (Levitas, 2005: 234).

Emergence of Community Cohesion and its linkage to 'self-segregation'

A generic concern with social cohesion became transformed to a specific policy agenda focused on Community Cohesion following the civil disturbances (popularly referred to in the media as *riots*), which occurred in the northern cities of Bradford, Burnley and Oldham in 2001. The Home Secretary's response to these disturbances was to immediately set up an Interdepartmental Ministerial Group on Public Order and Community Cohesion, chaired by John Denham. This group's mandate was to report on what the government should do in order to minimise the likelihood of further outbreaks of such urban disorder, and in a complementary way to advise on how to build cohesive communities. Due to the scale and level of the group's general scope, it is fair to say that it had a national strategic remit.[5] At the same time, the Home Secretary also established a more tactical and narrowly focused Community Cohesion Independent Review Team, chaired by Ted Cantle, to review the views and opinions of different interests in the towns affected by the disturbances and beyond. The significant output from this team was a report entitled *Community Cohesion: A report of the Independent Review Team* (Community Cohesion Independent Review Team, 2001), also often referred to as *The Cantle Report*.

Interestingly, while Denham had a strategic remit, his report nonetheless drew heavily on the local reviews commissioned in Burnley and Oldham after the disturbances and on a seemingly prescient study of urban demography and intergroup relations in Bradford commissioned shortly before the riots there, a report carried out by Sir Herman Ouseley (Burnley Task Force, 2001; Oldham Independent Panel Review, 2001; Ouseley, 2001). These three reports cumulatively identified three key agendas that underpinned the urban unrest: ethnic segregation, limited cross-cultural interaction and the absence of shared identity and values. As government policy developed, the issue of 'self-segregated' settled South Asian minority ethnic communities (often specifically defined as Muslim, then and later) and their alleged persistence in living within parallel cultures became central to the framing of emergent policy.

In setting this narrow agenda, *The Ouseley Report* on the situation in Bradford, which preceded the Burnley and Oldham reports, did much to establish the image of a dramatic and threatening society with its emphasis on segregation and the *fear* that supposedly was characteristic of urban life in Bradford (see Alam and Husband, 2006). This report opened with an overview entitled 'Removing fears'. The reinforcement of fear as reality was most explicitly established in the reader's mind on the first page where 7 of the 13 paragraphs start with the word *fear* itself. *The Ouseley Report*, coming as it did from an author with the authority of the ex-chair of the Commission for Racial Equality, did much to establish the conflictual and fear-laden vision of inner-city Britain that was to become the dominant conception of ethnic relations over the following year. Indeed, in a range of later policy initiatives dealing with security and cohesion, one of the principal drivers was a demonstrable and calculated exploitation of fear (Denney, 2009).

Residential segregation was a dominant theme within the Oldham report, and the Burnley report similarly concluded that 'the Asian and White communities live separate and parallel lives and have very few ways of learning from and understanding each others' cultures and beliefs' (Burnley Task Force, 2001: 7). These heavily rehearsed themes became widely visible in the British mass media and in the political debate following the 2001 riots. It is not surprising, therefore, that the issue of segregation and the existence of ethnic communities operating within 'parallel lives' became central to the highly influential Cantle Report:

> Whilst the physical segregation of housing estates and inner city areas came as no surprise, the team was particularly struck by the depth of polarisation of our towns and cities. The extent to which these physical divisions were compounded by so many other aspects of our daily lives was very evident. Separate educational arrangements, community and voluntary bodies, employment, places of worship, language, social and cultural networks, means that many communities operate on the basis of a series of parallel lives. These lives often do not seem to touch at any point, let alone overlap and promote any meaningful interchanges. (Community Cohesion Independent Review Team, 2001: 9)

Given this range of 'findings', most of which are clearly problematic, it is useful to explore possible ensuing remedies, usefully assessed by Robinson (2008), who argues:

This short section of the Cantle Report provides a précis of the official storyline that emerged to explain the 2001 disturbances: residential segregation leads to social isolation and limited cross-cultural contact, which allows misunderstanding and suspicion to flourish and can lead to inter-community tensions and violence and disorder. If we invert this storyline, we can see a route map out of this dystopian world of community conflict. What we need to do is challenge the 'them' and 'us' attitude apparent in such situations and develop common goals and a shared vision. To this end, greater contact should be promoted between different communities by tackling the residential segregation that promotes separation in schooling, employment, service and social life. (Robinson, 2008: 19)

However, in his later account of the development of Community Cohesion, Cantle (2008) argues that we need to be careful in disaggregating differing definitions of segregation, and notes that:

At one *extreme*, segregation has been described as 'parallel lives', a concept first established by the Independent Review Team [chaired by Cantle].... This demonstrated that physical separation of BME [black and minority ethnic] households in distinct housing areas had become underpinned by a complete lack of contact between people from different communities. Social and economic ties had lessened, or ceased altogether and there was little or no contact of any sort between different groups. (Cantle, 2008: 16, emphasis added)

On this basis we may conclude that Cantle regards the condition of 'parallel lives' as an *extreme* instance of segregation, and yet a few pages earlier, when he is describing the *normative* condition of British multi-ethnic cities, he offers this picture:

Even within the multicultural cities, there is evidence of considerable levels of separation, to the extent that the relationship between communities might also be characterised as one of 'parallel lives'. (Cantle, 2008: 14)

He then quotes British references in support of this thesis so that we can be sure that he is referring to Britain, and continues with a further supporting statement:

> The inner city 'ghettoes', mono-cultural schools, separate employment patterns and distinct faith and cultural associations, are simply seen as part of the natural fabric of many cities. (Cantle, 2008: 14)

We can see here the association of the need for Community Cohesion policies with a disturbing vision of multi-ethnic British cities that on its own terms offers an extreme picture of the levels of segregation, and feels additionally comfortable in talking about 'ghettoes', a term Wacquant (2008) would regard as entirely unsustainable in the British context.

The relative comfort with which the term 'ghettoes' is used here, complete with all the connotations[6] the word carries, is indicative of Cantle's alliance with elements of the MUD discourse; so much for being careful! However, Cantle does more than tactically suggest a need for Community Cohesion policies to become operational; he strategically frames this proposal with his own vision of multi-ethnic British cities that are seen through an extreme picture wherein the levels of segregation are deep and divisive.

As it was developed, this conception of 'the problem' of inner-city multi-ethnic Britain was negotiated within the 'double shuffle' of New Labour rhetoric and policy, and hence came to provide a concrete articulation of MUD and SID rhetoric. The central place of communitarian philosophy within the emergent definition of New Labour's social ideology gives a particular centrality to the role of shared values, and shared identity in providing the foundations for viable civility among a disparate population. Shared values, and their perceived absence, in the 'apparent' ethnic segmentation of contemporary urban Britain provided a fertile site for the identification of recalcitrant difference among Britain's marginalised populations as defined by their ethnicity, religion and urban working-class *marginality*, namely, those categories without linkage to the labour market and often those with *negative* linkage as they are perceived to take from the state and the taxpayer.[7] Thus, the rhetoric of 'the enemy within' that had been so central to the MUD logics of Thatcherism found new expression in relation to the developing debates around inner-city England.

The social upheavals of 2001 gave a new reason to focus on ethnic diversity. The reality of ethnic diversity had never become a non-

---

issue within Britain, since, apart from anything else, continuing flows of inward migration to supplement the established minority ethnic communities along with new flows of asylum seekers had kept British immigration (control) and border policy as a recurrently vital issue for the British population. Sporadic media-generated moral panics (Critcher, 2006) provided peaks of political conflict around ethnicity that tended to ratchet up exclusionary border policies while reaffirming the inherent marginality of Britain's settled minority ethnic communities.

The 'riots' of 2001 provided a new stimulus to a political re-examination of Britain's commendable progressive development of a distinct form of multiculturalism, embedded in anti-discriminatory legislation and normalised in much state and organisational administrative routine. Racism had not been eliminated in the last five decades of the 20th century but its translation into discrimination had been rendered considerably more difficult, principally due to operational British anti-discriminatory legislation and policy (Husband, 2003). Meanwhile, and in many ways, the social and cultural fabric of British life had been extensively transformed through the emergence of distinct, robust and complex minority ethnic communities (Eade, 1997; Keith, 2005, Loury et al, 2005). The majority population of white Britons had substantially accommodated to the *de facto* multi-ethnic reality that was Britain despite 'race' remaining powerfully embedded in the British social imaginary (Taylor, 2004). Routine interpersonal, multicultural civility was no guarantee that around specific issues white majority sentiments could not be energised to reflect and support ethno-nationalist sentiments that were heavily informed by historically embedded racism (Kiernan, 1969; Jordan, 1986; Grewal, 1996), itself becoming apparent with the arrival of migrant labour from the new member states of the EU from Eastern Europe following their accession (Pollard et al, 2008). The riots, however, provided an opportunity to rehearse the British values of decency and tolerance in relation to their betrayal by the supposedly unassiminable alien-ness of the minority ethnic urban youth that became a focus of attention following the riots. Flint (2009) makes the important point that the 'colonising of civility' by the government, that became so central to Community Cohesion, was part of a long tradition of the state seeking to domesticate the behaviour of its populace, and that a similar process was being addressed to working-class communities in Britain. The 'broadening, deepening and widening' ambitions of the Labour government's Respect agenda, to address anti-social behaviour in everyday life, could be seen as a variant on this process (Respect Task Force, 2006).

It is noteworthy that the Burnley, Oldham, Ouseley, Denham and Cantle reports developed their analysis on the basis of consultation and gathering evidence. Systematic social scientific data was not commissioned and played only a modest role in the construction and validation of the 'self-segregation'/'parallel lives' script that came to dominate the policy agendas of Community Cohesion. Indeed, as Robinson (2008) notes:

> The final report of the Community Cohesion Panel (2004), for example, which had been set up to work with and advise ministers, reported that, despite its best efforts, including requests to government departments and agencies, it had not been able to acquire information that allowed it to 'take a really informed view about patterns of segregation and integration' (2004, p 17). The panel was therefore forced to 'rely on anecdotal and limited information' (Community Cohesion Panel, 2004, p 17). However, this did not stop it going on to recommend that a 'suite of policies be developed in response to segregated neighbourhoods' (Community Cohesion Panel, 2004, p 17). (Robinson, 2008: 24)

In fact, there is a significant, if contested, body of research literature which provides a much more complex and dynamic understanding of patterns of ethnic population distribution in urban Britain, rendering notions of 'self-segregation' at the very least suspect, and probably spurious (see, for example, Dorling and Thomas, 2004; Simpson, 2004, 2007; Simpson et al, 2009; while Robinson, 2008: 23-9 provides a useful overview). Finney and Simpson (2009) in particular offer a measured exposure of the inflated rhetoric and spurious interpretations that have formed such a significant part of the discourse on self-segregation and parallel lives.

The continuous flow of guidance from central government to local authorities since the reports of 2001 has made Community Cohesion a ubiquitous agenda across the activities of the local state. Whether in relation to schooling or the delivery of area-based initiatives (ABIs), the extant responsibilities of the local state have been suffused with policy statements and guidance documents aimed at building Community Cohesion into their routine practice (see, for example, LGA et al, 2002). Thus, for example, the 2005 White Paper, *Improving opportunity, strengthening society: The government's strategy to increase race equality and community cohesion* (Home Office, 2005), integrated the area of

Community Cohesion with the extensive extant 'race' equality agenda, thus mainstreaming cohesion as national policy.

The government's concerns with inner-city Britain and the priority to be given to Community Cohesion received a further significant jolt through violent outrages with the bombings in London on 7 July 2005. The reality of 'home-grown' terrorism constituted a major reconfiguration of the intersections of ethnicity, religion and urban diversity. The threat of social disturbances from that time onward has been catalysed by the language and logics of the global 'War on Terror'. The transnational linkages of resident settled minority ethnic populations (and quite specifically Muslim populations) renders the construction of 'parallel lives' suddenly and dramatically more problematic. Interfamilial connections and the sporadic visits that may follow from them now situate visits to Pakistan as potentially suspect when viewed through the lens of Al-Qaeda and terrorism. Added to this, the cyclical flow of Imams is made problematic when framed by the political concerns around the propagation of 'Islamic fundamentalism'.

The relationship between the global and the local is further complicated when the wished-for common values and common aspirations of community cohesion are defined through a shared national affiliation. These associations, alongside meanings of citizenship and identity politics, become questionable when events in Palestine and Afghanistan register, and have a depth of meaning, among the banal daily concerns of resident Muslim British citizens. The transformation of the salience of Islam for majority non-Muslim citizens and for Muslim British citizens that had taken place following the events of 9/11 had already had a considerable impact in constructing different perspectives on British international relations within the British population (discussed more fully in the next chapter). The taken for granted complexities of lives lived within diasporic and transnational identities, then, does not fit happily with the simplistic nostrums of the current discourse on citizenship (Alam, 2006; Alam and Husband, 2006).

The London bombings generated a radical shift in the potential agendas that might be addressed through a concern with Community Cohesion. The notions of a segregated and detached Muslim community, living parallel lives, that had been so successfully constructed following the riots of 2001 were now re-energised and focused through the lens of 'home-grown terrorism'. We were no longer invited to consider the 'peculiarities' of Muslim communities in our midst simply because it may contribute to civil unrest in major multi-ethnic cities. The agenda now became infused with the notion that these communities may export their violence, on a catastrophic scale, to any location in

Britain. This perspective was then reinforced by the subsequent attacks in London and Glasgow and by the arrest of those accused of planning further attacks.

This concern with inner-city urban Britain was given an unanticipated propaganda boost when Trevor Phillips, head of the Commission for Racial Equality (Britain's major statutory body for the promotion of ethnic equality and harmonious community relations), produced a heavily reported address that presented the current situation in the most stark terms. Phillips claimed that:

> Some districts are on their way to becoming fully fledged ghettoes – black holes into which no-one goes without fear and trepidation, and from which no-one ever escapes undamaged. The walls are going up around many of our communities, and the bridges … are crumbling…. The aftermath of 7/7 forces us to assess where we are. And here is where I think we are: we are sleepwalking our way to segregation. We are becoming strangers to each other, and we are leaving communities to be marooned outside the mainstream…. These marooned communities will steadily drift away from the rest of us, evolving their own lifestyles, playing by their own rules and increasingly regarding the codes of behaviour, loyalty and respect that the rest of us take for granted as outdated behaviour that no longer applies to them. We know what follows then: crime no-go areas and chronic cultural conflict. (Phillips, 2005)

Whatever his intentions, a statement such as this coming from the head of the government's own body for promoting community relations, and spoken by a black male, was incendiary in the immediate aftermath of 7/7. The domestic capacity for civil unrest that had already been very effectively attached to inner-city Muslim youth was now framed in the strongest possible terms by the assertion of the emergence of fragments of British society whose allegiance lay elsewhere and whose values were alien to those of mainstream Britain. The link between segregated Muslim communities and the growth of home-grown terrorism was explicitly made by Phillips in this same speech:

> In the weeks following 7/7, Commission personnel and more importantly, the thousands of folk we support in communities around the country, were concentrating on three crucial tasks:

encouraging communities to come forward with information that would help us to tackle the threat of terrorism;

reassuring communities from which the perpetrators of the 7/7 and 21/7 outrages came, that they should not be the targets or scapegoats of retribution; and

combating the divisions that these events threatened to open up within communities, and preventing those who would exploit those divisions for racist or Islamophobic purposes from doing so. (Phillips, 2005)

Regrettably, in the same period as Phillips' intervention, an opportunity for a more balanced view of the situation was lost when the House of Commons, Home Affairs Committee report (2005) *Terrorism and community relations* sought to address the linkage between counter-terrorism and Community Cohesion. While seeking to make a more explicit link between Home Office policies on counter-terrorism and Community Cohesion, and explicitly arguing for a recognition of the relevance of Community Cohesion initiatives at the local level for successful counter-terrorism strategies, this report failed to address the contribution of material inequalities in contributing to potential radicalisation. In McGhee's (2008: 62) words:

... the Home Affairs Committee has rejected explanations that linked terrorism to social exclusion in their report. Instead the Committee, following the Cantle Report, emphasized the importance of cultural factors....

Perversely, in the same year the government's *Improving opportunity, strengthening society* was launched (Home Office, 2005). This document offered a much more balanced view in recognising the implications of social and economic exclusion as contributory factors to the development of extremism. This recognition of material concerns was also linked with an explicit recognition of the marginalised circumstances of long established white working-class communities; indeed, a significant element in this policy is directed at addressing the perception of preferential treatment and the resentment felt by such communities toward minority communities perceived as being unfairly privileged. A strong focus that came out of this policy was a concern with local level leadership, which of itself fed into the 'good'

Muslim–'bad' Muslim discourse (Spalek and Imtoul, 2007; Lambert, 2008). The practical policies aimed at addressing local leadership and addressing 'community relations' initiatives were of course much more easily funded than any fundamental assault on the reproduction of structural class inequalities in Britain.

Although there was now a clearer understanding of the necessary linkage between counter-terrorism and Community Cohesion policies, in both of these areas a conceptual and economic neglect of the possible socioeconomic determination of the sense of exclusion felt by members of Britain's Muslim population continued to result in a focus on the challenge of '*their*' cultural differences, differences which had to be addressed at the local level. Notwithstanding statements from within government which offered a wider understanding of the relevance of economic factors (see, for example, McGhee, 2008: 70-1, 90-107) the self-segregation/parallel lives mantra was persistent, and provided a distorted framework for both policies.

Similar sentiments around terrorism were echoed in 2007 when Sir Cyril Taylor, a government adviser on education, was reported to have said: 'the concentration of ethnic minorities and religious groups in certain schools had created a "strategic security problem" … allowing significant numbers of ethnic minority children to lead virtually separate lives was fuelling extremism and harming academic standards' (*Mail Online*, 2007). It should be noted that Muslim schooling figured not only as an issue of security, but schooling, along with the veil, arranged marriage and other manifestations of Muslim identity were a contemporaneous concern within British political discourse; the issue of Islam and terrorism was being debated within a context in which the 'cultural challenge' of the Muslim presence in Britain was being simultaneously rehearsed in other areas of government policy.

However, the reality remained that Community Cohesion was now clearly infused with the priorities and logics of counter-terrorism. A conflation, for example, previously rehearsed by Baroness Amos in her 2006 address in opening the Labour Party's debate on Community Cohesion where, while talking of 'Suicide bombers with broad Yorkshire accents', she developed her argument about the need to engage with Muslim communities (cited in Finney and Simpson, 2009: 108).

Following the London bombings the government established the Commission on Integration and Cohesion, with a remit to examine the factors that contribute to the raising of tension, segregation and conflict, including evaluating the role of labour migration and asylum seeking. When the Commission reported in 2007 *(Our shared future)*, the issues of immigration and fundamentalism remained salient, and the concerns with isolationism, segregation and separation that were so visible in the Denham and Cantle reports again proved central to the offered analysis. However, while segregation and parallel lives remain key to the examination of the forces undermining Community Cohesion, the political heart of the report is shaped by an invocation of Blairite communitarian resolve with suggestions that the government should support a national vision of integration and cohesion and promote a 'shared futures' campaign. The 'assimilationist' trajectory of striving for a newly found common ground in a shared national identity along with the communitarian emphasis on mutual obligation is framed in this report by an emphasis on 'what binds communities together rather than what differences divide them' (Commission on Integration and Cohesion, 2007: 43). Thus, in its foundational values and policy agenda this report can be seen as both an implementation of the cumulative British retreat from multiculturalism and a powerfully unobtrusive contribution to advancing a nuanced assimilationist discourse. A sense of this politics is apparent very early in the report where one word underlines this retreat. In sketching out its initial view of the society it seeks to promote, the report states that it sees such a society as being a place where: 'people are committed to what we have in common rather than *obsessing* with those things that makes us different' (Commission on Integration and Cohesion, 2007: 3, emphasisis added).

The insertion of the word 'obsessing' tellingly indicates a political discourse turning its face away from a *rights*-based politics of difference to a more assimilationist agenda of cohesion defined through a future of shared values and opportunity as opposed to one which is built on diversity, equality and the eradication of inequalities (see the discussion of rights and citizenship in Chapter Six, this volume).

Our shared future distances itself from vulgar versions of the self-segregation rhetoric, noting that excessive coverage about residential segregation serves to spread a view that the whole of England is spatially segregated and that it overstates and oversimplifies the reality, leaving us 'sleepwalking into simplicity' (Commission on Integration and Cohesion, 2007: 3). However, as Kalra and Kapoor (2008) note, the report 'takes up the far more problematic notion of people living 'parallel lives' (Kalra and Kapoor, 2008: 6). In their paper Kalra and Kapoor seek to track the ways in which the policy debate around segregation has moved from an earlier concern with desegregation as a way to promote *material equality* to a current discourse which sees desegregation as a means to remove *cultural difference*. They argue that:

> The parallel lives discourse relies on the establishment of a stable whiteness against which the destabilizing effects of the Muslim 'other' are negatively attached. By entering into this terrain, any potential arguments about equality attached to desegregation are subsumed by a necessity for cultural homogeneity or for reducing the gap between the white and the other. (Kalra and Kapoor, 2008: 7)

Despite its acknowledgement of the different contributions that a diverse population may make to a shared future and despite its much more nuanced account of the possibilities of diverse co-existence, it remains the case that *Our shared future* focuses on ethnic and religious differences so that the question of social inequality becomes marginalised within the report. When we look to the recommendations within the report and to the subsequent government response and guidance, we can note the focus on social contact, and specifically intergroup contact, across religious and ethnic identities. The fact that Britain saw a growth in class segregation over the period of the most recent Labour governments (see Chapter Six, this volume) is conveniently neglected by this emphasis on Islam and culture.

The social psychology of the *contact hypothesis* is an ever-present sub-text in the language of Community Cohesion. Unfortunately for its latter day proponents, the rich literature on social contact points to the importance of the *conditions* under which contact takes place (see Pettigrew and Tropp, 2005). During the years of ethnic segregation in South Africa, or in the Southern States of the USA for that matter, there may well have been frequent and routine intergroup contact, but the social relations that defined the contact were intrinsic to segregation. As Letki (2005) notes, 'efforts to revive social cohesion through ... inter-community relations are misplaced if they under-emphasise material deprivation, crime and low community socio-economic status' (Letki, 2005: 24).

The strategic submergence of class inequalities that is inherent in the emergence of Labour Party policy around Community Cohesion means that even as a policy based on the limited aspirations of promoting improved intergroup relations, Community Cohesion is a two-legged stool. Seeking to promote Community Cohesion, while presiding over an increasing polarisation of the wealthy and the marginalised, is an act of political schizophrenia, which is almost admirable in its wilful ignorance and necessary suspension of disbelief. As political ideological practice, however, it may be considered successful in being a constituent element of New Labour's retreat from the pursuit of equality.

Community cohesion and its ideological baggage

A core ambition of this chapter has been to put the concept of Community Cohesion into its historical and political context. As we said in Chapter One, this book does not set out to provide an evaluation of the implementation of these policies but rather to explore the implications of their coexistence and their impact on British ethnic and religious relations. A key feature of this process is to reveal the inherent ideological properties of these two policies as they have been developed in the last decade. In the case of Community Cohesion, this chapter has sought to reveal the ideological baggage that has been built into its definition and implementation.

Community Cohesion as we saw earlier in this chapter was, in the British case, defined in distinction to social cohesion as having a specifically minority ethnic focus, and to be significantly detached from concerns with equality which were seen as the proper focus of social cohesion. Thus, as McGhee (2003: 393) observes:

> By focusing in the main on opening up channels of communication, on generating a culture of respect through attempting to encourage commonality – in place of division, what is observable in community cohesion discourses and programmes is a partial repression of 'conflict' achieved through discursively placing unwanted characteristics outside of the debate.

In its essentials this is a continuation of the *two Britains* politics that we saw developed within Thatcherism. There is a willingness to acknowledge some people and some political agendas as within the consensus of *Third Way* imagination but those who do not fit within this imaginary of democratic concern are consequently, and literally, peripheral. And, if, on occasion and for whatever reason, they do enter into consideration it is by definition as an aberrant problematic violation of the norm. As we have seen in relation to the citizenship debates, their deviation provides an opportunity to robustly reassert the norm. And as Flint (2009) demonstrates, the concern about establishing a normative set of values and behaviours for minority ethnic groups in Britain is transparent in government documentation, including 'the use of migrant information packs as a mechanism to achieve the micro-regulation of social interactions' (Flint, 2009: 135).

Thus a core achievement of Blairism was to erode the significance of class and to remove class conflict from the political agenda. Class, and class conflict in particular, was seen as the neurotic concern of *Old Labour* that had so effectively kept the Labour Party in the wilderness of political opposition for so long. Community Cohesion provided a discursive package that effectively detached minority ethnic communities, and specifically Muslim communities, from their disproportionate marginalisation within the class spectrum in Britain. Their problem became defined as being predominantly located within *their* cultural and religious distinctiveness, not within or due to structural determinants and forces.

Equally the language of Community Cohesion was co-opted into the political purposes of Blairism's commitment to civic renewal and a neo-nationalist reassertion of national identity defined through shared core values and history. Translated into the political shift from discourses of plural multiculturalism to those of assimilationist citizenship, Community Cohesion became the Trojan Horse which rendered illegitimate the identity politics at the heart of multiculturalism. But, given the national political elite's assertion that *multiculturalism had failed*, the anodyne, behaviourally oriented policies that spontaneously flow from the narrow construction of Community Cohesion have been politically congenial. They facilitated a refusal to engage in a self-critical exposure of the structural conditions that might have contributed to both the struggles of multiculturalism and the continuing demographic concentration of minority ethnic communities. Like class, 'race', and to a much greater extent anti-racism, has been effectively banished as a conceivable political agenda within government policy. Relegated as an unfortunate episode that flourished prior to the ascendancy of New Labour, racism, along with class-based exclusion, has been effectively sidelined in the pragmatic expression of Community Cohesion policies. Thus while 'race' hatred and Islamophobia have been capable of political and practical recognition, as the regrettable expressive behaviour of a minority of lumpen white citizens, the state has itself actively promoted a programme of categorical stereotyping of Muslim communities through the ways in which it has formulated and implemented its policies on Community Cohesion. It is *their* perceived self-segregation, and *their* wilful pursuit of parallel lives that has defined the purpose and the method of Community Cohesion policies.

The focus of the research that lies at the heart of this analysis has been on the experience of the local state in seeking to implement central government policy. Of course, this does have implications for our understanding of the outcomes that may be discerned as policy becomes practice. But it would be foolish and naive to enter into this process without first critically examining the political context within which this policy has developed. Consequently the aim of this chapter has been twofold: to provide the reader with a synopsis of that background, and to make explicit the fact that Community Cohesion is a *profoundly* ideological construction. Thus the question is not so much how successful have Community Cohesion policies been, but rather what is their political nature.

Notes

[1] Less well known are the 'race riots' which occurred in places such as Liverpool and Cardiff during 1919. Rising postwar unemployment fuelled the clashes between white and black communities partly resulting in the repatriation of some 600 individuals. See National Archives (nd).

[2] Similar sentiments have continued to feed into 'race relations' rhetoric and policy. For example, immigration policy, process and impact as well as, in particular, the ideals which underpin 'citizenship tests', all serve to suggest there is a proto-nationalist ideology supporting, perhaps subtly and unwittingly, conceptualisations of Britishness, diversity and integration.

[3] Given the political juxtaposition of anti-racist practice against 'softer' forms of 'persuasive' attitudinal approaches (Husband, 1991), we are clear that non-racist practice would require the antecedent operation of systemic anti-racist initiatives.

[4] The report of the Community Cohesion Independent Review Team (*The Cantle Report*, 2001), the 2002 *Guidance on community cohesion* produced by the Local Government Association et al and *The Ouseley Report* (2001) on Bradford.

[5] However, as its remit was driven by recent civil disturbances, it gave this, and other reviews, a focus that took local 'crises' to the level of national review with a propensity to neglect the substantial achievements of interethnic co-existence that had been achieved in other British cities.

[6] See Wacquant's *Urban outcasts* (2008) for a powerful critique of the use and abuse of the term 'ghetto'.

[7] 'Welfare cheats/scroungers', single mothers, large families, asylum seekers and others not connected explicitly with the labour market are often defined as unreasonable drains on the nation's resources; in particular the construction of this definition is often assisted by the tabloid press.

THREE

The prevention of violent extremism

Introduction

In the previous chapter we explored the unique development of the British version of social cohesion as it became conceived and emerged as Community Cohesion. In this chapter we seek to provide a similar understanding of the emergence of counter-terrorism policies in Britain following the London bombings of 7 July 2005. In tracking this development we will again see that this particular policy did not emerge in a policy vacuum, but that rather it was developed within a framework shaped by past experiences of terrorism in the UK, and by other instances of civil crisis. Again, the centrality of Britain's Muslim populations to the specific shaping of this policy is outlined. The transition from the initial formulation of Prevent, in CONTEST I, to its reshaping, following the critical response to its early roll out, in CONTEST II, reflects the problematic nature of this policy. Recent government reports on the operation of Prevent provide a further basis for exploring the inherent difficulties that have emerged as Prevent has been implemented in the context of parallel Community Cohesion policies.

In order to place this policy process into a wider context the issue of the ways in which the terrorist threat comes to be popularly understood is explored, and the symbiotic relationships between the media, the government and terrorists is opened up for consideration. In a similar vein the relation between the specifics of counter-terrorism and the wider growth of perceived threats to security as a many headed problem is discussed through a brief exploration of the 'securitisation' of urban policy in general. Again, the intention is to place our understanding of the specifics of Prevent within a wider framework. The chapter closes with a discussion of the tension between security and civil freedoms and the significance of the assault on support for human rights principles for our understanding of both how the political process of putting Prevent in place, and evaluating its impact, has been shaped by these wider issues.

Emergence of British counter-terrorist policy post the London bombings

Hennessy (2007a) recounts that the British have been depicted as having the habit of going into major changes (such as accession to the European Economic Community in the 1970s and the Human Rights Act of the late 1990s) 'as if under an anaesthetic' and only much later do people comprehend the significance of the huge constitutional changes that have been introduced. In this context, and in speaking of what he calls the 'protective state' of intelligence and security, he observes that:

> ... the construction of the wider protective state since 2001 falls into this 'anaesthetic' category. Parliament, public and the press have yet to appreciate fully either its scope and magnitude-in-the-round or its long-term significance to our systems of government and the kind of country we are. (Hennessy, 2007b: 6)

There is something of a paradox built into this analysis, since although the organisational and policy changes in the British management of British security since 9/11 have been extensive in their nature and ramifications, they have also been accompanied by a remarkable openness in the public disclosure, through government publications, of the workings of the British security system. The intense secrecy about the structure and operational workings of the British intelligence that was characteristic of the 'Cold War' period has now been replaced by what appears to be a remarkable transparency. As Tebbit (2007: 74) commented, 'Much has been published recently, by the Government and by informed "insiders"[1] about the nature of the threat from international terrorism *and the strategies to counter it*' (emphasis added).

A major demonstration of this openness can be found in the remarkable candour of the 2006 White Paper, *Countering international terrorism: The United Kingdom's strategy*, which outlines the nature of the challenge in blunt terms:

> The Government assesses that the current threat in the UK from Islamist terrorism is serious and sustained. British citizens also face the threat of terrorist attacks when abroad. Overall we judge that the scale of the threat is potentially still increasing and is not likely to diminish significantly for some years ... as the tragic attacks of 7th July, 2005 have

shown, it is not possible to eliminate completely the threat of
terrorist attacks in this country. (HM Government, 2006:8)

This explicit judgement of the security risk presented by contemporary
terrorist outrages signals a marked shift in the conception of the nature
of the threat that the British population faces, and hence of the remit it is
invited to present to the 'protective state' in order to guarantee its safety.
In the epoch of the nuclear Cold War, the potential scale of the assault
was catastrophic but, given the capacity for retaliation (the essence of
the philosophy of 'deterrence'), the likelihood of such an attack was,
as a consequence, relatively small. In the current era of Al-Qaeda and
terrorist attacks, the scale of the loss and damage that may be inflicted,
while still horrendous, is not on the same scale as nuclear war. However,
the likelihood of such attacks successfully eluding the security services
is quite high. Small cells of terrorists operating with considerable
autonomy and requiring minimal infrastructure and munitions make
them hard to detect and eliminate. The fact that random death is the
essence of terrorism additionally means that the potential targets are
innumerable, and interchangeable. We are all targets. These realities
define both the challenge faced by security services and the sense of
exposure felt by the British population. It is consequently the necessary
logics of intrusive and extensive counter-terrorist surveillance that
requires the public to be made self-consciously aware of their own
vulnerability, and hence likely to see the sense in under-writing the
counter-terrorist strategies developed by *their* 'protective state'.

The logics of Cold War hostilities were framed by a state-to-state
dynamic in which intuiting the intentions of 'hostile' states formed a key
part of the intelligence brief. In contemporary Britain the intentions
of Al-Qaeda-inspired terrorists are relatively transparent but specifically
identifying these enemies remains a tenaciously elusive and problematic
task. (The nature of Islamic terrorist threats worldwide has become
increasingly complex, and we should note that the use of the catch-
all term 'Al-Qaeda' suggests political and organisational homogeneity
that is belied by the reality; see, for example, Esposito, 2002: 18-25;
Cesari, 2004: 100-9; and especially, Bonney, 2004). Particularly with the
emergence of 'home-grown' bombers the threat cannot be assumed to
be external. And the remarkable 'normality' of detected home-grown
terrorists undermines any simple 'identikit' construction of the proto-
terrorist that can guide intelligence and surveillance (Cantor, 2009).
Consequently, we are all potentially suspect and therefore legitimate
targets for surveillance. Well, not quite. Given the faith-based nature of
jihadist terrorism, Muslim communities have been specifically identified

as targets for the attentions of the multiple agents of the protective state as surveillance has now extended well beyond the finite number of employees of the intelligence services.

It is this intersection of the high probability of terrorist attacks and the ubiquitous reach of the necessary logics of counter-terrorism which brings the consensual support of the public into sharp relief. As we have noted, all citizens may legitimately regard themselves as potential targets of lethal terrorist attacks; the question remains whether they reciprocally perceive themselves to be the legitimate targets of intrusive intelligence surveillance. In this context, the contemporary greater openness[2] in discussing the nature of the terrorist threat *and* of the security response cannot be seen as innocent of political intent. The British public are increasingly, and in many ways, being drawn into the apparatus of the protective state as peripheral agents of the intelligence community; as teachers, lecturers, community workers and neighbours they are invited (expected/required) to remain vigilant for any behaviours that may be an indication that a fellow-citizen may be a terrorist. And of course they are themselves subject to the same intrusive environment of surveillance. Public support for both of these realities is a central agenda of legitimating the new protective state.

However, the elements of this protective state did not leap *ab initio* from any security vacuum. Britain and the British have a long experience of the operation of state security, and the relatively recent experience of Irish Republican terrorism in mainland England has provided a fruitful foundation for the post-9/11 evolution of the current protective state (see Hillyard, 2006). From the late 1960s the emergence of 'The Troubles' in Northern Ireland had a significant impact on the security of mainland Britain. The pursuit of IRA terrorists in Northern Ireland involved major intelligence activity and, in the words of Hennessy, 'the stimulus the IRA had given to surveillance techniques generally has proved of great value in combating jihadist terrorism' (Hennessy (2007b: 30). Not least is the use of CCTV, now developed to such an extent that the British have become the most visually monitored population in Europe (see House of Lords: *Surveillance, citizens and the state*, 2009). 'The Troubles' also demonstrated how specific violent outrages can radically shape changes in law and policy, a feature that was repeated with the 2001 urban disorders in northern England and the social cohesion agenda.

The lethal bombing in Birmingham on 21 November 1974, by the Provisional IRA, resulting in 24 deaths and the injury of nearly 200, spurred the then Home Secretary, Roy Jenkins, to rush the Prevention of Terrorism Bill through Parliament which included provisions 'which had now become acceptable although they would not hitherto have been so' (Jenkins, 1991: 393). The Act rendered the IRA a proscribed organisation, empowered the police to detain terrorist suspects, without charge, for 48 hours on their own authority, and for a further five days subject to getting the authority from the relevant Minister of the Crown. The Act also allowed the Home Secretary to exclude from Great Britain citizens of the Republic of Ireland where he had reason to believe that they were involved, or likely to be involved, in acts of terrorism. The incursions into the exercise of established liberties under British law, which were concretely enabled by this Act, demonstrated how terrorism is capable of spreading its negative impact through the repressive legislation and related policies that it provokes. And, in a comparable way, the fear and outrage among the wider public that is also generated by terrorist violence, contributes to shifts in popular opinion, and even values, that serve to facilitate the legitimacy of the state's repressive reactions.

So, too, in 2001, following the atrocities of 9/11, an extensive Anti-Terrorism, Crime and Security Act was rapidly passed through Parliament. Elements of this Act, such as deporting foreign nationals to countries with poor human rights records, were in violation of the European Convention on Human Rights. However, in the urgency of 2001 this was not a sufficient hindrance to its parliamentary passage. The House of Lords, in December, 2004, subsequently overturned this legislation as being incompatible with the European Convention on Human Rights and discriminatory as it only applied to foreign nationals. The government then countered this with legislative finesse, invoking 'non-derogating' control orders in the Prevention of Terrorism Act 2005. The report of the House of Lords/House of Commons Joint Committee on Human Rights (2010) provides a worrying account of the struggle of the judiciary to counter the British government's attempts to circumvent international human rights principles and judgements. As we shall see below, the government has found the role of the judiciary in protecting the rule of law a significant irritation, as they have sought to press through counter-terrorism measures.[3]

Interestingly, as Tebbit (2007) has illustrated, the first major and explicit government policy statement on counter-terrorist policy after 9/11 came from the Ministry of Defence in the form of *The strategic defence review: A new chapter* (HM Government, 2002), a major review of the UK's defence strategy and plans. The 'New chapter' provided an explicit account of the military input to counter-terrorism and, as such, was an early contribution to the evolving interagency coordination that has become a dominant feature of British counter-terrorism structures and planning (see Hennessy, 2007a; Tebbit, 2007). While recognising that the fight against militant Islam could not be won by force alone and while asserting that it is preferable to engage the threat through action overseas 'in their own backyards', rather than at home, the 'New chapter' is clear that the military should be available to be called on for specialised elements of protection at home. In asserting this, the Ministry of Defence was consolidating the relevance of its own internal priorities in so far as planned UK Rapid Reaction Forces would necessitate 'improved communications, intelligence, command and control capabilities, strategic and tactical transport, campaign logistics' (Tebbit, 2007:85) while becoming equally relevant to counter-terrorist activities. In this the Ministry of Defence were providing an early example of a general phenomenon,[4] whereby a wide range of partisan actors seek to maximise their own interests by capitalising on the exceptional context provided by this fetid counter-terrorist political environment (for example, the police, security and surveillance technology companies and policy advisers).

In preparing the 'New chapter', the Ministry of Defence, along with other government departments, would have already been on a rapid learning curve initiated by three civilian major emergencies that came with the millennium, what Mottram calls 'the three F's' (Mottram, 2007: 45), referring to the extensive *flooding and fuel crises* of 2000 as well as the *foot and mouth crisis* of 2001. These events demonstrated the complex interdependencies that are characteristic of modern society. And this 'triple whammy' of F's was, as Mottram (2007) argues, particularly effective in revealing the current lack of prior preparedness for interagency action in dealing with such emergencies. Given that, as we have noted above, there could be no absolute guarantee of preventing terrorist outrages, the nature of crisis management and its need to respond to major civil crises was recognised as having clear synergies with the preparedness necessary, not to stop terrorist outrages, but to be capable of efficiently responding to their aftermath. Thus, the Civil Contingencies Act 2004:

> … swept up and revised existing emergency powers and civil defence legislation, fusing them, in a single statute, with the generic capabilities needed to deal with the consequences of a terrorist assault on people, infrastructure, essential services and systems. (Hennessy, 2007b: 13)

The Ministry of Defence's 'New chapter' and the extensive range of agencies and ministries involved in the production of the Civil

Contingencies Act 2004 valuably underline the importance of not arbitrarily encapsulating any understanding of Britain's emerging protective state over the last two decades within a perspective confined to intelligence and policing. Even in the very brief sketch presented here it is apparent that 'risk awareness' is entering into a widening public sphere of debate where an expectation of state competence to intervene and manage crises is rehearsed and refined. So, too, individual agencies have become increasingly sensitive to the necessity of developing rehearsed and sophisticated capacities to operate coherently that go well beyond simple contingency plans. Routine interdepartmental and interagency operation has become a dominant *leit motif* of the protective state. Anti-terrorist legislation continues to evolve, as, for example, with the Terrorism Act 2006, but the core structure has been clearly laid out in *Countering international terrorism* (HM Government, 2006).

As outlined in that document, the government's counter-terrorism strategy, known as CONTEST, has a structure that reflects the four elements at its heart: *prevention, pursuit, protection* and *preparation*. Hennessy (2007b) provides a valuable, and informed, schematic outline of the organisational structure laid out in CONTEST that is drawn on here. He points out that by 2006 (Hennessy 2007b: 27) each of the four elements was accountable to its own ministerially led committee or TIDO (Terrorism International Defence and Overseas), comprising of civil servants, the intelligence community and the military, reflecting the interdepartmental/interagency ethos noted above. Each of these in turn is accountable to an overarching Strategy and Delivery TIDO, chaired by the government's security and intelligence coordinator. Additionally, the integration of the 'four P's' is further facilitated by three wide-ranging TIDOs that span the activities of the 'four P's'. These are: 'TIDO – Communications', which widely ensures compatibility and coherence in communications; 'TIDO – Overseas', which ensures joined-up thinking across strategy; and 'TIDO – Research and Development', which deals with counter-terrorist equipment and techniques. Thus, the focus on collaborative working outlined in, for example, the thinking behind the Civil Contingencies Act 2004 and the Ministry of Defence's 2003 White Paper, *Delivering security in a changing world* (HM Government, 2003), is evident in the structure for the management of the new protective state.

The 'four P's' provided a logical distribution of responsibilities for addressing the differing issues that are real and potential in the context of contemporary international terrorism. As the updated policy of CONTEST II (HM Government, 2009: 13) succinctly phrased it:

> CONTEST is intended to be a comprehensive strategy:
> Work on *Pursue* and *Prevent* reduces the threat from
> terrorism: work on *Protect* and *Prepare* reduces the UK's
> vulnerability to attack.

Prepare addresses the challenge of ensuring an adequate organisational
and resource capacity to be able to address the consequences of a
terrorist attack. This is an agenda that was given particular emphasis by
the inadequate response capability that was fulsomely demonstrated in
the case of the 'triple whammy' of the 'three F's' as discussed above. Of
course, it is clear that adequate preparation is contingent on an accurate
understanding of the potential nature and scale of the terrorist attacks
and their immediate and long-term consequences.

Protect addresses the protection of the public, key national services
and British overseas interests. The long history of responding to
Irish Republican terrorism has provided a significant basis for the
development of current policy and practice.

Pursue addresses the challenge of pursuing terrorists and those who
sponsor them. This agenda is highly dependent on cooperation between
intelligence agencies at home and abroad. Not only is 'intelligence'
critical to this task, but where, for example, pursuit involves action
across different state jurisdictions, diplomatic and legal matters will
need to be addressed.

Prevent is the TIDO most central to our concerns here. Although
it would be naive and unhelpful to believe that this agenda can be
understood in its operation independently of the other 'three P's',
Mottram provides us with a succinct outline:

> The 'Prevent' element of the Government's counter-
> terrorism strategy identifies three principal strands of effort
> whose breadth illustrates the extent of the challenge:
>
> 1. Tackling disadvantage and supporting reform –
>   addressing structural problems in the UK and overseas,
>   such as inequalities and discrimination.
> 2. Deterring those who facilitate terrorism and those who
>   encourage others to become terrorists – changing the
>   environment in which seeking to turn others towards
>   extremism and terrorist violence can operate.
> 3. Engaging in the battle of ideas – challenging the
>   ideologies that extremists believe can justify the use of

violence, primarily by helping Muslims who wish to
dispute these ideas to do so. (Mottram, 2007: 50)

In discussing these three elements of 'Prevent', Mottram (as the previous
Security and Intelligence Coordinator of TIDO Strategy and Delivery,
and subsequently Permanent Secretary, Intelligence, Security and
Resilience in the Cabinet Office) argues that tackling disadvantage
and supporting reform 'is a huge task with uncertain payback in
counter-terrorist terms' (Mottram, 2007: 50). Part of his justification
for this conclusion is that in the UK those who become drawn into
terrorism are not themselves particularly disadvantaged in educational
or employment terms. This may be true of the individual terrorist, but
it is hardly true of the communities from which they are drawn. The
situation of many Muslim minority communities in Britain places
them, as a collectivity, within areas of high multiple deprivation where
their children are frequently located in poorer, less well-resourced
schools (Loury et al, 2005). While there is social mobility within these
communities, with movement out of the inner-city areas (Simpson,
2004; Finney and Simpson, 2009), it remains the case that disadvantage,
discrimination and Islamophobic prejudice and violence remain all too
frequent facets of life for many of Britain's Muslims. Consequently,
Mottram's (2007) qualifying phrase to his initial conclusion somewhat
undermines his confident assertion that: 'the impact of perceived
discrimination affecting them or others in encouraging alienation
is difficult to judge' (Mottram, 2007: 50). Quite so. The evidence
suggests that terrorists are driven by a commitment to an inclusive
shared religious/political identity. The social psychology of intergroup
behaviour robustly demonstrates the radical shift in perspective and
behaviour that follows from an individual conceiving of their actions
as being driven by their conscious perception of intergroup events,
rather than in interpersonal terms (Capozza and Brown, 2000; Brewer
and Hewstone, 2004; and see Chapter Four, this volume).

It is for this reason that events in Palestine, Afghanistan and Iraq
are relevant to proto-terrorist sentiments, as are the circumstances of
Muslim communities in inner-city Britain.[5] However, government
policy that seeks to sustain an arbitrary *cordon sanitaire* between foreign
policy and the internal policies of counter-terrorism can only be kindly
described as naive wishful thinking. In January 2009 Gordon Brown's
security and counter-terrorism minister, Lord West of Spithead, offered
up an insight into the previous regime's view on this matter. He is
reported in *The Guardian* as saying: 'We never used to accept that our
foreign policy ever had any effect on terrorism....Well, that was clearly

bollocks. They [the Blair administration] were very unwilling to have any debate about how our foreign policy impacted on radicalisation' (cited in Booth, 2009). Speaking of the then current Israeli assaults on Gaza he also noted, 'The business in Gaza has not helped us at all in our counter-radicalism strategy' (Booth, 2009). The same article reported the head of MI5, Jonathan Evans, as saying that the Israeli action had given extremist groups in the UK more ideological ammunition while community groups working with young Muslims reported that the Israeli action had set back their efforts by years. It is interesting therefore to note that according to the more recent CONTEST II: 'Unresolved regional disputes and conflicts', particularly those of 'Palestine, Afghanistan, Bosnia, Chechnya, Lebanon, Kashmir and Iraq' (HM Government, 2009: 41), are identified as one of the four strategic factors that may shape the rise of terrorism and therefore must be addressed.

Comments such as these indicate the impossibility of ring-fencing the counter-terrorist activities of Prevent from the domestic impact of British foreign policy. The transnational and diasporic connectedness of members of Britain's Muslim populations gives them an organic linkage to events taking place beyond the territory of the UK. For some, this linkage is mediated by ongoing familial connections with family and friends in their original country of ancestral heritage (regardless of their generational location among their settled 'immigrant' community). Thus, for example, US bombing of targets in the Federally Administered Tribal Areas (FATA) bordering Afghanistan is not necessarily a distant and barely significant event for those British citizens who still have relatives there. And, more generically, the reciprocal face of Islamophobia has been the complementary consolidation of Islam as a salient shared identity. As social identity theory (Capozza and Brown, 2000) suggests, an external threat presented to members of a group with pronounced and shared markers of identity has a recognised capacity to further promote in-group identification.

Perhaps one of the most important markers of shared group identity among Muslims, regardless of schism or sect, is the notion and the actuality of *Ummah*, the global, quasi-diasporic 'community of believers, Muslims' (Bonney, 2004: xxvi). Islam and being Muslim functions at a trans- or supranational level and while echoing some features of 'diaspora' (Werbner, 2002), it also exists beyond an original 'national' space. For Muslims, although there is a pull toward the cities of Mecca and Medina, there is no 'homeland' as such. Nevertheless, what *Ummah* is, how it is shaped and affected has both personal and group dimensions. Indeed, as Werbner notes:

> Being a Muslim *diasporan* does not entail an imperative of
> physical return to a lost homeland. It enables Pakistanis
> to foster and yet defer indefinitely their fulfilment of the
> myth of their return back home, while asserting their
> present responsibility for fellow diasporan Muslims – their
> membership in a transnational moral, religious community,
> the *umma*. (Werbner, 2002: 12)

The spiritual and humanitarian realities and ideals that are interwoven
into the idea of *Ummah* enable Muslims to look beyond identification
along lines of nationality and, in theory, ethnicity. A British Muslim,
therefore has commonality with Muslims in Australia, Sudan, Pakistan
or the US. When Muslims learn of global Muslim hotspots – whether
in relation to conflict or catastrophe – there may be a very real sense
of connection that fosters sympathetic and empathetic responses.

Construction of Prevent and its focus on Islam

As we shall see below, the introduction of Prevent presented challenges
for local authorities and met with a range of negative responses
from within Muslim communities and elsewhere. The introduction
of Prevent, and the roll out of the first phase of initiatives under
the Pathfinder programme, met with considerable resistance from
Muslim communities who resented the ways in which they had been
specifically stigmatised, and from local authority staff who had political
and operational concerns about the Prevent agenda. Responding to
these experiences, in March 2009 the government produced *The United
Kingdom's strategy for countering international terrorism* (HM Government,
2009), in which the Home Secretary (Jacqui Smith) in her Foreword
to the document, reported that:

> … the threat is always changing. New groups emerge and
> terrorists continue to develop new methods and make use
> of new technologies. Learning from our experience over the
> past few years, we have updated all aspects of our strategy
> to take account of this changing threat. (HM Government,
> 2009: 7)

In presenting this new policy statement the government acknowledged
that in the 2003 CONTEST strategy Prevent had been the least
developed strand of policy. Arguing that this 'completely revised strategy'
is based on 'a new analysis of the causes of radicalisation in this country

and overseas and on contributions from a wide range of Departments, agencies and community organisations' (HM Government, 2009: 58, para 7.11), CONTEST II asserts that over the next three years the Prevent element of this policy will have five main objectives. Namely:

> To challenge the ideology behind violent extremism and support mainstream voices.
> Disrupt those who promote violent extremism and support the places where they operate.
> Support individuals who are vulnerable to recruitment, or have already been recruited by violent extremists.
> Increase the resilience of communities to violent extremism.
> To address the grievances which ideologues are exploiting. (HM Government, 2009: 12, para 0.33)

Echoing the concerns of CONTEST I, this document notes that 'Because the greatest threat at present is from terrorists who claim to act in the name of Islam, much *Prevent* activity takes place in and with Muslim communities' (HM Government, 2009: 15, para 0.36). The reality behind this statement is argued in the extensive review in Part 1 of the document which seeks to outline the 'Strategic context' of the UK's current terrorism threat. A key issue in making sense of the critiques of Prevent, and of our data, is to maintain a critical balance in evaluating the specificity of Muslim–related terrorism, and the adequacy and proportionality of the responses to it. Indeed, in responding to the then extant critiques of Prevent, and perhaps also anticipating those that were to come, CONTEST II, follows this statement of the centrality of Muslim threat with a qualifying sentence, promising that: 'the principles of our Prevent work apply equally to other communities who may be the focus of attention from violent extremist groups' (HM Government, 2009: 81). It is not too cynical to suggest that while the *principles* of Prevent under CONTEST II might well apply equally to far right terrorist threats, the major body of Prevent work has nonetheless continued to focus on Muslim communities and Muslim citizens.

Significantly for our analysis here, CONTEST II (HM Government, 2009: 84, para 9.13) makes explicit links between community cohesion, 'race' equality and Prevent. It argues that extremists are less likely to find support in cohesive communities and reciprocally that communities which isolate extremism are likely to increase levels of community cohesion. Additionally it suggests that 'race' equality policies in challenging inequalities can contribute to addressing the grievances that feed extremism. In a section entitled 'Promoting our shared values' (HM Government, 2009: 87), these threads are linked together in a familiar communitarian concern about the shared values that must bind together both community cohesion and the rejection of extremism. What is more, in the initiatives outlined under the Prevent agenda, the basis for a confusion between projects that are under the imprimateur of Community Cohesion and those under Prevent is apparent. Anticipating one of the findings from our research, the different funding streams flowing from Prevent show a mix of agencies and departments that provide a structural basis for the inter- and multi-agency working that has become so central to Prevent. Additionally, the significance of the local context for providing both the territorial location and the specific interagency working that is central to CONTEST in general and to Prevent in particular is spelt out in Section 14 of CONTEST II, where it asserts that:

> Our revised *Prevent* strategy puts local delivery at its heart: the national strategy sets the framework, overall objectives and standards but we recognize that the way in which the objectives are met and the type of programmes that are required must reflect specific local circumstances. (HM Government, 2009: 139, para 14.03)

Given the focus of Prevent on potential radicalisation within local communities, this commitment to a form of subsidiarity at the point of programme delivery is a logical necessity. Indeed, our data below speaks loudly of the significance of the ownership of this challenge by the local authorities and of the critical relevance of their local knowledge and expertise for the delivery of both Prevent and Community Cohesion. However, it must also be said that our data shows an inability of central government to yield up this level of local autonomy. Often, our respondents complain of the weight of guidance coming from central government seeking to micro-manage these policies from the centre.

In sum, CONTEST II stands out as a clear statement of the government's response to their own learning curve as they seek to absorb their new knowledge about the nature of the challenge they face, and to react to critiques of their initial CONTEST policy and practice. CONTEST II is a document which continues the practice of providing considerable transparency into both government thinking around counter-terrorism, and into the structures and resources that they have put into place in order to meet the challenge of terrorist threat. However, this new policy was in no way adequate to stem the cumulative body of critiques that continued to build up around the Prevent agenda (see, for example, Kundnani, 2009a).

In March 2010, the Communities and Local Government Committee (CLGC) of the House of Commons (CLGC, 2010) produced a report entitled *Preventing violent extremism* which proved to be a robust assessment of evidence that it had elicited in reviewing the performance of Prevent. The conclusions of this parliamentary report provide a recent and supportive framework for the data that is presented in our analysis below. Questions around the reasonableness and proportionality of the government's response through Prevent in specifically targeting Muslim communities are widely visible throughout this report. The issue of the 'targeting' of Muslim communities within the Prevent programme receives wide coverage in the evidence taken and in the report's analysis. It is telling, then, that in its 'Summary' statement the report concludes that:

> ... the single focus on Muslims in *Prevent* has been unhelpful. We conclude that any programme which focuses solely on one section of a community is stigmatising, potentially alienating, and fails to address the fact that no section of a population exists in isolation from others. (CLGC, 2010: 3)

Three paragraphs later the report again underlines the dangers of this narrow focus on Islam, by concluding that:

> Regarding the Government's analysis of the factors which lead people to become involved in violent extremism, we conclude that there has been a pre-occupation with the theological basis of radicalisation, when the evidence seems to indicate that politics, policy and socio-economics may be more important factors in the process. (CLGC, 2010: 3)

The CLGC report (2010) addresses the many accusations against Prevent seeking to assert the policy as a vehicle for spying on the Muslim communities in Britain. Indeed, the evidence reproduced in that report, and published elsewhere, provides substance for that charge. What is interesting is that when in the report Charles Farr, Director General of the Office of Security and Counter Terrorism (OSCT), seeks to refute the charge, it appears that the essence of the rebuttal is based around definitions of 'support' and spying:

Clearly if someone is involved in activity which suggests they are being drawn into the world of violent extremism, such as ... browsing a chat room or operating in a chat room, which is clearly one of those which encourages violent extremism, if that activity stops short of something which is illegal under the Terrorism Acts, notably TACT 2006 [Terrorism Act], that is the sort of person we would expect to get referred to Channel, not to criminalise them but precisely to avoid them criminalising themselves. That process by any reasonable definition of the term 'spying' and certainly by the definition in UK law does not amount to spying. Spying defined by the Security Service Act makes it absolutely clear who does covert operations. Channel enables the referral by people for the purposes of crime prevention to a group comprising of local authority and police members. That person is not then, as it were, subject to surveillance, they are provided with support which is precisely intended – I repeat – to stop them being, as it were, drawn into violent extremism and thence into the criminal justice system. (CLGC, 2010: 16, para 35)

One of the major sources of concern around the implementation of Prevent has been the fear and resentment within Muslim communities that the local authority personnel and other partners in Prevent have become by default an insidious infrastructure for surveillance which is routinely spying on their community. Spying is a very emotive term, but then a sense of being placed under routine observation through which the innocent actions of your daily life may be given a totally unjustified, but seriously threatening, meaning by strangers is itself alarming. When this perceived scrutiny is taking place within the context of a heightened public anxiety around terrorism, and your community has been specifically labelled as the potential source of future terrorists, then such concerns have a powerful legitimacy.

The routine collection of information that takes place across the many actors involved in the Prevent partnerships, as revealed in the interviews for this project underpinning the analysis and findings within our text, may not indeed involve 'covert' action, but it does nevertheless constitute a reporting back on the behaviour of identified subjects; in terms of the casuistry of the OSCT quoted above this is, if not spying, then certainly intrusive surveillance. The referral of young people into the Channel element of Prevent is, for example, dependent on observation, judgement and transmission of concerns to cognate authorities, reports that may emanate from a wide variety of sources feeding into Prevent partnerships.

Given these realities and this concern it is significant that the CLGC report cannot dispel these criticisms as unfounded. In fact their judgement is similar to the Scottish legal system's verdict of 'not proven'. In conclusion, they state:

> ... we cannot ignore the volume of evidence we have seen and heard which demonstrates a continuing lack of trust of the programme amongst those delivering and receiving services. Based on the evidence we have received, it is not possible for us to take a view. (CLGC, 2010: 18, para 40)

They go on to suggest that if the government wish to improve public confidence in the Prevent programme then they should commission an independent investigation into the allegations.(Certainly the House of Lords, (2009) Constitution Committee report, *Surveillance: citizens and the state*, makes uncomfortable reading in this context).

Importantly for our analysis presented below, in reviewing the relationship between Prevent and Community Cohesion it is significant that the CLGC report (in Section 5) underlines the degree of overlap and confusion surrounding the interaction of these two policies. Anticipating the evidence from this study, the report asserts in its 'Summary' statement that:

> We agree with the majority of our witnesses that *Prevent* risks undermining positive cross-cultural work on cohesion and capacity building to combat exclusion and alienation in many communities. (CLGC, 2010: 3)

One of the core aspects of activity that may foster greater levels of social cohesion, then, is posited as being undermined by Prevent. Indeed, the report goes on to assert:

> Despite significant efforts by Government to clarify that *Prevent* focuses on al-Qaeda terrorism (as opposed to Muslims *per se*), Muslim communities have felt unfairly targeted and branded as potential terrorists. The strategy has contributed to a sense of frustration and alienation amongst Muslims which may increase the risk of making some individuals more vulnerable to radicalisation. (CLGC, 2010: 11, para 21)

Thus this parliamentary review of the roll out and impact of the Prevent policy has produced a very troubling, if not exactly damning, account of its misconceived policies and perversely negative consequences.

Not to be left out of the parliamentary scepticism surrounding the nature and efficacy of Prevent, the House of Lords/House of Commons Joint Committee on Human Rights of March 2010 raised serious doubts about the credibility of the nature of the threat which the government so assiduously rehearsed as legitimating the raft of counter-terrorist strategies it had put in place. In their unambiguous words:

> Since September 11th 2001 the Government has continuously justified many of its counter-terrorism measures on the basis that there is a public emergency threatening the life of the nation. We question whether the country has been in such a state for more than eight years. This permanent state of emergency inevitably has a deleterious effect on public debate about the justification for counter-terrorism measures. (House of Lords/House of Commons JCHR, 2010: 3)

In sum, the Prevent agenda emerged as a response to a very specific perception, interpretation and analysis of reality. This reality was shocking and reasonably understood as presenting a new challenge to the security of the population of the UK. The development of the response did not, however, take place in a policy vacuum but rather built very heavily on the recent British repertoire of responding to terrorist threats. It also took place in a world that had been radically reshaped by the events of 9/11 and more specifically by the fetid politics of the 'War on Terror' which followed. The specifics of Prevent which concern us in this analysis have therefore developed within a context which is widely described as the *securitisation* of civil society (Hughes, 2009). Infused into this context has been the very particular identity of the Muslim population of the UK. As the CLGC report accurately pointed out, the *de facto* reality of Muslim involvement in the bombings, and the global significance of Islam-related terrorism, put this population centrally within the concerns of counter-terrorist strategy and delivery. The problematic issue that followed has, however, centred around the appropriateness and proportionality of the responses that have been developed. The media have undoubtedly been significant players in the way in which the nature of the threat and the characteristics of the Muslim communities have been represented. As we shall see below, mass media (in particular news and current affairs genres) have been assisting in the construction of an Islamicist terrorist threat with a variety of actors who have vigorously pursued their interests in shaping British counter-terrorist policy.

Muslims, the media and terrorism

Media and representing diversity

While we have observed above a range of evidence pointing to the current social construction of Islam as alien and potentially threatening, we should also look to some form of understanding of how this state of affairs has come about. In Chapter Four we shall give some attention to the historical relations and the attendant imagery that has contributed to the current manifestations of anti-Muslimism. But here we need to enquire how it is that a demographic reality which indicates that Britain is *de facto* an implacably multi-ethnic society, with a particular spatial dispersal of the population by ethnic and class criteria, becomes translated into a heavily politicised discourse in which multiculturalism as a principle and practice of managing diversity has become vilified (Kundnani, 2007b; McGhee, 2008); while at the same time a neurotic form of neo-nationalism, following the internal growth of national devolution and the post-colonial loss of status on the world stage, has all but equated a legitimate reproduction of ethnic diversity as an assault on Britain's national integrity (Fekete, 2009). One key player in this process is the mass media.

In relation to the concerns with social cohesion and counter-terrorism that are at the heart of this text, the mass media continually emerge as central and necessary to the processes that create a consensus defining both popular and elite understandings of the dynamics of immigration and integration. At the same time, the mass media shape the definition of intergroup relations that in turn feed into affirmations or assaults on ethnic and gendered identities. Mass media take part in the setting of a framework for understanding the state of national security, thus channelling a persuasive legitimation for counter-terrorism measures that would previously have been regarded as 'un-British'. A brief examination of each of these phenomena is therefore useful as a means of further establishing and filling out the nature of the context within which policy is constructed and operates.

Mass communication theory and research has a long history of looking at the ways in which the media impact on their publics. One widely employed conception refers to the distinction between the *agenda setting* and the *framing* functions of the media. Agenda setting refers to ways in which the media, through an emphasis on some issues and not others, helps shape a narrow consensus on what are the most salient concerns of our time. Framing processes emerge as a consequence of the *manner* in which the media contextualise these issues and provide a limited repertoire of ideas and stories which enable the population to try to make sense of these issues. Thus, for example, in 1974 Hartmann and Husband demonstrated how immigration became a powerful agenda in public discourse framed by a language of 'colour' and of 'threat', rather than, for example, with a reflection on the desperate demand for labour required in re-energising postwar Britain and its economy (see Scheufele and Tewksbury, 2007, for a valuable review of the relevant literature).

Thus, agenda setting and framing is a filtering process whereby the media, through their own internal routines and priorities, create a narrow range of news and other 'stories' which provide accounts of current events that necessarily narrow and situate the public's cognitive understanding of them (Reese et al, 2001). They construct an effective consensus about how the events *should* be understood which both shapes future reporting and which predisposes their audience to find further use of this framing as non-problematic. Through processes of agenda setting and framing, then, centred, normative and *reasonable* positions are achieved and, furthermore, rendered real, realistic and, of course, unbiased. In the British context, however, there is a wide body of research literature which has cumulatively indicated how the media have provided powerful, and partisan, accounts of the development of Britain as a multi-ethnic society (see Hartmann and Husband, 1974; Troyna, 1981; Law, 2000). There has been an incestuous feedback loop between British politicians' 'playing of the race card' in seeking popular electoral advantage and the media's reflexion, and exacerbation, of this discourse. Of course, the media are not monolithic in the coverage of issues and while selective perception on the part of media audiences play a significant role in shaping the impact of the media, the pragmatics of media production are key (see Downing and Husband, 2005). Furthermore, we are familiar with what Hall et al (1978) referred to as *primary definers*, namely those elite people[6] who have privileged access to the media. At the same time, these elites are sourced by the media as an aide to establishing, qualifying and often developing news items, thus disproportionately shaping content. Some reportage is sensationalist and explicitly seeks to engage prejudiced sentiments, while other reportage, by merely excluding other voices, reproduces a narrow conception and messaging of 'race relations' in crisis. The current greater visibility of 'minority' persons in the media has been no guarantee that minority voices are in fact given a representative hearing (Campion, 2005). The reporting of Muslims in Britain has been marked by exactly this form of conceptual distortion and prejudice (Poole, 2002; Richardson, 2001; Poole and Richardson, 2006). Indeed, as Kundnani notes:

> Since September 11, media attention has focused on Muslim fundamentalists in the UK, such as Abu Hamza al-Masri, of Finsbury Park mosque, and Sheikh Omar Bakri, leader of the Al-Muhajiroun group, who have become household names. Yet for all the pages devoted to their 'links' to al-Qaeda, little effort has been made to place their antics in the wider context of British Islam and point out how small their respective followings are. (2002: 74)

Karim (2000) has provided a telling analysis of the news reporting of conflicts in the Balkans, Caucasus, the Middle East and elsewhere which revealed the continuing vitality of long established stereotypes and imagery in contemporary reportage involving Muslims. Poole (2002) valuably extended this analysis with a focus on the media representation of British Muslims, while Richardson (2001) found Muslim voices substantially excluded from British domestic reporting of Islam. More recently research has indicated that news coverage has focused on social tensions and raised questions about the loyalty of Muslims to Britain, with terrorism being a recurrent theme (see Poole and Richardson, 2006). A 2008 report by Moore et al found news coverage of British Muslims had increased significantly since 2001, with a peak in 2006, but remaining at high levels in 2007 and 2008, a finding they related to the increased coverage of terrorism and terrorism-related stories. Reflecting the concerns of van Dijk (1993) with the role of elite discourse in its capacity to have privileged access to being heard in the media, Jackson (2007) traces the elite construction of 'Islamic terrorism' as an issue in political and academic discourse, echoing the international construction of social capital noted earlier in Chapter Two. Additionally, in a 2009 pilot study of the British press reporting of minority ethnic communities, Firmstone et al (2009) found that terrorism was the dominant issue in headlines relating to minorities, and that tabloids had a significantly greater referral to terrorism than broadsheets. When the analysis examined the reportage within the body of the texts, terrorism was the second most frequent issue, with political decisions and debates on regulation for minorities and migrants dominating. This again points to the salience of immigration and border policy in the British public sphere and underlines the relevance of nationalist sentiments in contextualising the perception of Muslims and Islam. Where Muslims were present in analysed texts, the report showed that they were overwhelmingly referred to in relation to terrorism. And in those few cases where Muslims were given a direct voice as speakers in the story, in over half the cases (55 per cent) they were associated with terrorism. No other religions were associated with terrorism within the analysed texts.

Clearly, then, there is a disconcerting amount of evidence which indicates the partisan and partial way in which Muslims and Islam are (re)presented in the 'Western' media in general, and specifically in British media. In drawing on this literature in order to better understand the significance of the media in shaping the political response to Islam and to the reproduction of specific forms of anti-Muslimism, it is important to keep in mind the ways in which wider national ideologies framing cultural diversity, and specific national experiences with minority ethnic communities, may themselves shape the reporting of Islam and Muslim communities. As has been apparent in the accounts above, and as will be clearly explicit in the empirical data to be reviewed below, immigration and integration remain complexly intertwined in the policies and rhetoric of both community cohesion and counter-terrorism, with the media continuing as an active agent within these agendas. From the early work of Hartmann and Husband (1974) onwards, there has been an accumulation of research demonstrating the ways in which the mass media provide a *definition of the situation* (Berger and Luckmann, 1966) whereby popular understandings of interethnic relations become framed by a few dominant conceptions of how the main players should be defined (white/British/ *'us'* versus immigrants/asylum seekers/blacks/Pakistanis/Asians/Muslims/ *'them'*), and how the relationships between them should be conceived. Whoever the 'us' happens to be is presented as centred, neutral and harmless but often being taken advantage of; the 'them', however, are 'taking our jobs', 'a burden on the state', agents who corrupt or pollute our culture, criminals and terrorists who are a threat to our security and way of life. The complexities of the linkages between media representations and their impact on individual beliefs and values, and public opinion in general, must be recognised (McQuail, 2005; Georgiou, 2010), but equally the role of the media in shaping understandings of British ethnic relations, and of terrorism, cannot be neglected. In the interviews reported below, respondents speak of their anger and distress at the way in which the local and national media have emphasised the terrorist potential of their local Muslim communities. Staff and councillors who are actively engaged in seeking to promote harmonious community relations feel undermined by the repetitive power of the news media.

We have already noted above the ways in which the stereotypical portrayal of self and others may be a core element of anti-Islamism, and it is appropriate to signal the key role of the media in supporting and undermining personal and collective identities. Studies of media content routinely demonstrate the exclusion of the minority ethnic person and their voice from an equitable presence within the varied sectors of the media. In multi-ethnic societies, the news media typically present the interests and values of the dominant majority (in terms of ethnicity, gender, class and [dis]ability) as the norm against which others are portrayed and judged (van Dijk, 1991, 1993; Downing and Husband, 2005). Even where media systems actively seek to recruit a diverse workforce, the power of established professional and institutional routines can prove to be exceedingly resilient in reproducing the dominant framework (see, for example, Campion, 2005). Not only news, but entertainment media also present distorted, and distorting, images of difference which impact on personal identities (Malik, 2002).

Thus, in recent years the media representation in Britain of the antagonism between 'British' and 'Muslim' identities has impacted on both Muslims and non-Muslims alike. However, in the contemporary media environment, minority ethnic communities are not contained within a media system that is entirely controlled by or aimed at the majority populations alone. With the growth of substantial domestic minority populations, and with the transnational capacity of new media to address the interests of diasporic communities, the media options of minority communities have in many cases increased dramatically. The notion of a single and unifying public sphere within which all citizens may participate in a dialogue, and be given equal access to be heard has long been a naive ideal type (Husband, 2000; Silverstone and Georgiou, 2005). As a result, minority communities have found themselves capable of constructing a media environment which reflects their own hybrid identities, with media which provide an alternative perspective to that disseminated by the hegemonic national media (Georgiou, 2006; Bailey et al, 2007; Husband and Moring, 2009). This provides succour to those who are rendered invisible, or vilified, in the majority media, while it is also a source of anxiety to sections of the majority population who experience this as a loss of their traditional taken for granted pre-eminence. The case of *Al Jazeera*, an Arab news channel available in Britain, provides a case study of this phenomenon (Miles, 2005) where its framing of news from outside of the prevailing Eurocentric world view resulted in it being seen as lacking in objectivity.

Additionally, new media formats and models, principally facilitated by the internet, provide a major resource for the liberation of individuals and collectivities from the constraints of the traditional ownership and control of the media. For Muslim populations globally and in Britain, this transformation in the media infrastructure has opened up new channels for expression (see, for example, Eickelman and Anderson, 1999; Rigoni, 2005). Of course, for those concerned with the restrictive reproduction of some notion of an 'authentic' British culture and identity, such media freedoms may be unwelcome. For security services, however, the radical expansion of access to a wide range of Islamic sources has proved worrying, and has invited surveillance and attempts at regulation through proscription. An interesting case where concern with Muslim media use is clearly apparent, is in a placement-based Economic and Social Research Council (ESRC) project entitled 'Communication Streams and Radicalisation'. It outlines its purpose as being "to conduct a study of radical weblogs ('Blogs') over the period of the placement, as well as to provide more general advice and assistance on RICU[7] business. The nature of this study is somewhat sensitive. Consequently, the exact aims and outcomes of the project will not be publicised" (www.esrcsocietytoday.ac.uk/).

Media and counter-terrorism

Finally, for our concerns here, we need to acknowledge the centrality of the media to the very operation of terrorism. There is an unavoidable sense of incestuousness when we explore the relationship between the terrorist and the media. While there appears to be a minor industry in contesting the definition of terrorism, there is a recurrent acknowledgement that contemporary terrorism especially requires the oxygen of publicity in order to function:

> Terrorism is a form of 'communicative action' (Karstedt) which is played out in front of an audience. That audience provides the oxygen that allows the terrorists to generate and maintain momentum; modern media, including access to the internet, can ensure that key messages and events have immediate impact. (CLGC, 2010: 160)

The power of terrorist outrages lie not primarily in the extent of the initial damage itself, but rather in the perceived threat that this damage may be inflicted on the target population *again* at any time in the future. The reach and power of terrorism lies particularly in this multiplier effect of the anticipation of future assaults among the target audience. In reality, only a relatively few may be the victims of such future violence, but all of the target population may realistically consider themselves to be potential victims. In modern terrorism as in politics more generally, then, the media are a powerful element within the terrorist's strategic repertoire of resources (Norris et al, 2003; Barnett and Reynolds, 2009) and as such, media outlets are regularly exploited and in some cases, perceived to be co-opted into or explicitly involved with acts of terrorism. Not only may terrorists reasonably expect the news media of the target population to cover their activities, but by strategic leaking of taped material to other sources they can seek to guarantee alternative media routes to access potentially supportive audiences.

As CONTEST II (HM Government, 2009: 43, para 5.15) succinctly spells out:

> Contemporary terrorist organisations design, conduct and record their operations with a view to publicity. On violent extremist websites films of terrorist attacks are routinely combined with other pictures from conflict areas which record the suffering of Muslim communities. Al Qai'da's ideology forces local events into a global narrative; technology constructs and illustrates that narrative and conveys it to a global audience.

This statement from the government's own policy document not only identifies the potential power of the media but also inherently accepts the linkage between Muslim communities in Britain and elsewhere. The local narrative only has global meaning because of globalised sensitivities whether these be a non-religious moral repugnance at inequalities brutally reproduced, or a faith-based affiliation with fellow members of the *Ummah*.

As Hoffman (2006) has argued, the internet can be exploited to avoid government censorship while at the same time providing a quick and efficient means of publicity allowing sources and producers of material to remain anonymous. The power of 9/11, and of 7/7 in Britain, was very considerably manufactured through the impact of the television and media coverage which so directly put the wider population in touch with the horror of these events. The statement from CONTEST II above may point to those sources that it defines as 'violent extremist websites', but the reality of the contemporary media environment is that material placed on such originating sites very rapidly finds its way onto a wider range of websites, and in edited form onto the mainstream media.

We might enquire if there is nothing that the media can do to resist being co-opted into this amplification of the initial event. There is in fact a significant literature which has explored just this relationship (see, for example, Norris et al, 2003; Kavoori and Fraley, 2006; Barnett and Reynolds, 2009), and while it addresses the responsible ways in which news media have sought to limit their exploitation by the terrorist, it remains the case that the professional identity and practices of journalism make them vulnerable to the publicist agendas of the terrorist. In many ways, terrorist events fit very closely to the established professional *news values* (McQuail, 2005) which determine and help select which events become translated into news. In terms of the public interest function of the news media, it is clear that it is a responsible action to ensure that the public is informed about threats that they may potentially experience. However, as Nacos has observed:

> ... as the move from news-as-information to news-as-entertainment continues, especially in television, media organizations seem increasingly inclined to exploit terrorism as infotainment for their own imperatives (ie ratings and circulation). More than ever before, terrorists and the media are in a quasi-symbiotic relationship. (Nacos, 2007, quoted in Barnett and Reynolds, 2009: 35)

Finally we must note the relationship between the media and the state's interest in counter-terrorism. The state's response to terrorism may impinge on the previously unquestioned freedoms of the majority population. Consequently, a critical challenge for the government of the day is to sustain the support of the population for their counter-terrorism actions. This may include providing the population with clear information about the nature of the counter-terrorism response, but it will also require maintaining the population's sense of imminent threat. There is at this point a perverse intersection of the interests of the terrorist and those of the government: both need to maintain an active sense of the possibility that everyone is a potential target of threats which have a credible likelihood of succeeding. The incursions into the established civil liberties of citizens require those same citizens to accept the legitimacy of these assaults on their liberties as a necessary trade-off of security against liberty. Consequently we see the government maintaining a high visibility for its counter-terrorist activities, and a political willingness to sustain a sense of a high level of threat. Thus, for example, CONTEST II (HM Government, 2009: 99) argued that 'Prevent depends on a shared understanding of the threat. We need to develop a consensus about this, often by encouraging more discussion about it'.

It is perhaps therefore not surprising that Richard Mottram[8] (2007) should note in his review of *Protecting the citizen in the twenty-first century* the importance of a coherent communications strategy. This would be required to challenge the communication strategies aimed at radicalising potential terrorist supporters in Britain while also addressing the disparate needs of members of the public. This has included the creation of Regional Media Emergency Forums working in liaison with Local Resilience Forums that 'have led to the development of closer working relationships between all stakeholders in co-ordinating, developing and ultimately delivering information to the media and thence to the public' (Mottram, 2007: 63). Part of this process is of course concerned with maintaining public support for the state's development and implementation of counter-terrorism measures. With the increase in surveillance of all citizens, the targeted surveillance of Muslim communities, the use of stop and search, and even the interpretation of counter-terrorism provisions to stop citizens taking photographs of traditional tourist attractions, there is a concrete insult to the sense of individual freedoms which have been historically nurtured as part of the British self-image. These practices have impacted directly on many citizens and have caused concern and outrage within sections of the British media. There is here then a specific challenge to the government in seeking to promote its counter-terrorism strategies while maintaining public support for their implementation. As Monar has said in his review of European Union (EU) counter-terrorism strategies:

> ... the fight against terrorism demands considerable resources and may involve measures that are likely to cause significant domestic opposition because of their invasiveness. Governments will find it more difficult to justify diverting resources to the fight against terrorism and to justify invasive measures if the public perceptions of the threat are rather low. (Monar, 2007: 301)

In the state's response to terrorist threat, the management of communication flows is recognised as a significant challenge: the ideological propagandising of the terrorist is contested by both the organised media management of government, and by the routine editorial policies of the national news media. At the same time, the activities of both maintain the terrorist threat as a significant element of concern in the public sphere: they give it publicity. And, as Monar has noted, the state has a vested interest in sustaining a sense of realistic threat. More generally, the media are very significant elements in the processes of identity formation and defence. At the same time, the contestation over the politics of difference (Taylor, 1992), framed within the continuing debate around the death of British multiculturalism, is fought out within the contemporary national and transnational media environment.

Counter-terrorism in the wider context of securitisation

As, with community cohesion, where we sketched the value of locating that specific policy within the wider framework of government policy, so too with the specifics of counter-terrorism policy we can see synergies with other government policies that have implications for the facilitation of the public's acceptance of the intrusive reach of the 'preventive state'. We have already noted in Chapter Two the extensive interpenetration of policies around immigration and those of Community Cohesion. We can now extend this to note their mutual deeply interwoven status in the discourses of 'securitisation'. As Noxolo and Huysmans (2009b) note, the issues of threat and security have become widely extended to issues that are well beyond the immediate remit of terrorism. Specifically they note the

> ... introduction of the concept of 'securitisation', in which the focus is moved away from the idea of objective threat and towards the discursive moves and negotiations through which an issue or a social group becomes defined as a security issue. (Noxolo and Huysmans, 2009b: 2)

The notion of securitisation raises questions about the forces that shape the emergence of specific definitions of threat and of the appropriate and necessary responses to it. The literature on securitisation points strongly to the relevance of the international context in which threat and security have become both a political issue and a social and economic terrain in which a large number of players are seeking to pursue their own vested interests. At an international level we have seen the integration of immigration and border policy into a securitisation discourse with attendant extensive European collaboration developing a collective policy framework (Grewcock, 2003; Huysmans, 2006). At the level of the nation Hughes (2009) points to the development of the new specific policy field of 'community safety'. He argues that:

> ... across increasing numbers of contemporary states, it is possible to discern a formal, territorialized, 'community-based' preventive and safety infrastructure, epitomised by the government technique of the local, multi-agency community and preventive partnership. This relatively new preventive and safety sector cuts across traditional boundaries of crime control and social policy in complex and volatile ways. (Hughes, 2009: 17)

With varying degrees of zealotry, or cynical despair at another policy innovation, the technicians of this new syncretic policy employ a language replete with such terms as 'mobilisation', 'responsibilisation', 'active citizenship' and 'community self-government'. For some this is an opportunity for innovation (Johnston and Shearing, 2003) while for others it smacks of authoritarian communitarianism (Scraton, 2002). For Hughes (2009: 17), however, it remains 'a terrain of unfinished contestation and unstable governance', with the potential for progressive or regressive policy outcomes as yet undetermined. Within the context of the operation in England of local area agreements the weaving of securitisation agendas into the field of community safety has produced an interagency nexus in which contradictory trajectories and contested power claims are likely to be routine.

In relation to this, Huysmans' (2009: 197) concern with the processes that securitise everyday relations through the circulation of 'unease' becomes critical where, for example, 'security practice is reworked in ordinary activity, such as negotiating one's belonging to various communities' (Huysmans, 2009: 97). Huysmans points to the double-edged argument of securitisation, which at one level through introducing *exceptional measures* (which may diminish your civil freedoms and impact on your perception of potential neighbours) claims to make you safe by allowing the security services to do what needs to be done. At the same time this discourse assures you that your daily life can continue as usual. In this way, the normality of daily life is a political goal of security policies, and its assumed unchanged continuation is a necessary ideological ploy in legitimating the security measures put in place to guarantee it. Consequently, Huysmans argues that:

> ... the everyday opens up as an important security terrain. The enhancement of social cohesion and community relations, aimed at sustaining the existing routines of life, can then emerge as a part of a national security strategy. (Huysmans, 2009: 199)

While at the level of politics and in the flexible manipulation of human rights principles 'exceptional measures' introduce radical changes in the fabric of the nation, the assertive reproduction of daily life, and of the norms that bind it, helps to desensitise the wider population to the securitisation of their world. As Huysmans (2009, 200) further argues:

> While claiming the need for exceptional decisions by the political leadership, in consultation with the security forces, the politics of exception constitutes ordinary human beings into habitual subjects, both as beings that desire to act routinely and as a demand upon them to indeed act that way for the purpose of securing their lives.

The logics and operational necessities of Prevent should therefore most certainly not be seen as a unique instance of the interpenetration of security with community policy. Securitisation has far reaching ramifications in permeating wide areas of policy and social life.

Thus, for example, urban planning can be seen to have been significantly impacted by this agenda. Atkinson and Helms (2007), for example, provide a text which offers a range of disturbing insights into the securitisation of urban planning and the urban space. Stenson (2007: 24) in this anthology speaks of the fact that:

> Increasingly with growing urban fears in the post-9/11 world, the governmental problems of city life and how to regenerate it are disproportionately coded under terms of security, crime disorder, and anti-social behaviour.

The discourse and practice of urban regeneration, for example, with the concept of 'place competitiveness', has positioned the notion of safety at the heart of urban planning. At the same time the widening of the gap between the wealthy and the urban poor, sometimes exacerbated by urban planning itself which has through specific regeneration policies created enclaves of affluent new neighbourhoods immediately adjacent to decaying inner-city communities, have produced new social tensions within cities. Managing anti-social behaviour through the introduction of Anti-Social Behaviour Orders (ASBOs), Curfew and Dispersal Orders became an integral element of the Labour government's perception and management of sustainable communities (ODPM, 2005). The promotion of the interests of the 'deserving' respectable urban achiever, and consumer, has been accompanied by a construction of a policy infrastructure to control and manage the unruly and marginal, who have been constituted through a vigorous MUD discourse that has emphasised their place outside of the communitarian homeland of sustainable communities (Coleman et al, 2005; and also the Special Issue of *Cultural Studies*, 2007, vol 21, no 6). As Hancock (2007: 63) notes, 'In the "new urban renaissance" the vision of "normality" is emphatically middle class where norms and lifestyle are concerned.' The criminalisation of elements of urban behaviour and the extensive securitisation of the urban environment came to be an unobtrusive, but radical achievement of the Labour administration. As Flint and Smithson (2007: 168) point out:

> The problematisation and criminalisation of previously non-criminal activities by young people has resulted in young people's citizenship rights being curtailed through the use of ASBOs and Dispersal and Curfew Orders (and Exclusion Orders in Private shopping centres) to prohibit young people's access to and use of public spaces.

In a further instance of the contradictions that may develop between disparate policies, the government's promotion of the night time economy as a key element in the regeneration of city economies and social life (DETR, 2000; ODPM, 2003) has perversely in many instances produced, or at the very least unwittingly encouraged, an alcohol-fuelled hedonist youth culture that has become associated with excessive drunkenness, and violence that deters the 'respectable' citizens from participating in this night time social environment. This disturbing outcome has received considerable attention from governmental and security agencies. As Smith (2007: 184) notes:

> The NTE (night time economy) is itself an ambiguous space simultaneously composed of both regulatory control strategies and deregulatory liberalisation policies. The paradox does not end there. Even the very social and technological measures brought in to pacify and civilise urban spaces and counter the NTE's undesirable

face are themselves, as will become obvious, riddled with contradiction.

Managing the urban social environment has become a major area of securitisation where the public has become inured through habit and self-interest to the securitisation of their daily life, where the circulation of unease has become routinely accompanied by the far reaching mechanisms of social control; there is, for example, considerable public support for CCTV cameras. Thus, far from being an exceptional encounter with issues of security and community, Prevent should be seen as but one particular aspect of a much wider and insidious phenomenon. The extensive growth of the security infrastructure in Britain is suggested by Stenson (2007: 33), who argues that:

> The 2002 Police Reform Act signalled the growing pluralisation of the provision of security across the boundaries of state commercial, and voluntary self-policing. Having eroded the provision of public guardianship in the form, for example, of park keepers and railway staff, in the name of state reform and efficiency, there are attempts to reinvent guardianship in new forms. By 2006 in the UK there was a record 139,000 sworn public police officers, matched by a similar number of commercial security staff and a projection of 25,000 community support officers (CSOs) ancillary to the police, and aided by an exponential growth in closed circuit television (CCTV) and other security technologies. The growth of the tax-funded world of security is matched by analogous commercial growth. By 2005, the commercial security industry employed about half a million people and had an annual turnover of £3-4 billion in the UK.

Issues of commercial advantage, extending professional territory and consolidating political powers, are mapped across the terrain of securitisation in general and across the nexus of Prevent and community cohesion specifically.

Prevent and human rights

In closing this chapter it is timely to consider the significance of the emergence of counter-terrorism as a major political agenda in Britain and other states worldwide. Counter-terrorism has not merely generated specific strategies which seek to annul the political purpose of the terrorist assaults and to pre-empt the terrorist's capacity to carry out their violent intentions. Counter-terrorism has also created a new political sensibility as states have responded to the challenges they have faced since 9/11. A core of this new sensibility has been a radical shift in the balancing of human freedoms guaranteed by the state against the state's invocations of special powers in countering terrorism. Since the construction of the emotive 'War on Terror' following 9/11, the world has seen a most regrettable erosion of a consensus on the inalienable nature of human rights guaranteed through international treaty and declaration. As Hicks has argued:

> Everywhere human rights activists are confronting a sea-change in what might be called the presumptive norm in international affairs that prior to September 11, 2001, saw adherence (or at least the pretence of adherence) to international human rights standards as generally desirable.... In contrast, today the primacy of respect for international human rights standards, and the legitimacy of striving for their realization and protection, is routinely challenged and questioned in word and deed by governments of all kinds, democratic and undemocratic alike. Because the rights of human rights defenders have been and are being violated, we are all less safe. (Hicks, 2005: 209)

In the British context, CONTEST II asserts in its statement of principles that: 'We will continue to regard the protection of human rights as central to our counter-terrorist work in this country and overseas', and that 'our response to terrorism will be based upon the rule of law' (HM Government, 2009: 13). However, the reality is lamentably at odds with this aspiration. As the government argues later in CONTEST II:

> A fundamental challenge facing any government is to balance measures intended to protect security and the right to life with the impact they may have on the other rights that we cherish and which form the basis for our society. (HM Government, 2009: 57, para 7.06)

Quite so, and it is likely that people with different experiences and different values may place the point of equilibrium between these interests at quite different points. As a complementary community study across the five authorities (Alam, forthcoming) has indicated, there is a widespread concern with crime and security at the local level, and it is apparent that nationally there is a good deal of popular support for surveillance cameras and some other aspects of counter-terrorist activity. However, we must remind ourselves that members of Muslim communities have been the principal target of these policies and therefore, as the CLGC report (2010) acknowledged, are likely to have a quite different sense of the legitimacy of the current balancing of these priorities. Additionally, the diversity of identity, status and local residence within the Muslim population is likely to create different perspectives within this population.

As we have already noted above, the construction of Al-Qaeda and the 'War on Terror' as some quantum shift in the challenge facing the contemporary world, with its pernicious penumbra of the fundamental ideological conflict between Islam and the West, has facilitated a politics of extreme threat which has nurtured anti-democratic defensive responses. The international collusion in the use of torture has had a corrosive impact on the self-regard which can nurture a confident defence of human rights. 'Extraordinary rendition', a combination of spin and *Newspeak*[9] for illegal abduction and removal from your space of legal entitlements, compromised states in facilitating the exporting of individuals for torture and legal non-existence. States retreating from their traditional support for human rights, as they pursued counter-terrorism strategies in the post-9/11 world, have attracted international concern and critique (Wilson, 2005; Cole and Lobel, 2007; Bonney, 2008). The UK has not escaped this concern, and although Gearty (2007) noted that while the UK did not on the whole embrace the language of the 'War on Terror', he nonetheless notes the pressures being brought on the judiciary by the executive to accede to new repressive measures:

> This amounts to a shift in sensibilities from anxiety about the repressive nature of such proposals to proud justification of them, an assertive transformation that has been laced with contempt for those who in the words of the Home Secretary Dr John Reid just 'don't get' how little the old rules matter any more. (Gearty, 2007: 353)

As the judiciary has acted as an attempted restraint on the executive's assault on British and European law, the strength of the government's resolve has been expressed forcibly as:

> … members of the judicial branch have been subject to withering critiques from senior government ministers; some of the comments have been unprecedented in their fierceness in the British political context (Gearty, 2007: 354)

In Britain, as elsewhere, the development of counter-terrorism strategies has therefore not merely represented an organisational response of security forces to address a new challenge, it has also involved a significant, and possibly radical, assault on the conception of human rights that have heretofore provided a consensual basis for the relationship between citizens and the state. There has been not only a substantive erosion of individual freedoms as counter-terrorism strategies have moved from government legislation to local implementation, there has also been a significant erosion of respect for fundamental human rights. A key feature of this process has been the international consensus on the 'negotiability' of human rights principles. Just as anti-immigrant and anti-asylum seeker rhetoric and policies have enjoyed a wide European consensus, so too the erosion of support for human rights has been nurtured by an intergovernmental complicity. As Beck (cited in McGhee, 2008: 20) has phrased it:

> Under the spell of terrorist threat, a lawless space has opened up which permits what was recently forbidden, a double carte blanche in interstate relations. Each state can combat its domestic enemies as 'terrorists' with the blessing of the international community and the human rights violations of allies are treated with discretion and thereby facilitated.

Conclusion

This chapter has sought to provide a broad context for our later understanding of the data generated in this research project. In particular, it has sought to provide a basic introduction to the development of the Prevent agenda that is a core concern of this analysis. Additionally it has paused to open up for scrutiny the nature of anti-Muslim feeling in the hope that this data will be seen in the context of the specific history of British Muslim relations, and in relation to the specific conditions applying in local towns and communities.

The data we explore is derived from qualitative interviews undertaken in major metropolitan authorities in West Yorkshire, each with their own ethnic mix and their own trajectories of social change. At the same time, however, the understandings that people have of this context is significantly framed by the media's construction of popular conceptualisations of current events. The British media have not been a neutral vehicle for representing the experience and presence of Muslim people in Britain. Anti-Muslimism, in its multiple forms, has been nurtured by the media environment in post-9/11 Britain. One reason for the partial vision provided by the British media has been the discourse emanating from the British political community, and from elite social commentators. In looking at the experience of the local authority personnel in implementing central government legislation and guidance it will be important to keep in mind the political and moral environment within which they have had to operate, including a pervasive national erosion of a commitment to unassailable individual human rights.

Notes

[1] These insiders included those intimately involved in the development of the new British 'protective state', such as Sir David Ormand, UK Security and Intelligence Coordinator, Permanent Secretary to the Home Office/ Director GCHQ (Government Communications Headquarters) as well as Richard Mottram, former Security and Intelligence Coordinator and later Permanent Secretary, Intelligence, Security and Resilience in the Cabinet Office. See Ormand (2003, 2005); Mottram (2006).

[2] Indeed, the publication in March 2009 of CONTEST II: *The United Kingdom's strategy for countering international terrorism* (HM Government, 2009) continued this strategy of remarkable openness in outlining both the nature of the threat and the counter-terrorist response to it.

[3] See also McGhee (2008: Chapter 1) for a distressing account of the government's convoluted series of strategems aimed at defying legal objections to their draconian measures to exclude and control suspected terrorists.

[4] The inherent wisdom of this competition for resources is reflected in the reality of the increased budgets. 'Between 2001 and 2008, the size of the Security Service doubled, GCHQ's Terrorist Team grew significantly and additional SIS resources have enhanced frontline counter-terrorism operations overseas. Since its formation in June 2003, JTAC, the UK's centre for the analysis and assessment of the level and nature of the threat from international terrorism has grown 60%. Since 2006, the number of police personnel dedicated to counter-terrorism work has grown by over 70%' (HM Government, 2009: 64, para 8.04). The cost of the key deliverables in

the Prevent Delivery Plan for 2008/09 alone totalled over £140 million (HM Government, 2009, 83, para 9.09).

[5] At the same time we should note that the ideology and aims of Al-Qaeda, and other similar groupings, are not related solely to Western foreign policy, but also have linkages to the internal divisions in politics and theology across Muslim states as well as broader schools of thought, interpretation and tradition.

[6] By elites, Hall et al (1978) refer to those with authority, including politicians, academics as well as those who are posited to be 'experts'.

[7] RICU is the Research, Information and Communication Unit within the Office for Security and Counter-Terrorism (OSCT), based in the Home Office and also funded by and answerable to the Foreign Office and the Department for Communities and Local Government.

[8] At the time of writing, Mottram was Permanent Secretary, Intelligence, Security and Resilience, in the British Cabinet Office.

[9] Newspeak is part of a fictional language introduced in George Orwell's novel, *Nineteen Eighty-Four* (1949). In short, Newspeak is a reduced and simplified, but ultimately, disempowering version of English used by a totalitarian regime to maintain control through presenting easily consumable information while at the same time, discouraging alternative views, opinions or ideologies: 'thoughtcrimes'.

FOUR

Anti-Muslimism

Introduction

In the previous chapters it has become apparent that for both of the policies under discussion here, Muslims, and the expression of the Islamic faith in Britain, are central to the conception and delivery of these policies. Consequently this chapter will pause in advance of moving on to present the data from this study in order to briefly explore the antipathies that may be attached to Islam and Muslims. These policies have not emerged and fed into an attitudinal vacuum in which the Muslim faith stands as a neutral entity awaiting appraisal by the British public. On the contrary there is a long association between Britain and the Muslim world that has laid down a rich tapestry of beliefs, values and attitudes.

In recent years we have become familiar with the term 'Islamophobia' as a descriptor of the antipathies that may be present within non-Muslim populations and which may shape their behaviour toward Muslims. As we shall see shortly, Halliday (1996) has coined the term 'Anti-Muslimism' as a means of encouraging us to carefully consider our understanding of the elements that may be present within this notion of Islamophobia: a term often used casually and without reflection to describe the relationship between Muslims and non-Muslims. Thus, in this chapter we will prepare ourselves for an appropriately sensitive understanding of the data that is to follow by engaging in an examination of the elements that may constitute Islamophobia.

We will begin with an account of the emergence of the term Islamophobia in the British context and then proceed to follow Halliday in deconstructing this term in order to better understand the elements that may be interacting in shaping people's perception of contemporary events, and possibly driving feelings of antipathy, and even hatred. This will be followed by a brief excursion into some of the literature from social science which can be very helpful in enabling us to have a fuller understanding of the internal dynamics of Islamophobia. Not only is this literature helpful in developing our understanding of the complexities of intergroup dynamics, it is also essential in reaching an informed competence when seeking to intervene in managing the relations between Muslims and non-Muslims, an activity that is at the heart of both of the policies which concerns us.

Anti-Muslimism defined and revealed

Having looked at the ways in which Muslim communities have become defined as the focus of two major governmental policies, and in anticipating the analysis of the data that is to follow, we now consider the phenomenon of Islamophobia. Bringing into focus Muslim identities and Muslim communities does not of itself constitute a discriminatory act motivated by prejudice. Nor is the recognition of challenges faced by Muslim communities and the majority ethnic populations in seeking to establish an equitable basis for co-existence as British citizens reckless trouble making. The literature on ethnic and intergroup relations provides a global basis for appreciating the sensitivities and political dynamics that may be present as different populations defined by ethnicity, faith and national identities come to adjust to new conditions of co-existence. In the current British context it is important to keep in mind the normality of such processes of adjustment. But hostility to Islam and to Muslims most certainly does exist and in the context of an argument such as this we would do well to take the time to understand it and its implications.

In the British context there is something of a consensus that the concept of Islamophobia took off with the publication in 1997 of the Runnymede Trust report *Islamophobia: A challenge for us all*. This report resulted from the formation by the Runnymede Trust of a Commission on British Muslims and Islamophobia. It was launched in November 1997 by the then Home Secretary, Jack Straw, and thus had the imprimatur of official recognition. The report contained 60 recommendations directed at, among others, government departments, local and regional statutory agencies, the media and the third sector. Specifically, the report provided a definition of Islamophobia as having eight constitutive components. These were:

1. Islam is seen as a monolithic bloc, static and unresponsive to change.
2. Islam is seen as separate and 'other'. It does not have values in common with other cultures, is not affected by them and does not influence them.
3. Islam is seen as inferior to the West. It is seen as barbaric, irrational, primitive and sexist.
4. Islam is seen as violent, aggressive, threatening, supportive of terrorism and engaged in a 'clash of civilisations'.

5. Islam is seen as a political ideology and used for political and military advantage.
6. Criticisms made of the West by Islam are rejected out of hand.
7. Hostility toward Islam is used to justify discriminatory practices towards Muslims and exclusion of Muslims from mainstream society.
8. Anti-Muslim hostility is seen as natural or normal.

This description of Islamophobia clearly contains familiar echoes of the imagery and values that are encapsulated in the literature on Orientalism, and point to the current reworking within contemporary national anxieties of well established cultural tropes. At the same time, the identification of the 'clash of civilisations' discourse (Huntington, 1996) and the fear of terrorist outrages points to quite specific contemporary phenomena. As a policy-directed initiative, this report had the benefit of the standing of the Runnymede Trust as a credible and responsible source alongside the immediate association with government support. It initiated a significant public debate and while it was not universally greeted with acclaim, it could be argued to have had a significant impact in placing anti-Muslimism on the political and policy agenda.

This report was of course published prior to the events of 9/11, and a subsequent reconfiguration of the Commission on British Muslims and Islamophobia, independently of the Runnymede Trust, and chaired by Dr Richard Stone, was able to report on a very changed social and political environment. This report, *Islamophobia: Issues, challenges and action* (Smith et al, 2004), was able to look back at both the implementation of the recommendations of the previous report and comment on the impact of 9/11. Its findings were not comfortable. At the launch of the report, Dr Stone was quoted as saying:

> The Government has not taken on board in a deep way the anti-Muslim prejudice in this country.... There is now renewed talk of a clash of civilisations and mounting concern that the already fragile foothold gained by Muslim communities in Britain is threatened by ignorance and intolerance. (Casciani, 2004)

Iqbal Sacranie, the Secretary General of the Muslim Council of Britain – a body claiming to represent British Muslims – added further weight by stating:

> We have been witnessing a relentless increase in hostility towards Islam and British Muslims and it is clear that existing race relations bodies have been either unable or unwilling to combat this phenomenon effectively. (Casciani, 2004)

This second report was a blunt and negative judgement on the aspirations embedded in the recommendations of its predecessor. Clearly the terrorist assaults of 9/11 provided a vivid and potent empirical support for the anxieties of non-Muslims who had embraced the earlier manifestations of anti-Muslimism. It gave them apparent legitimacy and as we have seen above, the response of the state was to confirm this judgement through their implementation of counter-terrorism policies that quite explicitly identified Muslim communities as the seat of an internal threat. For Muslim communities, these same strategies of stop and search, of surveillance and of house raids, provided concrete evidence of the institutionally anti-Muslim nature of the British state. The issues of the balance achieved in establishing an appropriate and proportionate policy response, raised in the previous chapter, was very much the issue as counter-terrorist policy interfaced with populist hostilities toward Muslim populations in Britain. This is particularly relevant as, over the last decade, the British National Party (BNP) has successfully increased its presence in local and European elections. More recently, we have seen the emergence in 2009 of the English Defence League, a single-issue organisation who claim to be against militant Islam, and who mobilise through populist street-based demonstrations. The recognition of the active political mobilisation of anti-Muslim sentiment must be factored into any account of Islamophobia, and of the experience of members of the Muslim faith in Britain.

A new dynamic had been constructed in which the legitimate anxieties of all citizens faced with potential terrorist violence had been mutated into an oppositional dialogue between the majority community as the potential victim and the Muslim communities as the potential perpetrator. The indiscriminate nature of terrorist violence provided a common agenda for all citizens to affirm their revulsion toward terrorism. In the media and throughout much of the political discourse, focus lay unwaveringly on those who spoke in support of jihadist terror. For the majority non-Muslim population, however, Muslim abhorrence at the un-Islamic and inhuman nature of terrorism was lost or rendered invisible.

Two parallel discourses have taken place in Britain since the domestic bombings of 7/7/2005 and the subsequent attacks in London and

Glasgow; one has been to engage with the threats posed by potential terrorist attacks and their prevention, while the other has been to monitor and condemn the recurrent expression of Islamophobia in Britain and elsewhere. The responses have been predominantly carried out by different actors, using different modes of access to the public sphere, and have engaged different audiences. It can be argued that there has been a truly frightening but at the same time ironic self-segregation of opinion makers addressing quite opposed parallel cultures: the culture of securitised xeno-nationalist Britain alongside the Britain of civil liberties and a recognition of multiculturalism as a demographic reality. (see Field, 2007, for an account of the changing nature of Islamophobia in Britain, pre- and post-9/11).

Concerns around Islamophobia from Muslim communities as well as liberal majority individuals and organisations have had limited visibility within the national public sphere and national politics. The concern with terrorism has, on the other hand, been predominantly expressed through the voice of the white majority, has predominantly spoken to an assumed majority white audience and has been an agenda at the heart of mainstream politics with open access to the national public sphere.

Manifestations of anti-Muslimism are now tracked by national and international bodies. The European Monitoring Centre on Racism and Xenophobia (EUMC), for example, produced two reports in 2006: *Muslims in the European Union – Discrimination and Islamophobia* and *Perceptions of discrimination and Islamophobia: Voices from members of Muslim communities in the European Union.* Both reports provide comparative quantitative and qualitative accounts of the prevalence of Islamophobia within the EU. More recently, the new form of the EUMC, the EU Agency for Fundamental Rights (FRA), has produced a study of the experience of discrimination by Muslims within the EU (EUFRA, 2009) which found that one in three of the Muslim respondents stated that they had experienced discrimination in the previous 12 months. This report usefully reveals the complex interaction of ethnicity, age and religion in the determination of discrimination which underpins our concern with the complexity of anti-Muslimism outlined above. Additionally, we should note that in a world of blogs and new media, Islamophobia Watch (www.islamophobia-watch.com) is but one manifestation of interest groups wishing to engage in contesting the definition and extent of Islamophobia.

While there continues to exist a vital debate about the nature and implications of Islamophobia (see, for example, Allen, 2007; Malik, 2010; Sayyid and Vakil, 2010), the perception of members of Muslim communities that they are being subject to vilification and discrimination on the basis of their faith remains powerfully present in contemporary British life. Recent data would also seem to sustain the legitimacy of their belief and experience. Through a memorandum sent to a House of Commons select committee on the impact of the Prevent strategy, the National Association of Muslim Police is reported to have stated:

> Never before has a community been mapped in a manner and nor will it be….The hatred towards Muslims has grown to a level that defies all logic and is an affront to British values. The climate is such that Muslims are subject to daily abuse in a manner that would be ridiculed by Britain, were this to occur anywhere else. (Davies, 2010)

Just as concerning are reports from various quarters indicating noticeable rises in the phenomenon at the level of attitude and perception (Doughty, 2010) as well as linkages with arguably more measurable and concrete rises in hate crime and physical violence against Muslims (Githens-Mazer and Lambert, 2010; see also Blick et al, 2006; Choudhury, 2007).

Deconstructing Islamophobia

In Chapter Two we discussed the racialisation of the discourse of community cohesion through the way it was, from its initiation, specifically related to minority ethnic communities and their perceived characteristics. In order to develop our argument further it is now necessary to revisit that phenomenon and open it up in order to reveal more clearly the dynamic relationships between 'race' and faith, and what over the last decade we have come to uncritically call 'Islamophobia'.

As a short-cut way of signifying a generalised prejudice against Muslims and their faith the term 'Islamophobia' has acquired a frequent and often unthinking usage in popular, and academic, debate. It provides an efficient way of seemingly describing, and more dangerously explaining, a widespread social phenomenon. However, such uncritical usage is likely to make the term itself a contribution to further misunderstanding. It is necessary to break down this seemingly homogenous phenomenon in order to better understand the multiple processes that may be in play in shaping contemporary British responses to Islam and to Muslims' presence here.

Halliday (1996), writing before 9/11, provides a very helpful resistance to any simplistic conceptual conflation. He prefers to use the term 'anti-Muslimism', and while it may not flow off the tongue with the ease of Islamophobia, equally it does not invite any assumed psychological *phobia* as the primary explanatory mechanism driving opposition to Islam and Muslims. His argument is that we must deconstruct our understanding of any specific instance of hostility to Muslims and Islam in order to reveal the quite particular mixture of forces that have shaped its emergence and nature. For Halliday:

> … anti-Muslimism is a semi-ideology, that is a body of ideas that, like gender or racial prejudice, is often articulated in conjunction with others that have a greater potential to function independently. (Halliday, 1996: 160)

From this perspective Halliday is explicitly opposed to the reductionist simplicities of Huntington's (1996) 'clash of civilisations' thesis which sees contemporary opposition to Islam as an inexorable expression of some primordial historical force of enmity between Islam and (Western) Christendom. Halliday acknowledges the relevance of history as a specific element in contributing to the shaping of contemporary hostility, but requires that we ask 'why' and 'how' it is that a specific rhetoric has emerged in a particular way in the current context. In developing his analysis he makes a distinction between 'strategic' and 'populist' strands of anti-Muslimism: the former being related to nuclear weapons, oil supplies and terrorism, while the latter are related to issues of immigration, assimilation and cultural practices (veiling, for example) which, significantly, *arise from the presence of Muslims* within *Western societies.* Using this framework he demonstrates how different historical experiences intersect with specific recent national engagements with those realities that are integral to the concrete experience of the strands of strategic and populist anti-Muslimism.[1] We can see, for example, how the issue of the veil has become a vehicle for rehearsing categorical distinctions between 'European values' and Islam in different contexts (Kastoryano, 2006; Amiraux, 2007).

In the British case we must of necessity acknowledge the particular history that has provided some of the deep cultural eddies that underpin our *contemporary social imaginaries* (Taylor, 2004) with regard to Islam. In that context we can note the early encounters with the difference of Islam that was shaped into oppositional conflict through the 'Crusades' into the Holy Land. We might also note that this too was a strategic conflict in which religion was but one part of the mix, as was obvious by the Crusader sacking of Christian Constantinople. A century later and beyond, the power of the Ottoman Empire came to be a key feature of the construction of conflict and enmity between Christian and Muslim Europe, although Britain did not experience either the domination of her territories or the proximity of Islamic power that was typical of many other European countries. By the late 19th century, Britain's imperial presence in Muslim countries in the Middle East and elsewhere provided yet another experiential basis for the consolidation of a national construction of difference. By the early 20th century, the particular power relations that framed popular and elite perceptions of the cultural practices of occupied peoples had become co-opted into an 'Orientalist' (Said, 1978) understanding of Islam. This was not the first, nor was it the last time that ethnic and national characteristics were seen as synonymous with traits of Islamic practice.[2] The First and Second World Wars provided further deeply flawed forms of encounter with the difference of Islam that contributed to the accumulated British repertoire of belief about Muslim peoples.

While we must recognise the potential of historically laid down beliefs and values about Islam, we should not reduce them to a homogenised and shared European experience. For example, Britain, unlike France, did not have a historical experience of significant parts of her territory being occupied by Muslim conquerors; nor did it have the bitter experience of decolonisation from a Muslim country that was experienced by France in relation to Algeria. And, as Marchand's (2008) analysis has revealed, the German experience of 'Orientalism' was not homogeneous but was modulated in relation to internal political and religious agendas that changed over time. Any simplistic invocation of a homogeneous 'European' Orientalism must of necessity provide a misleading contribution to any account of anti-Muslimism.

Nor should we assume that Muslim peoples have been construed only in negative terms. The learning and sophistication of Muslim societies has been valued and respected at points in European and British history and as with other peoples that have been subjected to British domination, there has been the ambiguity of attraction and repulsion that such circumstances typically engender. Not only has Muslim science and arts been critical to the Renaissance and later British thought and creativity (Hobson, 2004), but so too the British (male) sexual imagination has not been sufficiently obstructed by Islam in their sexualisation of Muslim women for European tastes and appetites. Young (1995), in his book *Colonial desire*, revealed both the fluidity within English identities and the fantasies of inter-racial sex that permeated the colonial experience. Kabbani (1994), meanwhile, exposes the same intermingling of denigration and attraction in the Western construction of its image of 'the Islamic East' (see also Hyam, 1991). The complex interplay between what were the domestic normative constructions of class and gender hierarchies, and their expression and reinterpretation within the British Empire as revealed by authors such as Inden (1992), Grewal (1996), Hubel (1996) and Cannadine (2002), indicate precisely why Halliday's assertion of the importance of the specificity of the historical context is always relevant to any understanding of anti-Muslimism. Thus, we should be careful to note that if anti-Muslimism can draw on historical cultural deposits that can help to legitimate contemporary prejudices, so too are there veins of respect, attraction and a particular familiarity with elements of Islam that can also feed positive attitudes.

When we briefly look at the British variants on strategic anti-Muslimism through the prism of international events, we can note that while the OPEC oil crisis of the early 1970s had a global impact in generating hostility toward the Arab and Iranian world, despite our dependence on external fuel supplies, the potency of the hostility in Britain was not perhaps as intense as it was in the US. However, the Iranian revolution and the end of the Cold War introduced new strident voices in Western politics, identifying 'fundamentalist Islam' as a new global threat; the green peril of (especially 'radical' or 'fundamentalist') Islam was poised to replace the red peril of Communism. The Gulf War of 1990-91, and now more particularly the British engagement in Iraq and Afghanistan, have provided quite specific foci for rehearsing notions of primitive ungovernability, and of a distant but real threat to British interests. Of course, 9/11 was the moment of crystallisation of Muslim alien-ness at which point perceived cultural, racial and psychological differences fused into an enhanced and overarching 'fundamentalist' Islamic threat.

As Allievi (2005) has pointed out, across Europe in the 1960s and 1970s Muslim immigrants were very largely defined in terms of their ethnic or national identities, rather than through their religious affiliation. The shift in redefinition depended on a number of factors, including the increasing visibility of local crises involving Muslims (in for example, Bosnia, Palestine and Chechnya), the increasing immigration of peoples with whom the majority had no prior contact and the changing dynamics within the traditional national faith communities, which contributed to the increasing definition of migrant and minority communities in terms of their Islamic faith in the 1980s and later. In the case of Britain, the internal escalation of perceiving British citizens in terms of their religious identity, rather than their ethnic identity, that had taken place with the Rushdie Affair was ratcheted up significantly by 9/11 and more particularly by the bombings in London of 7 July 2005. These acts of terrorism on British soil most powerfully tied the international context of Al-Qaeda and fundamentalist jihad to the domestic security of all British citizens. As we have seen above, the development of the counter-terrorism agenda quite explicitly identified the Muslim population as the focus of concern, making faith/religion (Islam) rather than ethnicity the primary focus of attention. The historically accumulated imagery of the Arab world and of Pakistani peoples was readily available to permeate the emerging definition of the situation[3] (Berger and Luckman, 1966; Hartmann and Husband, 1974). Thus if we wish to employ Halliday's distinction between strategic and populist anti-Muslimism we must take the time to trace the uniquely British, and perhaps within that the English, Scots, Irish and Welsh, trajectory of events and politics that have shaped our construction of this ideological package of belief and feeling.

Looking more specifically at the significance of Britain's domestic economic and political context we can note that Britain in the Thatcher period underwent a radical shift in its social structure and identity. Traditional industries that provided extensive employment for skilled and semi-skilled labour became obsolescent. Not only did whole communities find themselves economically pauperised, they also found that the structural environment that had routinely made their culture rich and relevant was no longer in place. The social dislocation that attended this transition in the British labour market has left a raw trauma that continues to leave many dislocated from their history and culture. This is a collective psycho-social transformation that has contributed to the individualisation of peoples' relation to their world. It is a world of loss and disorientation that has been painfully sketched by Sennett in his examination of the shifting basis for constructing meaning and value in contemporary lives (Sennett and Cobb, 1972; Sennett, 1998, 2003).

The radical individualism that was promoted under Thatcherism was a British expression of a neoliberal ascendancy that transformed large swathes of the Western world. This was a world in which finance capital and the consumption patterns of those who prospered within it came to significantly define contemporary cultures. In the Britain shaped by New Labour's 'Third Way', the gap between the haves and the have-nots widened, although segments of the population were lifted out of poverty. In 2008, Harriet Harman set up the Independent National Equality Panel, which set about exploring relationships between a range of economic outcomes and a range of social backgrounds. The resulting report, *An anatomy of economic inequality in the UK*, was published in 2010 (Hills et al, 2010). One of its most revealing, but at the same time sadly *unsurprising*, findings is that income inequalities that sharply increased during the 1980s under Thatcher's free market nirvana have grown even wider. Additionally, Britain has higher levels of economic and resulting social inequalities than many other industrialised countries. Much of the economic inequality explored in the report is structural and systematic in nature, where sexuality, gender, ethnicity and locality, as well as class, appear to be highly significant markers of identity that influence economic outcomes.

Even in a world of prosperity for some, affluence has not necessarily been accompanied by contentment and security. The churn of the globalised economy rendered a 'job for life' increasingly speculative with middle-class families no longer feeling assured that their children would inherit their privileged place in the labour and housing markets. In what Beck (1992) aptly called 'the risk society', insecurity became the norm; equally, Elliott and Lemert (2006) have lamented the costs of individualism for contemporary social relations. British citizens now find themselves routinely bombarded in their homes with mail urging them to take out insurance on things that they previously would not have considered at risk: we are invited to insure the pipes that bring water into our homes; we are informed that it is prudent to protect our car insurance policy with further insurance; and, when or if we take out a mortgage, we are urged to take out an additional mortgage protection plan. This personal sense of insecurity, arguably combined with a 'fostering vulnerability' (Furedi, 2009: 97-9) that is incessantly being reified by the authority of corporations, their advertisers and, it has to be said, by politicians, their rhetoric and policy,[4] is in contemporary Britain a foundational backdrop against which national threats are etched.

Britain is not short of perceived national threats. The rise of internal nationalisms, and the attendant forms of devolution of powers, has done much to destabilise the hegemonic notion of British identity within the awkwardly titled 'United Kingdom'. For many, the EU continues to represent an intolerable threat to their national autonomy and their economy. For others, the national dependency on external suppliers for their fuel supplies is an increasing source of anxiety, as both the predicted peaking of oil supplies and the newly apparent belligerence of Russia as a controller of energy supplies provide concrete foci for generalised anxieties. An apparent radical increase in flash floods and other cataclysmic expressions of nature's power underlines a widespread, although contested, concern with global warming. Britain specifically is not short of concerns about threats to her security. As a small island with a big history Britain is still committed to strut on the stage of international affairs with the demeanour and *amour proper* of a big player. Consequently, Iraq and Afghanistan provide daily evidence of the risks taken by British troops and the cumulative economic costs of our commitment to play on the world stage. Currently the fragility of the British national economy is given a harsh and concrete focus as the economic woes of Greece, and the anticipated difficulties of Portugal and Spain, are presented as auguries for the potential collapse of Sterling and of the British economy.

As we briefly examine below something of the internal dynamics of anti-Muslimism as an ideology, and a psychologically underpinned expressive vehicle for identity maintenance, the contextual factors that provide the grist for this defensive psychological mill must be continuously borne in mind. The populist anti-Muslimism which is a response to the presence of the 'stranger' in the heartland of the majority's territory can clearly draw on social imaginaries that have their roots in centuries of stereotype formation and in concrete relations of dominance and subjugation. The contemporary neo-nationalist xeno-racism sketched in some detail by Fekete (2009) is very much a product of the painful rehearsal of historically based notions of national pride and national distinctiveness, brought into sharp relief by the all too obvious challenges to their objective status. As we have seen, these historical relations between the 'all powerful colonial powers' and their subject peoples were full of ambivalence and had deep ramifications into the psyche and culture of the majority society. And as post-colonial critics have eloquently pointed out, these same relations have reciprocally left a profound residue in the psyche and identity of the now resident, once migrant, minority populations in Britain. The perception of strategic and symbolic threats are themselves contingent on the existence of a collective 'we' who are threatened, and consequently one of the many links between strategic and populist anti-Muslimism lies in a floating construction of nationalism that can flexibly be exploited to provide affect and salience to the concerns of both. The insertion of citizenship, and its proper affiliation to a shared basket of (national) values, into the heart of community cohesion is but one expression of this need to stem the perceived threats to an embattled, but perversely elusive British identity. It does, however, further signal the marginality of Muslim British citizens. We could fruitfully remember that the Church of England has been the established faith in Britain and the Act of Succession of 1701 continues to exclude Roman Catholics from ascending to the throne. Faith as a critical indicator of national identity has a long and tortured history in Britain, including the use of faith as a marker of difference of minorities, as the experience of British Catholics and Jews indicates. The vehemence of the 'Rushdie Affair' for example was as much an incapacity to empathise with another faith, deemed alien, as it was a knee jerk defence of a particular construction of European modernity. The place of Christianity within the cultural construction of British identity has provided one basis for symbolic threat, as the global strength and internal visibility of Muslim communities challenge the quiet certitudes of British superiority that had been laid down over previous centuries.

Examining the dynamics of anti-Muslimism

Clearly our experiences of perceived threats to British wellbeing and security would require a much more extensive chronicling than the brief sketch provided here. However, any unravelling of the populist anti-Muslimism that has developed in Britain, and which is routinely implied in the term 'Islamophobia', requires a further revisiting of the historically based images and beliefs that are available in contemporary British cultures. This time they are creatively co-opted to fuel a much more emotive antipathy toward Muslims; specifically, Muslims 'in our midst'. This is the fetid dynamic of the *stranger* so graphically described by Bauman:

> The stranger undermines the spatial ordering of the world: the fought-after co-ordination between moral and topographical closeness, the staying together of friends and the remoteness of enemies. The stranger disturbs the resonance between physical and psychical distance – he is physically near while remaining spiritually remote. He brings into the inner circle of proximity the kind of difference and otherness that are anticipated and tolerated only at a distance – where they can be dismissed as irrelevant or repelled as inimical. The stranger represents an incongruous and hence resented 'synthesis of nearness and remoteness'. (Bauman, 1990: 150)

Given the historical embedding of the racial imagery of the South Asian located in Britain's long history of involvement in the Indian sub-continent there has, for example, been a robust repository of belief and feeling that has fed into the British response to Pakistanis since their arrival in Britain from the 1950s onwards. The *Paki-bashing* of the 1970s was one particularly violent and explicit expression of the negative capacity of this heritage. The market forces that initially brought this population to Britain as an essential supply of labour was from the outset accompanied by discriminatory exclusion in the labour and housing markets which contributed very significantly to the subsequent demography and community development of this (now former) migrant population (Deakin, 1970). Defined by their colour and ethnicity, the Pakistani populations resident in Britain were the objects of deeply embedded racist ideologies present in British culture. Racism based on notions of biological inferiority that owed their legitimacy to neo-Darwinian biological theory became complemented (and certainly not entirely replaced) by less vulgar and less embarrassing forms of cultural racism in the 1980s. In the crucible of Thatcherism's fusion of neoliberalism with rampant nationalism, a cultural version of racist argument emerged which found in cultural difference a presumed non-negotiable form of differentiation which made the ambitions of multiculturalism foolish and void. In Barker's words, within the logics of this 'new racism':

> Nations ... are not built out of politics, or economics, but out of human nature. It is in our biology, our instincts, to defend our way of life, traditions and customs against outsiders, not because they are inferior, but because they are part of different cultures. This is a non-rational process: and none the worse for it. For we are soaked in, made up out of, our traditions and culture. (Barker, 1981: 23)

Thus a key element of the 'new racism' is its underpinning of contemporary socio-biological theory, which provides an apparent academic legitimacy for our 'natural' inclination to prefer our own, driven as we are by the inherent logics of our 'selfish genes' (see Barker, 1981; Gordon and Klug, 1986). As Kundnani (2001) argues, the normalising of xenophobia as human nature has introduced a powerful and new element into British racism. The populist language of kith and kin provides a flexible category for inclusion and exclusion from the national 'imagined community' (Anderson, 1983), where again history plays a critical role in enabling some immigrants (Australians, white Africans) to be non-problematic while others (Somali or Sudanese refugees, or Pakistani British citizens) are self-evidently *not one of us*. By employing this consensual language of the new racism, politicians, tabloid journalists and 'decent' white Britons are able to start their objection to the presence of immigrant communities with the phrase

'I am not racist, but ...'. Identifying the alien-ness of the *stranger* and confidently asserting their illegitimate presence in our midst has become a spontaneous and non-problematic expression of the rights of the concerned British citizen, and it has become a familiar part of the public rhetoric of members of the 'liberal left' in Britain as much as of the right and far right (Kundnani, 2007a). Vulgar biological racism is certainly not dead and its expression is heard explicitly in 'race' hate speech and in the coded euphemisms of the educated racist who has the competence to employ discursive strategies that allow everyone to know what they mean without having to say it (see Barker, 1981, on 'discursive deracialisation'). However, kith and kin xenophobia provides a powerful complementary discourse that addresses the language of identity and community through the lens of threatened self-preservation. As Kundnani points out, 'a combination of colour, cultural and kith and kin racisms can all co-exist, mutually reinforcing each other' (Kundnani, 2001: 53).

The neurotic politics of border policy and anti-immigrant sentiment, infused by an anxious xenophobia, has continued as an unbroken, and powerful, theme in British domestic politics from the heights of Thatcherite neo-nationalism to the communitarian-informed discourses of immigration and citizenship generated by Blunkett and others within the Blair and Brown governments (Back et al, 2002a; Solomos, 2003). In this context the old imperial notions of the difference and inferiority of South Asian peoples merged with their proximity, and continuously growing population, to find a new focus on their religion as the demonstrable and, quite literally, fundamental source of their difference. Colour and national heritage did not become irrelevant, but it was now their religion that was salient in defining the non-negotiability of their difference as 'strangers in our midst' and, if not already, then potentially as 'enemies within'.

The changing self-definition of young people of Pakistani heritage to foregrounding their ownership of their Muslim identity was one of the consequences of the majority societies' fixation with Islam (Alam, 2006; Alam and Husband, 2006), and reflected a response to the experience and behaviour of their parents. In the dialogic nature of intergroup identity formation and maintenance, the increasing salience of the Islamic background of South Asian citizens for majority ethnic Britain reciprocally changed the positioning of their faith within the self-image of the objects of anti-Muslimism. A body of research has examined this shifting nature of self-identification within the British Muslim population. Writing in the latter part of the 1990s, Samad (1998) reports an empirical study demonstrating the shifting salience of the Muslim identity among young 'Pakistani' people in Bradford (see also, for example, Gardner and Shukar, 1994; Shaw, 1994; Archer, 2001; Werbner, 2002). Reflecting the complexity of identities that Halliday and many others would require that we keep in mind, in tracking changes in 'Islamic identity' the literature has clearly shown the intersection of an Islamic sensibility with the re-positioning of men and women within Muslim communities along with the development of intergroup, politicised Islamic identities in relation to the majority populations. Thus, in following the developing argument below, we must remain vigilant in avoiding the adoption of essentialised images of the Muslim *and* majority populations.

The British anti-Muslim sentiments of the 1980s and onwards have been developed within a continuation of the British political scene's fixation with forms of immigration linked with labour and asylum seeking. The centrality of anti-immigrant sentiments within British political life in the postwar years is well documented (Layton-Henry, 1992; Malik, 1996; Pilkington, 2003; Solomos, 2003); its continual vitality in the British public sphere shows that it may be capable of shifts in nuance, but its centrality in framing British ethnic relations has not waned (Kundnani, 2007a; Fekete, 2009). Thus, populist anti-Muslimism in the British context is, as Halliday suggested, an ideological construction that is interwoven with other ideologies of nationalism, racism and gender. Phillips (2007), for example, provides a subtle understanding of the intersection of gender politics with critiques of multiculturalism and with Western ethnocentric postures of defence for Muslim women. That religion should be capable of occupying such a central role in the 'othering' of British citizens is ironic in the context of the relatively secular nature of British society.

Excluding the Muslim communities in a country where Christian church attendance has become a vestigial activity of a practising minority tells us a great deal about the nature of current British nationalism. Christianity is not a shared practice of the majority population, and indeed in terms of knowledge of the Bible it is not necessarily even a shared element of cultural knowledge. It is, however, a deeply historically embedded element in the imagined community of Britishness, and now can best be shared as a collective characteristic through a common opposition to another faith. In social psychological terms, Christianity has become a significant *criterial attribute* that defines the boundary between the British 'us' and the alien 'them', and frames intergroup comparison and competition (Turner, 1987; Oakes, 1996). The publicly visible devout adherence to the outward forms of their faith that is apparent in significant portions of Muslim communities stands as an unwelcome critique of the superficiality of much of the majority populations' faith. Consequently it hardly takes a Freudian analysis to see the benefits of defining such adherence to *their* faith among Muslims as fundamentalist and radical. There was a time when those who expressed their faith in a seamless way throughout the many facets of their life were called devout. Now, if you are a Muslim you are at risk of being labelled a 'fundamentalist' and may be suspected of being 'radicalised'.

A self-conscious adherence to a Christian *tradition* of faith as an integral part of British identity is complemented by the ubiquitous permeation of Christian imagery and reference throughout British culture. Thus, faith as an element of collective identity is far from alien to a British national sensibility. Consequently, an *alien* faith is not merely another signifier of difference; it is a highly salient and emotive basis for exclusion from the national collective. We have already noted the deeply sedimented historical beliefs and imagery which serve to render Islam as patently non-British within the national psyche. To this we can add the impact of the 'War on Terror' and the British state's explicit signalling of Muslim identity as being of itself a *prima facie* basis for surveillance.

Britain has three decades of experience with significant anti-racist legislation, and there is a normative awareness across the population that racism may attract legal penalties, and is best expressed judiciously depending on the context. However, there is no comparable national historical experience of a legal and administrative framework signalling the unacceptability of religious intolerance (religious discrimination regulations came into force in 2003 and the Racial and Religious Hatred Act was passed in 2006). The same inhibitions are therefore not in place and the new protective state's (Hennessy, 2007a) rhetorical and policy assault on Muslim communities has done much to facilitate a contrary tendency, namely, a confidence and comfortable self-righteousness in signalling the unacceptability of Islam as a faith and Muslims as communities within British society. As a result, Britain has seen a potent interweaving of strategic and populist anti-Muslimism.

In addressing, if not exactly answering, Halliday's questions of *why* and *how* in relation to the current formation of anti-Muslimism in contemporary Britain, it is exactly issues such as these sketched above which must be taken into consideration. Anti-Muslimism serves contemporary personal and political needs and its power lies not in the internal coherence of its discourses, but rather in the eclectic possibilities for co-option to different agendas that this semi-ideology provides contemporary British society.

Theorising the dynamics of anti-Muslimism: Werbner (2005)

Something of the internal flexibility and complexity of anti-Muslimism can be revealed by pragmatically employing a form of analysis outlined by Werbner (2005). Drawing on psychodynamic insights, she proposes that there are three internal logics to all forms of racism, including anti-Islamism. There is a drive by the majority toward:

- *Self-purification:* to physically eject or eliminate the threatening 'other'.
- *Subordination:* a need to denigrate and differentiate the 'other' in order to physically exploit them.
- *Assimilation:* a need to eliminate the 'other' through the destruction of their culture.

Werbner further suggests that as there are three logics of racism so too there are three complementary archetypal demonic figures that are conjured up by these racisms. Employing terms that can only be called unfortunate in their connotations, she calls these *the slave, the witch* and *the Grand Inquisitor* (Werbner, 2005: 7).

Her argument is that where exploitation and subordination are the underlying dynamics then, 'the fear is of the physically powerful, wild, out of control "slave"' (Werbner, 2005: 7). For Werbner, such 'slave' folk devils must be controlled and subordinated. In the context of contemporary anti-Muslimism it is not unreasonable to identify the 'slave' trope located in the inner-city South Asian youth populations. The progeny of the once much needed, and exploited, reserve army of labour that serviced the northern textile industry, and other harsh and poorly paid modes of employment elsewhere, these young men are now presented as the feared inner-city youth whose arrogance and streetwise style offends 'English' decency. The current heirs of the urban youth threat that has mutated from Cohen's (1972) 'Skinhead' folk devils, through the 'muggers' of Hall et al's (1978) *Policing the crisis* and the Afro-Caribbean 'Rude Boys' of Gilroy's (1987) *There ain't no black in the Union Jack*, are the young Muslim men in Britain's inner cities who find themselves portrayed as macho sexists, disdainful equally of their parents' moral constraint and of the majority rule of law. Living in 'self-segregated communities', they are presented[5] as the feral, criminalised, uncontrolled lumpen mass whose threat was made concrete in the riots of 2001. Soon after those events, politicians, journalists, academics and 'leaders' of all political and ethnic shades came to the same or similar conclusion: *steps have to be taken for they must be controlled!*

The need for such a specific historicising of the current stigma attached to Muslim male youth is underlined by Wacquant's (2008) comparative account of the very different symbolic environment constructed around US ghettoes and the French *banlieues*. The very British intersection of class, 'race' and religious sentiment around the moral panic over the contemporary inner city provides a quite specific context for the emergence and expression of anti-Muslimism in Britain. The inner city is both the locus of the perceived 'self-segregation' of Muslim communities and the domestic 'alien' territory where they pursue their 'parallel lives'. It is the feared natural terrain of the 'home-grown bomber' and the site of the much publicised police raids.

In a broader sense, we can see here also the 'realistic conflict' (Sherif, 1967; Brown, 1995) between the white working class and the Muslim communities who find themselves sharing a marginalised status within the distribution of wealth, health and status in contemporary Britain (Modood et al, 1997; Loury et al, 2005). For such white working-class communities, informed by a mix of historically embedded racist imagery that fuels the 'slave' status attached to Muslim 'strangers', and a nationalism that offers a compensatory status to offset against their class exclusion, anti-Muslimism offers a displaced target for their anger and distress. However, the sometimes inappropriate nature of this working-class response should not be allowed to obscure the fact that they too have historically and currently, faced state processes of 'civilisation', and that they have concrete issues of marginalisation which are negotiated in very specific urban and rural contexts where *their* threatened identities are defended. This underlines Halliday's emphasis on, among other things, the interplay of context, identities and specific issues.

In an opportunity society where a Labour government has predominantly followed the economic policies of Thatcherism, and where the middle classes have been actively nurtured at their expense, then the white working class has demonstrated a capacity for resentment at the *perceived* benefits that have been enjoyed by minority ethnic communities, a conclusion that is apparent in and drawn from our own data below. Their grievances are given legitimacy by the populist provocations of the tabloid press, by the elite polemics of social commentators, while social science too has found the circumstances of the displaced white working class a cause for concern (Dench et al, 2006; Dorling, 2009; Garner, 2009; Gillborn, 2009; Nayak, 2009). The resentment of settled communities who find themselves in real and imagined competition with once migrant communities has a well recorded capacity to be translated into racist, and in this case Islamophobic, prejudices.

Alongside the 'slave', Werbner defines the 'witch' folk devil as being:

> … highly assimilated, cultured, successful, wealthy…. The witch crystallizes fears of the hidden, disguised, malevolent stranger, of a general breakdown of trust. Of a nation divided against itself. Your neighbour may be a witch who wants to destroy you. (Werbner, 2005: 7)

Although Werbner herself sees the witch as having a relatively minor role within anti-Muslimism, it seems very probable that this is exactly the folk devil conjured by the resentment at the new Muslim economic and professional elite. No longer confined to their subordinate role as the hewers of wood and the drawers of water who serviced Britain's postwar economic recovery, Muslim communities have now experienced their own internal differentiation as children have succeeded in business and risen in the professions. As Finney and Simpson (2009) have shown, there is a new Muslim bourgeoisie whose comfortable straddling of both their British identity and familial culture constitutes exactly the ambiguity that infuriates distraught nationalist sensibilities. Following Werbner, it is reasonable to hypothesise that in current circumstances it is *their* difference that must be *made* explicit so that they can be clearly known as the cultural Trojan Horse that they are: hence the reification of religious difference as a vehicle for their ejection from the collective ethnos of the national body. Their perceived threat is subversive, their success is resented, their Britishness is not trusted. They must renounce their difference or have it expunged. The dynamics of employing the witch trope in the British context would, for example, set a limit on the efficacy of class mobility as a means of exiting from the traditional marginalisation of the urban Muslim population. Indeed it would suggest that such success might be the very trigger to processes of re-fencing the difference between the non-Muslim and Muslim populations.

Werbner's third archetypal folk devil she portrays as being rooted in a Western elite response to the rise of political Islam, and the perceived challenge it presents to the individualism and self-expression located in the Western secular state. It seems both appropriate and necessary to quote Werbner at a little length on this definition, principally because of the depth and context her definition provides:

> I have deliberately named this folk devil the Grand Inquisitor rather than using several more obvious epithets (the terrorist, the fanatic, the fundamentalist), the reason

being to draw attention to the reflexive fear Islam conjures – not (as in the case of the black mugger) the fear of physicality unbound, the Freudian id let loose, but the fear of the super-ego gone wild. European history is marked by the long struggle to escape the Grand Inquisitor, the domination of the church over the soul, the stranglehold exerted over the body. In this respect Islamophobia is like other phobias and racisms, an incapacity to cope not only with difference but with resemblance. At stake is not the battle between Christendom and Islam, as many Muslims believe. What is scary about Islam is the way it evokes the spectre of puritanical Christianity, a moral crusade, European sectarian wars, the Crusades, the Inquisition, the attack on the permissive society. (Werbner, 2005: 8)

There is then something distinctive here about this form of anti-Muslimism: it resides in the perceived challenge that Islam presents to the contemporary Western European, and distinctively British, experience of the struggle of individual freedoms in relation to Christian dogmas. It is also represented within the challenge that Islam, or indeed other faiths, present to the secular European polity. It is, in an uncomfortable sense, a case of seeing your own moral and cultural ambiguities laid bare through the lens of assertive Islam. Werbner is explicit in identifying the assertive, moral superiority of elements of political Islam. In denying the validity of other cultures and in presenting a polarised opposition between Islam and 'the West', these same elements provide a concrete basis for this sense of challenge and threat. Thus she argues that the Grand Inquisitor is 'a figure constructed by fearful elites which may nevertheless legitimise far cruder forms of biological racism' (Werbner, 2005: 8).

In this regard we can note that a core element in the assault on British multiculturalism has been exactly within this *Grand Inquisitor* mode. It has been an anguished cry for the protection of a self-evident, and therefore undefined, British identity which is seen to be under assault from the pernicious relativism of multicultural ideologues.[6] The argument that every culture except 'the British culture' has been given respect and protection within the pluralism that was at the core of British multiculturalism has been widely rehearsed in British politics and in the press. The invocation of 'political correctness', as multiculturalism's gagging of the free-speaking British citizen legitimately trying to assert *their* identity and *their* rights, became a ubiquitous and efficient means of undermining any attempt to defend multicultural principles and practice. Indeed for one commentator, multiculturalism provided a quite specific context for an assault on the integrity of the British working classes (Collins, 2004). Thus with a melding of cultural and class concerns we can see that the sentiments and values invoked through the *Grand Inquisitor* agenda and through the *slave* agenda are quite capable of merging in the specific context of the white working class who may frame their economic anxieties within the cultural concerns of their own distinctive forms of British nationalism. Again we can note the concrete context of the loss of social status, and of economic and financial security, that frames the disposition to take up these expressive intergroup positions.

At the same time the challenge to the ownership of moral authority and intellectual certainty presented by assertive Islam is felt by segments of the British elite in much the way that Werbner's depiction of the *Grand Inquisitor* would predict. Their status and their self-regarding sense of their destiny as the arbiters of the British cultural cannon propel them to vigorously contest what they see as this pernicious assault on the core values and identity of 'Britishness'. Notably, this elite is defined by class and cultural affiliation rather than simply by ethnicity. As Werbner suggests, a core element in this anti-Muslimism is a concern to protect the liberal freedoms and secularised public space that has been characteristic of the zeitgeist of the 'baby-boomer' cogniscenti. It is the moral certitude, linked with the collective adherence to religious observance, that is seen in elements of British Islam that constitutes the perceived threat to this elite's commitment to an individualised, and possibly relativised, moral universe.

Through Werbner's taxonomy we are invited to explore the particularities of the history and context that frame the emergence in Britain of specific modes of anti-Muslimism. Not only may different fragments of the majority population be particularly susceptible to specific forms of the anti-Muslim repertoire, but so too different actors can be anticipated to play active roles in the construction of specific folk devils and forms of hostility. The concerns of white working-class estate dwellers, who share many of the economic disadvantages experienced by Muslim communities, can be realistically converted into resentments at the *perceived* benefits enjoyed by these same Muslim communities. And, in our data below, the practice of 'myth busting' emerges as one of the successes of the local authority staff who have become adept at identifying new and varied forms of strategic Islamophobia/anti-Muslimism, as adjacent communities misinterpret the realities of local resource allocation.

It is in this context that the erstwhile 'slave' is also seen as an illegitimate competitor for scarce local government largesse. This 'slave' population can equally attract the ire of comfortable middle-class majority citizens, who have no direct contact with Muslim communities, but who nonetheless fear the assault on urban security that they see as being present within these 'parallel cultures' of which they are routinely reminded. Phillips' (2005) discourse about the 'victim culture' of Muslim communities may seek to inculcate exactly this kind of resentment at the perceived illegitimate claims of Muslims, the majority of whom, we should remind ourselves, are British *citizens*. Elites and others can react strongly to the perceived threat of Islam *per se* in a convulsion of anxiety about national identities and unstable cultural norms. Each of these constituencies of anxiety can become the target of quite specific political rhetorics, honed specifically for their consumption, both by localised campaigns of the BNP and by the anti-Muslim sentiments expressed by mainstream politicians.

Theorising the dynamics of anti-Muslimism: contemporary social psychological insights

While there is not the time to adequately develop the material further here, it is important to note that there is a substantial body of research and theory, found in the social psychological literature, which can provide a rich conceptual language for understanding the psychological dynamics that are likely to be engaged in the operation of the many forms of anti-Muslimism (see, for example, Douglas, 1995; Abrams and Hogg, 1999; Capozza and Brown, 2000; Dovidio et al, 2005).

Social identity theory (Tajfel and Turner, 1979), which has developed an extensive research literature, argues that people are motivated to maintain a positive sense of their social identity through their engagement in social groups. By a creative and active social comparison of one's in-group(s) with specific out-group(s), individuals maintain a positive self-identity. However, the creation of negative out-group judgements is by no means an automatic product of group comparison but, for example, is a function of such variables as the intensity of group identification, normative beliefs about group differences and ideological features of the social world (Turner, 1999). Thus the *psychology* of social identity maintenance takes place in a relationship to the objective world; and the beliefs and values that are brought to bear in making sense of it. Social identity theory is very much a social theory (Reicher, 2004); the situational determination of the specific triggering of intergroup salience is heavily supported in the research literature (see, for example, Capozza and Brown, 2000).

In a complementary way *integrated threat theory* (Stephan and Stephan, 1996; Stephan et al, 1999) provides a particularly fruitful perspective on anti-Muslimism by drawing on the distinctions between realistic threat, symbolic threat, stereotypes and intergroup anxiety. *Intergroup anxiety* refers to a personal anticipation of loss of control and of possible personal embarrassment when faced with an intercultural exchange. It is, then, a reasonable personal anxiety when contemplating ethnic diversity. However, when such personal anxiety results in avoidance of contact because of the anticipated loss of face, it becomes self-perpetuating. The existence of prior *stereotypes* about the strange 'other' feeds this anxiety, and provides post hoc justification for any avoidance action taken: it is *their* strangeness which has made this avoidance behaviour both necessary and appropriate.

Realistic threat and *symbolic threat*, however, are experienced as an intergroup phenomena, where the heightened sensibilities of intergroup competition can play a specific and amplificatory role (Tajfel and Turner, 1979; Abrams and Hogg, 1999). *Realistic threat* is comparable to Halliday's '*strategic* anti-Muslimism' being associated with economic, political and physical concerns. *Symbolic threat*, on the other hand, is comparable to Halliday's '*populist* anti-Muslimism', being focused on a concern with the in-group's cultural and moral integrity. The benefits of employing integrated threat theory, and other social psychological models, is that they can provide invaluable insights into the *psychological dynamics* that may underpin specific forms of anti-Muslimism. As the MORI poll commissioned as an element of the Commission on Integration and Community Cohesion's final report (2007) *Our shared future* revealed, a sense of realistic threat is a common element of intergroup sentiment in Britain.

Gonzalez et al (2008) have applied integrated threat theory to an illuminating exploration of attitudes toward Muslims. There is considerable research evidence to support the view that, in an intergroup situation, those with high levels of in-group identification are more likely to engage in a variety of group-level responses compared to the responses of low identifiers (see Ellemers et al, 1999). As Gonzalez et al (2008: 670) phrase it:

> The more people identify with their in-group, the more likely they are to be concerned about their group interests and to consider it important to preserve their own culture.

> Group identity functions as a group lens that makes people
> sensitive to anything that could harm their group.

Thus when we wish to account for the power of anti-Muslimism one of the first tasks is to enquire ,'How is it that specific in-group identities have been made salient, and how is it that specific out-groups have become accepted as the legitimate target for comparison and out-group hostility?'. This is entirely consistent with Halliday's perspective and underlines the significance of the discussion in the previous chapters of the manner in which Muslims in Britain have been constructed as a threatening presence and a focus of government policy.

What social identity theory can add to this process of revealing the nature of the development of anti-Muslim sentiments is a body of literature that can lay out the likely antecedents of specific *intergroup postures being developed* (Tajfel, 1981). When groups enter into a process of intergroup comparison in the context of group differences in status and power, then quite different perspectives on how the marginalised group may respond to their objective situation may develop depending on how they subjectively perceive this situation. *Is the differential in status seen as legitimate? Is it seen as stable? Can you conceive of it being vulnerable to pressure? Are the boundaries between groups permeable? Can you easily exit from your stigmatised group?* (Verkuyten and Reijerse, 2008). Factors such as this may determine whether the intergroup dynamics become shaped by a framework of conflict, of extensive efforts to leave the marginalised group (exit), or through social creativity (where the stigmatised group develops new criteria whereby they can maintain positive intergroup comparison, while not challenging their objective situation) (Abrams and Hogg, 1999).

In the British context the pervasive intersection of religious and ethnic identities means that for South Asian Muslims their *ethnic* identity is likely to remain a sufficient criterion for them to be identified as Muslim, even though they may be non-Muslim. The power of colour and historical colonial imagery to continue to fuel the stereotyping of British South Asian Muslims is a major barrier to their full acceptance in British life: a significant degree of impermeability is attached to their situation. However, as we have seen above, the Muslim communities in Britain have in recent decades acquired a quite distinct in-group sensibility that contributes significantly in enabling them to perceive their marginality as illegitimate. They are additionally aware of the historical progress that has been made in the political challenges to exclusion and marginality that have been made by ex-colonial peoples in confronting their treatment by majority populations. Additionally, their sense of an embattled identity exists within the wider context of a 'politics of difference' where it has become quite usual for identity groups to assert their rights: think, for example, of feminism, gay pride and the civil rights movement (discussed further in Chapter Six, this volume). Such sensibilities are of course internally mediated within these minority Muslim populations by gender, age and class variables. But passive acceptance of religious vilification and racial exclusion should not be regarded as likely socio-political perspectives held among Britain's Muslim populations. In this context social identity theory has much to offer in illuminating some of the likely emergent intergroup processes.

The research literature also indicates the ways in which the socio-political context may shape the development of perceived threat. For example, Sniderman et al (2004) demonstrated the power of symbolic threat in the context of the Netherlands. But the strong politics of difference expressed in the Dutch–Muslim cultural war, and the explicit rejection of multiculturalism that has dominated Dutch politics, would have provided the dominant discourse in the public sphere that would have made such a finding likely. As we have seen above the very visible and bitter debates around the 'self-segregation' of British Muslims and their perceived preference for living 'parallel lives' has similarly constructed a political environment in which symbolic threat has an over-determined salience in the British context. At the same time the continuing implications of the London bombings of 7/7 and further terrorist arrests gives a concrete base for a sense of perceived realistic threat that may not be so apparent in countries which have had no such terrorist outrages associated with Islam. Bizman and Yinon (2001) found that in the state of Israel, realistic threat, but not symbolic threat, strongly predicted out-group attitudes. Given the historical experience of Jews and the current political context of the Middle East, linked with the internally constructed sense of continuing vulnerability to external aggression, such a finding is hardly surprising. We may then conclude, echoing Halliday's (1996) injunction, that when we seek to explore the role of symbolic and realistic threat in shaping anti-Muslim sentiments we should expect in each instance to systematically explore the socio-political context in order to understand *how* realistic and symbolic threat comes to be configured in particular ways in specific locales.

This social psychological perspective also valuably underlines the fact that where realistic threat is experienced it is not the absolute extent of deprivation that one group suffers in relation to another, but that rather it is the perceived *relative* deprivation – a sense of deprivation in comparison with other persons or groups –that is significant

(Runciman, 1966; Walker and Pettigrew, 1984). Thus relatively affluent members of a majority group may resent what they perceive to be the benefits provided to asylum seekers not because the asylum seekers are better off than them, but because they are perceived as getting more from the state: *we pay taxes, they spend them!* Both social identity theory and relative deprivation theory pivot around issues of social comparison (Grant and Brown, 1995; Tropp and Wright, 1999), and insight into the social psychological processes underlying the subjective perception that fuels relative deprivation is highly relevant to any understanding of anti-Muslimism.

The explanatory power of social identity theory and integrated threat theory has been complemented by recent developments in social psychology that have explored the production and impact of social discourses that have shaped the construction of intergroup perceptions (Edwards and Potter, 2001; Billig, 2002; Wetherell, 2003). Thus the operation of the psychological processes of intergroup dynamics can be better understood through an appreciation of the specific definitions of the group identities and the language that comes to define their interrelationships. This has been a fruitful field of research for discourse analysis where language practices have been revealed as being central to the reproduction of relations of power and the legitimating of dominance and exploitation (Fairclough and Wodak, 1997). We have seen above the critical role of the media in framing events around terrorism and Islam within highly selective discourses and authors such as Burnett and Whyte (2005), Beck (2002) and Zedner (2006) have examined the construction of terrorism discourses.

Recently, Tileaga (2007), in a valuable analysis, employs this research tradition in exploring the manner in which discourses construct the dehumanisation and delegitimisation of out-groups (Tileaga, 2007: 720):

> According to Opotow, 'moral exclusion occurs when individuals or groups are perceived as outside the boundary in which moral values, rules and considerations of fairness apply' (Opotow, 1990a, p 1). The term 'delegitimization' has been introduced as a very important social psychological process that permits moral exclusion.

The processes of dehumanisation and delegitimisation that are reviewed by Tileaga point centrally to one of the key processes in a specific form of intergroup dynamic that radically shifts the relationships between the two parties involved, namely, it renders one of them as outside of the normal range of moral affinity, as fundamentally 'not us'! This is what we have experienced in the impact of extreme Islamophobia. It is the correlate of the accumulated and interactive impact of the 'War on Terror', of the 'clash of civilisations' discourse in its many varieties, of the 'othering' that is implicit in the normalisation of 'securitisation' and of the permeation of these discourses by a historically specific British form of Orientalism and stereotyping of Islam. In intergroup dynamics, this discourse legitimates the construction of fundamental divides between 'us' and 'them' whereby the 'them' are not only different and inferior but are seen as being outside the pale of our routine moral writ. This provides a framing of the 'limits of tolerance' discourse (Blommaert and Verschueren, 1998) within a radical rejection of any common ground between the virtuous 'us' and the threatening and contaminating 'them'. The psychological logics and power of delegitimisation outlined by Tileaga is given a wider political context, and significance, when linked with Mouffe's (2005) account of the replacement of adversarial, left–right politics by a juxtapositioning of moral categories of 'good' and 'evil', and of 'freedom' and 'fundamentalism'. It is argued that this process of 'evilisation' forecloses on debate and limits contestation.

From a more positive perspective, social psychological research has shown the relevance and the power of a quite different discourse in shaping intergroup relations: specifically, the significance of a commitment to a philosophy of multiculturalism. Research has shown that the endorsement of multiculturalism is related to out-group attitudes (see, for example, Verkuyten, 2005; Wolsko et al, 2006). Holding a positive commitment to a multicultural ideology, which regards cultural diversity as good for society, has been shown to be a key ideological aspect in the context of immigrants and minority cultures (Verkuyten, 2006). Berry (2006) has argued that multicultural policies try to facilitate a feeling of confidence among people living in a plural society which includes a sense of trust and security in 'the other' and in one's own identity. In simple terms, belief that mutual coexistence can be positive and mutually rewarding has an impact on the construction of specific intergroup postures: positive cooperative, rather than negative, ones. Thus, for example, Verkuyten (2005) found that the more Dutch participants endorsed a multicultural ideology the more likely they were to evaluate the Muslim Turkish out-group positively. Gonzalez et al (2008) have provided a rich empirical analysis of the interplay of such positive sentiments toward multiculturalism with expressions of subjective and realistic threat. In their words:

> The endorsement of multiculturalism was indirectly associated with prejudice, namely through its associations with symbolic threat and stereotypes. Individuals who endorsed multiculturalism more strongly perceived less symbolic threat and had less negative stereotypes. Multiculturalism was also negatively related to realistic threat. (Gonzalez et al, 2008: 680)

The significance of these findings is particularly poignant when we note the extensive retreat from a commitment to multiculturalism as mapped above, and the complementary weakening of commitments to human rights principles which frame and give political leverage to such commitments.

Thus, in sum we can see that in any attempt to understand the nature of anti-Muslimism there is to be found within social psychology a range of theoretical and empirical tools which will significantly extend our understanding of the processes that may be engaged in any specific instance of Islamophobia. This literature may not simplify our understanding, but it will make our understanding of the challenges to be faced in challenging its existence more realistic.

It is appropriate that Halliday identifies anti-Muslimism as a pseudo-ideology since this focuses our attention on the nature of anti-Muslimism as a system of beliefs, values and practices that have substantive political import as well as a socio-political derivation. From this perspective we can benefit from the sort of analysis sketched above where we have sought to trace the historical origins of anti-Muslimism in past intergroup relations, and to track its current permeation of different cultural sites. We can deploy sociological understandings of current demographic and structural realities in order to map the current context which gives specific forms of anti-Muslimism their resonance and political relevance. However, in order to develop a more nuanced understanding, it is necessary to employ a social psychology which can provide us with an account of why anti-Muslimism can be so inflected with the 'bloody-mindedness' that is so characteristic of homo sapiens' intergroup hostility. Accounts of anti-Muslimism expressed in sociological terms, as an ideological construction, can too often leave out of contention the strongly emotive and irrational content of Islamophobia, that, like Werbner's account, needs to reflect the psychodynamic notions of defensive psychological mechanisms such as projection and suppression. All such routes of understanding are necessary if we are going to be able to draw valid and applicable policy insights from the data.

Conclusion

This chapter has sought to open up our understanding of the complex nature of Islamophobia, and of the dynamics which may shape it. Rather than seeing it as some homogeneous process driven by an expression of 'natural human prejudices' we can see it as a multilayered ideological construction which in every instance must be understood in its specificity. In the British context the particular Orientalist sediments that may be found within British culture have a quite distinct historical trajectory, and their cooption into contemporary sentiments of anti-Muslimism are mediated by the religious (Islamic), ethnic, gender and class identities of the target populations. As Halliday has pointed out, this specifically anti-Muslim content of Islamophobia exists in a dynamic relation with other ideologies of hierarchy and exclusion. The work done by these interacting belief systems does much to make the populist expression of anti-Muslimism seemingly reasonable and legitimate. However, the introduction of psychological insights into our understanding provides an additional dimension to our appreciation of the political potency of such beliefs and feelings. They point to the affective power of anti-Muslim sentiments when they become integrated into the negotiation of intergroup dynamics. At this point we see anti-Muslimism as not only some product of an over-socialised shared belief system, but as being also a vehicle for maintaining self-esteem and in-group identity. The fusion of the socio-political and the social psychological dynamics provides a qualitatively different understanding of the resilience and potential political potency of anti-Muslimism.

Notes
[1] While our discussion here is focused on the British situation we should keep in mind the very particular manifestations of anti-Islamic sentiment and practice that is taking place in other European countries (see, for example, Fetzer and Soper, 2005; Modood et al, 2006).

[2] See, for example, Steet (2000), for a useful account of the interplay of Arab ethnicity and Muslim religious identity in *National Geographic's* representation of the Arab world.

[3] See also EUFRA (2009) for a demonstration of the intersection of ethnicity, age and religion in shaping the discrimination experienced by Muslims in Europe.

[4] The development of a personal and state form of insecurity has been particularly frequent during the 'credit crunch' as well as the fuel crisis and protests of 2000 onward, not to mention the rhetoric of violent (often inner-city and/or knife) crime as well as, of course, the various aspects of terrorism, both at home and abroad.

[5] See Hussain and Bagguley (2005) for an illuminating account of the response to the 2001 disturbances.

[6] The international nature of 'white backlash' to multiculturalism has been valuably explored by Hewitt (2005).

FIVE

The experience of managing Community Cohesion and Prevent

Introduction

The purpose of this chapter is to present the reader with an account of the insights that can be derived from the interview data collected from the research outlined in Chapter One. The preceding chapters offered a wide framework within which this data may be understood, and provided an account of the context within which Community Cohesion and Prevent have developed in the British policy arena. The broader national and international political context within which these specific policies should be located has also been sketched in order that the material below may be seen as an integral part of wider social and political trends. Additionally a range of academic analytic concepts have been introduced so that the specific examples provided below may be read in relation to an explanatory language that will inform the conclusions drawn in the next and final chapter.

The insights outlined below do not tumble out of the data as a wonderfully coordinated pre-structured story. Following the rationale outlined in Chapter One, each of the themes presented below has been identified by a careful mapping of the evidence coming from across all the interviews. Consequently there is always a question of how best to present this collection of findings as a cumulative whole that provides a story that can be justified by the data from which it is drawn. The simplest way to present the data would have been as a listing of each of the themes as a single item under a separate heading, so that these building blocks could then be assembled in any way that the reader chose to make sense of them. However, the findings are not in fact a random collection of discrete 'facts', but rather they can be seen as elements in a story that can be made sense of in terms of the context sketched in the previous chapters. Thus, in presenting the data below, the findings, outlined under discrete sub-headings, have been deliberately put in an order that will hopefully help the reader see the connections between each element. That there should be such linkages follows from the fact that this data represents a reflection of the ways in which the local authority personnel interviewed in this study sought to make sense of the challenge they experienced in trying to apply these two central government policies at local authority level. To a significant degree they share a common institutional and professional environment, and are governed by a shared political context in which legal and organisational constraints on their actions have much in common. Consequently it is reasonable to expect that their responses will have a degree of common coherence.

The first three sections below – *Managing Community Cohesion and Prevent, The local state and central government* and *Policy overload and local discretion* – tell us something of the **organisational context and response** at the local level to the introduction by central government of these two policies. This section opens up our understanding of something of the dynamics between the local state and central government as they are filtered through the implementation of these two policies. The data presented here introduces us to an understanding of the pressures experienced by local personnel, and to something of the organisational and personal resources they draw on in making sense of central government's expectations. This provides a necessary understanding of the organisational context within which the following actions and experiences are shaped.

The next section explores the **political impact of Prevent** as we explore *Prevent as politically problematic* and some of its implications for the implementation of Community Cohesion. This section reveals the significant hostility that was generated by the introduction of Prevent and the extent to which implementing it at local state level constituted a personal and organisational challenge. This section introduces the data which demonstrates the extent to which the Prevent agenda permeated the operation of Community Cohesion, and resulted in a problematic *intersection of Prevent and Community Cohesion*. This then becomes a significant factor in shaping the experiences that are revealed in the subsequent sections.

The next section, *Implementing Prevent and Community Cohesion* explores the implications of the management of *Funding* for our understanding of how resistance to Prevent had implications for the ways in which it was implemented while the issue of *The 'usual suspects'* indicates how concerns with security and community resistance interact in shaping the local authorities' engagement with local communities. The contested status of Muslim identities become central to this analysis, as the state's concern to distinguish between 'good' and 'bad' Muslims destabilises routine practices. This then has direct implications for the personal *experiences of staff in implementing Prevent and Community Cohesion*, where exploring *Prevent as morally problematic* reveals something of the fundamental shift in the working environment of local authority staff. The 'risk' that has become attached to working with Muslim communities, when they are framed by the national agenda of concern with security and counter-terrorism, is revealed as introducing a significant new dimension to community work. In a similar vein *The specific experience of Muslim staff* reveals the uncomfortable tensions that may be attached to Muslim personnel working in local authorities where they may be expected to assist in implementing a policy that is unpopular in the communities they serve.

The section, *Communities, identities, governance* presents a shift from a focus on the personal to a concern with *Community perceptions* of the implementation of these policies. The material presented here echoes the concerns with intergroup threat discussed in Chapter Four and provides some limited insight into how different communities perceive their relation to the local authority and to each other. This material feeds back to the prior discussion of the significance of local knowledge held by local authority personnel; in a discussion of *Myth busting*, how this expertise is employed in diffusing developing intergroup tensions is explored.

The final section continues this process of expanding the focus and explores the wider context where an exploration of *Interference from other government policies* reveals the impossibility of isolating one policy from the implications of other government actions. A discussion of *Community Cohesion, Prevent and inequality* identifies a concern that the actions undertaken under these policies may represent only a tokenistic means of addressing the underlying structural determination of inequalities that feed both radicalisation and intergroup tensions.

The data presented in this chapter thus offers a multilevel insight into the impact of attempting to implement both Prevent and Community Cohesion simultaneously at local authority level. In addition, the data presented below provides a cumulative picture of the ways in which, in their implementation, the Prevent and Community Cohesion programmes and rationales overlap and merge organisationally and at the point of delivery. There is clear evidence of the intrusive penetration of Prevent into the practice of Community Cohesion, often with explicitly negative consequences.

The reader might want to recall the discussion in Chapter One about the purpose of the interviews analysed here. It was not to evaluate the effectiveness of these policies at the point of delivery but rather to focus on the *experience* of trying to make sense of them at local authority level. In trying to remain true to the commitments undertaken when negotiating access to these authorities, the quotations have been deliberately selected in order to pre-empt any identification of their sources; the analysis, therefore, is presented in terms of the shared experience of these five authorities. Of course, in not being able to interrogate the differences between these authorities, a condition laid down in agreeing access, there is a necessary loss of an additional level of analysis. But the benefit is the remarkable openness and directness of the evidence made available through these interviews. The frankness and detail provided in the interviews has contributed significantly to the confidence that may be attached to the insights offered below.

As indicated above, the data is provided under a number of headings that will allow the account to remain true to the data, while not trying to stretch individual statements beyond the context in which they were made. Any linking analysis is given in the concluding chapter.

Managing Community Cohesion and Prevent: the organisational response

Before looking in more detail at the themes emerging from this research it is appropriate to briefly note the changing organisational context within which these two programmes were being delivered. The remit of this research explicitly excluded any comparative examination of the operation of the five participating authorities. Rather, the focus was to be on revealing common themes that emerged across all the authorities. Nor was the focus to be on the success with which each authority had implemented central government policies but rather it was to explore their experience of seeking to implement these policies. With this in mind it remains useful to note the organisational changes that were characteristic of the situation in each of the authorities at the time of the data collection. It would be fair to say that 2008/09 was a period where these authorities were engaged in widespread internal reorganisation as they sought to reconfigure their internal departmental structures in order to manage the mix of policy demands that were impinging on them. This reorganisation was shaped by the need to efficiently mesh the delivery of Community Cohesion and Prevent in the context of other government policy directives and specifically in the context of *Safer stronger communities* and *Our shared future*. In quite different ways each of the five authorities was reorganising their departmental structures in order to fit their management capacity to the challenge of delivering their *Strategic plan* in the context of the wider policy environment and their particular local area agreement. Before Prevent, or even Community Cohesion, departments with remits in regeneration, equality, community development, young people or housing had been carrying out functions that had now become central to the coherent articulation of Community Cohesion and Prevent; at the point of data collection, each authority was carrying out its own form of managerial and departmental restructuring in order to manage this nexus of competing agendas. This was a process to which much detailed planning and thought was being given, and it was clear that in each authority their own solutions were being evolved in relation to their own experience and perception of priorities. In some authorities the responsibility for managing Prevent and Community Cohesion was being effectively combined, both departmentally and operationally, while in others they remained distinct entities.

From an outsider's perspective it seemed likely that a central driver within this process was the new centrality of interagency working that had been driven by a number of agendas since the late 1990s, and was given impetus by the implementation of Community Cohesion and Prevent. Parallel departmental silos, each operating within a minimal engagement with the activities of other salient departments, was an anathema in the context of delivering Prevent and Community Cohesion. The extensive reality of interdepartmental and interagency working and the necessary coordination of overlapping responsibilities informed the reorganisation. Additionally a regional Cohesion Board of chief executives, operating within the Association of West Yorkshire Authorities (AWYA), supported by a Cohesion Group of senior managers, provided a network for sharing experience, best practice and the development of a coherent shared relationship with central government. Across the five authorities there was a real sense of considered engagement with the challenges faced in delivering these two policies in the context of all the other cross-cutting policy functions of the local state. Developing a coherent policy response at this time was not aided by the chronic ambiguity attached to the concept and process of Community Cohesion, nor by the indecent speed with which Prevent, and specifically the Pathfinder initiative, were introduced.

As noted elsewhere in this text the commitment and professional engagement of the senior managers interviewed was impressive. No one was overwhelmed by the cross-cutting agendas of these two policies, although there was a widespread recognition of the particular problems and sensitivities that came with managing both of these policies in tandem. Frequently in interviewing the senior managers, a strong sense of their fusion of their professional and personal ownership of the managerial task was underpinned by a strong identification with the local area. This was often accompanied by explicit pride in an extensive local knowledge of their local populations, and their distinctive differences and histories. An assertive confidence in their ability to manage these contemporary challenges very probably owed much to these personal biographies and this cohort's personal experience of the resilience of the local state apparatus in the face of central government initiatives. They certainly saw it as their task to make local sense of contradictory and ambivalent central government policy.

The interviews with the senior managers and the elected councillors (providing the local political governance) responsible for these two policy agendas revealed a range of managerial styles across the five authorities. In some it could be said that the councillors took a loose hold on the reigns of policy management, and that consequently it was the officers who were very much in control of developing and implementing policy. Elsewhere, however, councillors demonstrated a much more hands-on approach in their working with the lead officers. It is worth noting that party politics appeared to have little relevance to the councillors' understanding of their role in overseeing these policy areas. They routinely claimed that there were no directives coming to them through the party machinery which laid down party lines on how they should be discharging their duties in relation to these policies. Indeed, a broad interparty consensus on the ways in which the local authority should manage these policies was frequently invoked. For example, two councillors offered these opinions:

> 'I mean the Prevent, it's here where I come across it. There's nothing from the political party that's come out, it's just something that's sent down and we are having to process it and implement it.'

> 'I think areas such as we are speaking of now, I think calls for a greater deal of cross-party understanding, and I'm not aware of any issues.'

The absence of a visible, or 'edgy' party political agenda causing conflict in the political management of these two policies at local state level should not go unremarked. It is consistent with the ideological merging of political perspectives on immigration, security and the management of ethnic diversity across mainstream British politics already noted in Chapters Two and Three. While there may be differences within the rhetoric, and the models for action in specific areas, the over-arching framing of 'post-multiculturalist' British policies on managing diversity reflects a generic consensus. At local state level this did not mean that there was an absolute consensus about the manner in which these two policies should be implemented across all the local councillors with responsibility for these policies. But it did mean that these judgements could be held as personal perspectives, which could coexist with other differing views without there being any strong 'political' implications. Frequently shared criticisms of central government performance in the introduction of Prevent were complemented by a confidence in their ability to exploit local knowledge and expertise to make these policies relevant at the local level.

As might be expected, the councillors did not, on the whole, have the in-depth knowledge and managerial focus that was apparent in the interviews with the staff. They were uniformly comfortable with the responsibilities that they held, including having on occasions to be the 'flak catchers' when, for example, issues related to these two policies emerged as contentious news stories. As one councillor put it:

> 'It's my responsibility and I stand up to that responsibility;
> and as far as I'm concerned the buck stops with me.'

Given that CONTEST, and within that Prevent, is aimed at confronting terrorism within the UK, it is inevitable that security issues lie at its heart. Consequently there is a concern with the flow of information within its organisational structure, and a 'need-to-know' principle has been translated into three tiers of organisational activity. The most sensitive and exclusive group is the 'gold' group at the top of the hierarchy, with 'silver' and 'bronze' beneath. The restriction on the flow of information, and knowledge about 'what is going on' that is inherent in this process, has significant implications for those who are engaged in implementing Prevent. As we shall see below it has implications for those implementing Community Cohesion initiatives, for interagency collaboration, and it raises questions about communication and trust between senior managers and those at the operational level delivering the policies. For some of the councillors at least, the necessity of this regulation of information was entirely understandable and non-problematic. As one councillor stated:

> 'I'm more than happy that there is someone taking decisions
> that says this is sensitive; and we have to be careful in the

manner in which that information is handled. I've got no problem with that whatsoever.'

And another councillor who was worried about the fact that too much information leaked into the public domain said:

'What as a politician I want is to know that there is effective controls; I want to know that there's political control over it and if I'm satisfied that there is political control at a relevant level, that's fine with me.'

Thus at the time of this study the five authorities at the heart of the project were in different ways developing a new organisational structure that would, among other things, provide an efficient system for integrating their delivery of Community Cohesion and Prevent. At the time of the interviews with the senior managers these changes were in process. A parallel project could have fruitfully been carried out on the multilayered organisational structures that were emerging with some ongoing ambiguities about their operational implementation. However, as departmental structures and their relationships to each other changed at the managerial level, there was also a strong sense of the continuity of professional identities, competences and styles of working at the operational level. Within the five local authorities there were extant organisational units dealing with, for example, equality or community development or youth, whose activities were relevant to both of these agendas and whose management structures were undergoing varying forms of change. It could reasonably be said that at the operational level the skills and routines employed in delivering services would remain essentially intact whatever the organisational changes. Among both the management and operational staff there was evidence of strong professional identities tied to substantive experience within the authority. There were, in other words, strong communities of practice that were the filter through which the policy innovations were processed. 'Communities of practice' (Lave and Wenger, 1991; Burkitt et al, 2001) are highly resilient entities within which professional identities and routines of practice are reproduced and defended. Hence, it was in this context that individual biographies within the local authority shaped their response to these policies and their preferred mode of implementing them.

This organisational change, and the challenge of effectively implementing two closely linked but mutually problematic policies, was of course associated with anxieties and tension. As one senior manager put it:

> 'It's very difficult to sensibly organise a bureaucracy to make it a kind of organic thing that you might be able to do if you ran a small business.... And I think that those kind of structural inefficiencies, the length of time it takes things to happen, the prioritising of policy and strategy over pragmatism and delivery; and also obviously, we are working in a political environment.... But in the local authority things have to be mediated all the time through the Executive, but also through local politicians – particularly with issues like cohesion and community relations.'

There are in addition the personal dynamics of individuals having their own professional and political views about the policies they are required to implement which have implications for the smooth operation of organisations. The stresses taking place in these authorities as they introduced changes in their organisational structures of necessity placed a significant number of staff in a situation of having to accommodate changes in their working environment in one way or another. Where this is linked with the rapid introduction of new policies around Prevent it is not surprising that there was a potential for disagreement. As one manager responsible for such innovation said:

> 'People in my line of work have got personal views about these things, I certainly have, and personal commitments, and sometimes it gets very personal. You know, conflict – personal conflict, and levels of animosity personally directed at you, or that you unfortunately feel towards others.'

While this statement was particularly frank, across the interviews this melding of professional role with personal commitment and political views was frequently evident. The issues raised by the introduction of Prevent certainly made such personal perspectives highly salient.

The local state and central government

If the above section reflected on one set of relationships between central government and the local managers of policy implementation, then in this section we should record the wider constituency of opinion present within these interviews where there were strongly held views about the government and those politicians sallying forth to the regions to wave the flag. In the interviews there were specific anecdotes about the behaviour of politicians who, on making visits to local projects, were regarded as acting in ignorance of the local situation, or worse. Quoting these anecdotes would reveal too closely the likely sources, but the instances that were rehearsed with an equal mix of relish and outrage were disturbing.

At all levels, there is evidence in this data of a strong local disdain for the (lack of) expertise and (inadequate) working methods of their central government colleagues. One specific experience that exemplified this exasperation at the folly of central government action was the initial roll out of the early stage of Prevent where the process of initiating the programmes funded under the first stage of the Pathfinder programme was widely regarded as a classic instance of Westminster fecklessness. The time between the announcement of this element of Prevent and the start-up of the funded programmes was unrealistically short, and doubtless increased the pressure toward the funding of the 'usual suspects', a narrow range of people and organisations, often with prior contact with the local authority (see below). Additionally, the time between the commencement of these initiatives and the required production of reports on their progress was regarded as unfeasibly narrow. This was a case study in the imperatives of Whitehall political expediency overriding a considered collaborative engagement with the local authorities in developing a well-founded and realistically scheduled new programme of work at the local level.

More generally there were frequent comments from a range of sources questioning the competence of those in Westminster who develop the policies to be implemented at the local level. Partly this reflects the pride which many of these local professionals have in their local knowledge. They were therefore righteously aggrieved when they perceived policy being developed as a political expediency with little or no real knowledge of the circumstances on the ground. This is perhaps particularly so where there were authorities from within which there had been individuals convicted of a terrorist offence. It was suggested that there was a shared sense of collective hurt and shame in such communities that this should have occurred on their patch, and a sense of civic pride in taking responsibility for managing the consequences of this for the community and the city. Thus there was little scope for forgiveness when visiting politicians made crass comments, or when policy directives appeared to have been written by people with minimal understanding of local circumstances.

While local authorities may themselves be critiqued for the partiality of their knowledge of the specific circumstance of communities and interests within their locale, there is nonetheless strong evidence here of local authority personnel and councillors having a less than complimentary view of the competence of their Westminster 'betters'. Their own sense of greater competence, sustained by a sense of greater political legitimacy to speak on behalf of their local populations, is an intrinsic element in fuelling their assertive approach, evident in this data, to the local interpretation of central government policy.

Policy overload and local discretion

In interviewing individuals who as senior managers, councillors or field workers are located in particular and different situations in relation to local authority structures, and the implementation of the Prevent and Community Cohesion agendas, there is a sense of the mosaic of professional and personal experiences that contribute to the delivery of these policies at the local level. If the responses outlined in the discussion of the Muslim experience below were preponderantly driven by the experience of those delivering these policies, then in this section it would be correct to say that the focus is on those senior members of staff responsible for the management of these policies, for converting central government policy directives into local action.

An element in the interviews addressed the personal motivation that sustained individuals in carrying out work that was demanding and frequently stressful. It was very apparent that each individual came to the task at hand from within their own unique biographic trajectory. Some could be seen as grass-roots community workers with a continuing commitment to the values and professional working routines that came with that background. Very often individual managers found it easy to refer to values that sustained them in their work. Others were fascinated by the challenge of making sense of policy and practice at the local level, and others might reasonably be seen as people with a preference and gift for management, whatever their professional background. This cohort was very definitely composed of quite different individuals addressing a common challenge. Any stereotypical reference to local government management as some sort of homogeneous group of well-paid apparatchiks could not survive exposure to this cohort of individuals.

However, what they do share is a seriousness of purpose and an apparent personal commitment to serving their local communities and to making the policies work for the local communities, a feature that an outsider looking in could not help but be impressed by. In the authorities that formed the basis of this study the local authority structure had recently undergone, or were currently undergoing significant restructuring as the internal 'tiers', 'departments' or multiple internal divisions were reorganised in order to make sense of the management of a changing policy agenda set by central government. Thus the management of Community Cohesion and Prevent was taking place within an organisational structure that was itself in flux. This administrative and organisational environment might reasonably be seen as adding to the stresses that might be experienced by these managers in implementing these two policies within their authority.

With this context in mind it is then interesting to explore the ways in which these managers experienced the process of being the recipients of central government policy on Community Cohesion and Prevent. What came across to an outside observer was that central government had directed a veritable blizzard of guidance notes, consultation documents and other directives down to the local state in an attempt to micro-manage these policies from above. In reality this seemingly produced a situation where the only rational response at local level was to operate with a large degree of local discretion in trying to make sense of this overload. In relation to this, a senior manager said:

> 'It is hugely difficult to keep on top of the mass of government documentation, and I would challenge anybody to say that they were completely on top of it all.'

Another said:

> 'You get policy from different departments and it's not joined up and they've been banging on about joining it up for years, and all that seems to happen is that it gets to be even more complicated.'

The lack of coherence in terms of the policy documentation streaming out of government departments was also strongly argued by this respondent, who asserted:

> 'You've got the Home Office with their Prevent strategies and things like that, but the funding is coming out to Communities and Local Government, as well as every other department as it seems.'

They noted the additional complications that arose from the intersection of Equality and Migration agendas contributing additional streams of data that should theoretically be made into a coherent strategy at the local level, giving the example that:

> '... the government changes their minds, you know, keep changing their minds.... We just did an add-up, migration – EU migration and stuff, I think that last year about 80 different reports and guidance and research – all this stuff came out. You can't read it all. Even in the last week I've had three from DCLG around migration, and it's trying to keep up with this – constantly the government not getting a handle on it!'

A senior officer talking of central government policy said:

> 'There is that view that they don't mean it, or somebody in an office has got to do something: and they're just chucking stuff out seeing what works.'

On the implementation of Prevent an officer noted that:

> 'There's this massive file of recent information about PVE [Preventing Violent Extremism] essentially. There's been lots of information coming out in a quite relatively short space of time.'

And talking of the necessity of making local sense of the "stuff coming out from central government" a councillor said, referring to an imagined conversation with government ministers:

> 'Nobody's ever challenged you about this have they? And we're going to have to deliver your policy for you, and actually if you listen to us we might do quite a good job. Because delivering Prevent in XXXXX is going to be very different.'

The same speaker went on to assert that:

> 'So if you listen, we know that ultimately we're going to have, you know, we're going to have to do it, but we'll do it

our way. So if you want it done properly then please listen to us. Sometimes it's not please listen to us – it's please go away.'

And the final voice is that of a councillor who, in recognising the reality of the sentiments expressed above, said this of the staff in his authority:

'The officers work very hard to do what is requested of them. I mean there's a lot of pressure from government really; and all these rules coming down – 'You must do this, you must do that, you must do the other.' But I think that they cope very well with them at the end of the day.'

Statements like these point to a level of frustration at the failure of central government to have any understanding of what the implementation of these policies at the local level involves. There is a widespread feeling of disdain for the competence and insight of the politicians and policy personnel in central government responsible for finalising the conception and development of these policies. Prevent has attracted a specific level of outrage and resistance, but for both Prevent and Community Cohesion policies the interviews give an insight into a professional workforce confident in their local expertise and professional skills, who resent the attempt of central government to micro-manage their work. The strong sense of commitment and pride in their local knowledge and cumulative expertise was an implicit backdrop to the strong critiques of central government's management of the introduction of Prevent along with the flood of guidance and documentation on both Prevent and Community Cohesion. This sense of local self-regard and confidence was further nurtured through the regional structures that had been developed around cohesion and through the forums this provided for rehearsing their distinctive local politics and competencies. Ironically it seems that the very burden of guidance from Westminster created an environment in which exercising local discretion was the only viable option.

The interviews show a learning curve as the local managers, having managed the chaotic haste of the introduction of the first wave of Prevent funding through the Pathfinder programme, were increasingly developing their own control on the roll out of Prevent. This of course was also facilitated by the transition within the governmental definition of Prevent where, following CONTEST II, the ways in which funding was employed at the local level was much more within the control of the local authority. This in itself, of course, led to a further blurring of the division between Community Cohesion and

Prevent as more of this funding was explicitly diverted to the 'softer' Community Cohesion type activity. Although it has not been an agreed focus of this research project, it should also be remarked that the existence of organisational structures linking personnel from across the five authorities was significant in facilitating a collective dialogue about the challenges that they faced, and in sharing learning as they moved forward together in seeking to integrate the new demands of Prevent into existing practice. Perhaps also these networks provided a collective ownership of the problem that also allowed for a shared sense of responsibility for the ways in which policy became translated into practice. As one officer said:

> 'There's been a lot of strengths in those groups in terms of just the joint sharing of information … so it's been quite useful actually to know who to go to in other areas to say – 'Well, actually what are you doing?' – and sharing our policy approaches and things like that.'

Through such contacts and dialogues the sense of personal exposure is likely to be diminished, and a political as well as practical consensus to be developed. Certainly, there were a striking number of occasions on which members of staff, and councillors, spoke very positively of the strong stand that four of the chief executives had taken in robustly critiquing the initial governmental formulation of Prevent. This had provided a binding sense of a regional consensus which framed their response to Prevent within a political discourse that enabled them to refuse to collude with an ill thought out central government policy. It also provided a foundational position from which Islamophobia could be explicitly addressed as a problem lurking within, and around, the Prevent agenda. An early capacity to explicitly address this risk provided a space within which staff could express their own reservations; it gave a sensibility toward the feelings of Muslim communities that the staff could carry into their attempts to negotiate the introduction of Prevent into their communities. This was a principled political intervention with wide-ranging significance.

There was also over this period more feedback from the senior executives of the local authorities into the policy environment of Whitehall. Chief executives felt that, beyond the initial period of Prevent's introduction, their direct lines of contact with Whitehall had provided a valuable channel through which local knowledge and expertise was able to inform the development of government policy, and hence local practice. Through dialogue, in reporting back to the chief executives and in subsequent meetings with some of them, a strong sense was given of the local state's claim to their independence from central government. As one chief executive said:

> 'I think that there is a conventional view that the relationship between central government and the local government is one-directional, and it almost sees us as a department of the civil service, that is, just here as a delivery agent for central government policy. And I think that that misunderstands the role of local government. On occasion you could say that local government has misunderstood that role itself in the past. But I do think, when you look at areas of developing policy, the idea that all the policy can be shaped and sustained from a top-down approach from Whitehall is both wrong and almost nonsensical.'

The authority, and the legitimate leadership role, of the chief executives in representing a distinct tier of locally elected government was seen as critical in providing a channel of expertise in shaping government policy. Examples were given, including those of resisting persistent central government pressure, where the local government was able to insist on recognition of the complexity of issues on the ground, insights that had seemingly eluded Whitehall.

Prevent as politically problematic, and its implications for the implementation of community cohesion

The Community Cohesion policies that had been in place for some time prior to the introduction of Prevent had, to a significant extent, taken the form of a variant on traditional community work practice. Granted it was developed in response to the social disturbances in the North West in 2001, and they specifically targeted the Muslim community, and in Cantle's definition it sidelined the concerns with social inequality that was traditionally central to much community development work, but in its practical expression it preponderantly drew on traditional community work practice. Prevent, however, introduced a radical departure from the integrative ethos of Community Cohesion in that while it explicitly targeted the same Muslim communities, it approached them as the source of future 'home-grown' bombers. Its politics were quite contrary to the values and practice of community work and consequently the emergent problems arose from the perceived increasing interpenetration of Prevent and

Community Cohesion as practice. At the heart of community work is a willingness to engage with communities in an open and responsive manner. Frequently this is associated with a degree of empathetic understanding of the circumstances that shape the lives of the people in these communities, and a degree of willing advocacy on their behalf. The foundational basis for such work is the establishment of trust between the worker and those they are working with. The Prevent agenda was widely seen as necessarily threatening this link, and as compromising the independence of the community worker from processes of state surveillance. The local initiatives of Prevent came with strong 'top-down' regulation that was not consistent with the more flexible working rationales of community work. In particular the expectations inherent in the performance indicator NI 35[1] that came with Prevent were seen by many as a fundamental assault on the impartiality of traditional community work, placing the local authority in an unacceptably 'politicised' role in relation to its citizens. The politics of Prevent became instantly highly problematic, and problematic in different ways to different constituencies.

The quotations below are drawn from interviews with senior managers, councillors and those responsible for the implementation of policies at the operational level. They give a sense of the range of political objections to the introduction of the Prevent agenda.

> 'If we take the Preventing Violent Extremism agenda, after 7/7 the government was, if we're honest, pretty close to panic; understandably so. All of a sudden we – supposedly – had these potential terrorists all over the place in our communities. And some of the language used was pretty strange to say the least.... Something had happened which had shocked government into needing to react. But that reaction, because of the anxiety and because the information stream the government had at the time was from the security services and from the police intelligence, it was security-based intelligence; we got a very, very narrow view of the approach to preventing violent extremism.' (senior manager)

> '... which comes back to this Prevent thing. If you're going out into the streets with Prevent – *Let's prevent terrorism* – that's a strange way of putting it in people's minds: *Oh there's terrorism*, you know and its focusing the wrong way to me, is

that. I have to be honest about it. I just do think it's tending to create a focus that we don't want.' (councillor)

'But actually the cornerstone of our position is *we don't want your money on Prevent, and if you in government persist on requiring local government to be an agency of the intelligence service* – that was some of the demands placed on us like NI 35 and other such activities – and we said very loudly and robustly....' (councillor)

On the introduction of Prevent, the same councillor stated:

'I think it was just a piece of reckless rhetoric to meet a government in panic over the very terrible situation we found ourselves in.'

'Under the PVE Pathfinder programme there certainly was that feeling among most Muslim communities in XXXXX, although I think there was a trend across the country, that it was a very unfair assault on Muslim communities. You know, tarnishing everyone with the same brush ... when the Pathfinder programme came on board there was I would say hardly any organisations, Muslim organisations, and indeed non-Muslim organisations, that wanted to touch the money with a barge pole.' (senior staff member)

The quotes from senior members of staff below provides a perspective that identifies the nature of the resistance, and identifies it as a necessary challenge to ensuring a more open debate about its introduction:

'There has been some collective resistance and some suspicious people and that does extend to some colleagues in the authority as well. People have a different take on the agenda. Some colleagues feel very uncomfortable about us considering Muslim people all the time, some people want to keep thinking about the far-right activity which is important but, in terms of government policy, it's explicitly about *Al-Qaeda*; so it's trying to keep that focus and explain the context for that. So there have been a few points of resistance and concern. That's been helpful in many ways because it actually led to some quite open debates and discussions and perhaps we've not done quite enough in some ways and that's at various levels.' [senior staff member]

'I think that everyone felt uncomfortable with it. We got quite a lot of complaints from members of the community, not just the Muslim community, but community reps who were part of our local area agreement structure.' (senior staff member)

'The Home Office view is that violent extremism equals Islamic extremism, which we disagree with as you can imagine.' (senior staff member)

This sample of views about the introduction of Prevent indicates the depth of feeling with which a range of actors took objection to the very explicit targeting of the Muslim communities as the focus for anti-terrorist activity. While, as was apparent in many interviews, there was recognition of the necessity of confronting the threat that now faced the UK, there was at the same time a clear perception that the policy as developed, and certainly in terms of the rhetoric that accompanied it, was far too near to being Islamophobic.

In talking with the interviewees in this project it became rapidly apparent that for many people working at the operational end of delivering the Prevent agenda (that is, the more middle management and field staff), there was something quite distinctive about being involved in the Prevent agenda. Substantively this was based in the very particular politics of Prevent that specifically identified the Muslim communities of Britain as constituting a distinctive potential threat to national security.

As became strongly apparent across the interviews, for many individuals the politics behind the introduction of Prevent were deeply flawed and objectionable. As one senior councillor said:

'When the document came out from the Home Office I was aghast. I threw it out. I said we're not having this. It was racist. Quite clearly racist.'

A Muslim fieldworker said:

'I think that it's the same as other government agendas and focuses the spotlight on the Muslim community. Far-right

> extremism comes under terrorism, the focus isn't on far-right extremism.'

Statements like these point to the sense of outrage at central government's production of a policy that so explicitly extracted a particular faith group out of the body politic and subjected it to such an overtly damning construction of their place in British society. It was seen as racist, Islamophobic and discriminatory. It offended Muslim communities and Muslim staff because of its explicit targeting of Muslim communities, a sentiment shared by non-Muslim respondents. It also was greeted with suspicion and criticism by a range of Muslim and non-Muslim respondents for its related failure to provide an equal focus on the dangers of far right extremism. In these authorities that took reasonable pride in the anti-racist and equality programmes that they had developed over the years, this complaint was perhaps grounded in their sense of Prevent's violation of this hard-won area of competence and commitment. Not surprisingly a range of voices within the local Muslim communities were reported as having spoken out vehemently to express similar conclusions regarding this central government response to the London bombings.

The response from within the Muslim communities meant, as we shall see when discussing funding below, that there was considerable resistance from large segments of the Muslim communities to becoming involved in any aspect of Prevent work, including funded projects. For local authorities there was the very real fear that engagement in the rolling out of this programme would seriously jeopardise the good relations that they had painstakingly sought to build up with their own Muslim communities; this was indeed a well founded anxiety. For local authority Muslim staff members, there was a real sense that their standing within their own communities could be jeopardised by being seen to be involved in such a politically tarnished programme. This period, when the Prevent agenda was initially introduced, was marked by strong resistance from a number of quarters, and was the time at which four of the chief executives made their objections to aspects of it very clear to central government.

Nor can the activities of Prevent be hermetically sealed in community perception from other elements of the CONTEST agenda. Thus, for example, some of the activities under Pursue have had directly negative consequences for Community Cohesion programmes. Within the interviews there were strongly expressed views from within some of the authorities, but not all, that particularly the raids on Muslim communities by the Counter Terrorism Unit (CTU) were a source of grievance for local Muslim communities; one authority has a small Muslim population and a very different profile of ethnic diversity, when compared with the other cities, and this was quite reasonably reflected in their concerns and priorities. Nevertheless, examples where young Muslim men are arrested, held and then not subsequently prosecuted were focused on. The failure of the police to proceed to a conviction was seen as resulting in the local community seeing such raids as speculative and part of a policy of policing by suspicion, in the absence of adequate evidence. The respondents who raised this issue did so in strong terms and spoke of intense feelings of anger within the communities where such raids had taken place. For example:

> 'People make the assumption that local authority staff who work on Prevent will know exactly, if them arrests come in, why they happened: who the individuals were and so forth; and seek answers from us. And all we can do is actually give back to them what we're fed through CTU in terms of, *these are the key messages that need to go out.* But, actually some of them are not very helpful and communities will not understand. [They say] *Well if you've released them we want to know the full facts.* They won't understand some of the issues in terms of protecting the sources of information and if there's ongoing investigations. So that does have an impact and again it kind of knocks you back a couple of steps. Whatever progress has been made, something like that happens you know and people will think nothing's going to change, because we talk about this and that and so forth, but at the end of the day you're still going to go ahead and do that.'

Within the range of negative responses to the internal logics of Prevent recorded above, a conscious awareness of the insidious nature of Islamophobia can be seen: a recognition that the separating out of people by their religious identity and the attribution to them collectively of culpability for the current threat to security is, in the context of the 'War on Terror' and its variants, a foundational basis for anti-Muslimism. In the rejection of the targeting of Muslim communities within Prevent there is an implicit acknowledgement of the pre-existing potential for this population to be made into scapegoats, and subjected to potentially escalating levels of hostility. Particularly for the staff with an established professional experience of community work and the implementation of anti-discriminatory policies there is an accumulated knowledge of the power of symbolic and realist threat when constructed between adjacent communities. Thus, there is a specific concern that not only is the rhetoric surrounding the targeting of Muslim communities unbalanced, it is also dangerous.

The intersection of Prevent and Community Cohesion

Given this negative response to the introduction and implementation of Prevent we might anticipate that it had consequences for the implementation of Community Cohesion. In particular, given the evidence from the interviews of the managerial fusion of the two policies in some instances, and the routine close linkages between the two, there was every reason to anticipate interference between these policies when implemented by the same authority within their local communities. Indeed, the interviews provide a strong sense of the negative impact of Prevent as it permeates the communities' perception of social intervention from the local state.

Again, the examples offered below are from the statements of senior councillors with responsibility for these programmes, senior staff with responsibility for managing these programmes and staff involved in their implementation.

A senior councillor said:

> 'When you are required as elected representatives to gain the respect … of the community and drive through values: the values of education, care of the elderly, standards in life – a clean environment – basically promoting and encouraging the greater well-being of the populace; to also be the Big Brother that is actually spying on part of the community – then there is a contradiction.'

And echoing the discussion of the interparty consensus on these policies, discussed above, a councillor said of his authority:

> 'That position I've just articulated about cohesion and the Prevent agenda, and the contradiction, is a position held by all three main political parties in this authority. And very strong, and very solid is our united position.'

When referring to the relationship between the two policies, a senior officer commented:

'It's an obvious contradiction.'

A Muslim fieldworker stated:

> '… what the Prevent agenda has done for us workers is that it has to an extent alienated us further; and so that battle for trust and confidence has been hard to achieve.'

And, troublingly, one respondent (a manager) reflected:

> 'I could imagine that there's nothing that you can do in social cohesion that can't be perceived as − a front for Prevent.'

A councillor gave a more unequivocal response to the question of whether there was any impact of Prevent on community cohesion:

> 'Definitely, I would definitely agree with that. It's like you're talking with a forked tongue. That's the thing and the community's not stupid. They know what the public agenda is, what the government agenda is and they know that their Muslim community is under the spotlight, under the heat.'

A member of the fieldwork staff talking of the encroachment of Prevent expectations on their work said:

> 'So of course it's a difficult situation: information gathering/ collecting − then are we then a reporting centre? Are we then working outside our own remit, you know? And what's somebody going to do with the information? So how much control and confidentiality? All those issues arose.'

A fieldwork member of staff who spoke of the ambiguous line between Prevent and Community Cohesion, speaking in 2009, anticipated some of the concern of the Communities and Local Government Committee of the House of Commons report, *Preventing violent extremism* (CLGC of the House of Commons, 2010), in saying:

> 'The softer things within Prevent are cohesion, and your extreme terms of work − sort of CTU and the police and the area they interact in is actually Prevent. Now the understanding from the communities is that the extreme

area of Prevent is the Prevent that we all are working at all the time, ie, gleaning intelligence, looking for bombers et cetera. Now what the communities don't understand at this minute is that probably 75 per cent of that quotient of Prevent work is cohesion.... Not only do the communities not understand the agenda, but we officers, and even people in central government, even people at ministerial level are still grappling with what the Prevent agenda is.'

A member of the fieldwork staff asserted that:

'It's very hard for that kind of work to go on without kind of deconstructing or breaking down those monolithic ideas of a conspiracy; when the whole social agenda at the moment seems to be tilted towards trying to make Muslim people accountable, and in some cases, guilty for atrocities committed by people they've got no connection to. And that kind of way of winning hearts and minds, you now, your basic youth work, your basic community work, that's a really, really difficult thing to achieve at the moment.... And until you can get rid of the Prevent agenda in its current sense, and just go back to good old fashioned building bridges and relationships without that kind of suspicion, it will be very difficult to make inroads.'

Statements like these point to the consequences of the conceptual and operational overlap between Community Cohesion and Prevent. They speak of a frustration that the intrusive and insidious penetration of the protective state's security activities into the domain that was traditionally occupied by community work or youth work, now covered by Community Cohesion, has significant negative implications for the execution of this work.

However, there was not an absolute consensus that the Prevent agenda impacted in a consistently negative way on attempts to implement Community Cohesion initiatives. One councillor, for example, while accepting that specific instances of Prevent work could result in very considerable Muslim community disquiet, including public demonstrations, was also at pains to argue that on a banal daily basis this same community was as concerned about security as anyone else. This underlines the extent to which the securitisation of mundane urban life has become part of a taken for granted acceptance of fear, and its complementary security measures, in everyday life (Huysmans, 2009).

A further insight into how different respondents had different perspectives on the issue of Prevent was indicated in the response of a senior councillor who, when asked whether he believed there was any contradiction between the policies of Prevent and Community Cohesion, replied that he did not think that there was:

> 'Broadly speaking people do think that the more watching there is the safer they may feel, and in a sense – my sense is the Prevent agenda hasn't made working together appreciably more difficult.'

However, a few minutes later, when discussing how many of the staff implementing these policies felt there were specific contradictions between them, the councillor agreed with this perspective but then placed it into a wider category of routine contradictions between government policies:

> 'I can subscribe to most of what you've just said, but contradictions between policies are much more common than that!'

What we have here is evidence of how different experiential understandings of the potential relationships that may exist between these two policies can shape quite different readings of the situation. The councillor, who had earlier spoken of his comfort in having no great involvement in the details of Prevent, in his role as a senior councillor with responsibilities that covered both Prevent and Community Cohesion, had no experience of conflict between these policies. But when presented with evidence that members of staff who implemented these policies, and councillors elsewhere, reported such conflicts, accepted this to be a true reflection of reality. Another councillor, in a different authority, expressed the optimistic view, not shared by the fieldwork staff interviewed in that city, nor by their colleague, that since they had refused to sign on to NI 35 and had developed their own corporate response to Prevent, then there was no problem in implementing it.

It is indeed an unsurprising fact that different locations within the structure of the local authority often produce particular perspectives on the operation of the system and, with notable exceptions, the strongest and most consistent expression of a sense of the capacity of the Prevent agenda to undermine work within the Community Cohesion agenda comes from those more intimately linked to service delivery.

The Prevent agenda as perceived through the responses of the respondents in this study emerges as requiring actions on the part of local authority staff that they feel sit very uncomfortably with the relations of trust and openness that were previously seen to characterise traditional community work practice. The obligations on local authority staff to act as an arm of the intelligence gathering network of Prevent is seen as compromising their relationship with their clients. Additionally some of the activities carried out under CONTEST, for which these staff have no responsibility, nonetheless have strong implications within Muslim communities that subsequently affects the local authorities' relationship with these communities. Prevent, therefore, has introduced new and problematic stresses into the relationships between local authority staff and their client populations.

The ambiguity around the definition of Community Cohesion, noted in Chapter Two, and the considerable organisational overlap in the management and delivery of Community Cohesion and Prevent, has not surprisingly nurtured a blurred and permeable boundary between the two policies at the point of delivery. The statement quoted above – "I could imagine that there is nothing that you can do in social cohesion that can't be perceived as a front for Prevent" – is perhaps the most truly disturbing insight into the interpenetration of these two policies. The apparently reasonable proposal of the Communities and Local Government Committee report (2010), urging the separation of 'soft' and 'hard' elements of Prevent as a solution to some of the difficulties they identified in the overlap of these two policies, does not sit comfortably with the on-the-ground reality of interagency working at the local level. For example, when members of staff working on Community Cohesion report back information on 'community tensions', or the working of specific projects, they cannot be certain that it does not also constitute 'intelligence' for counter-terrorism.

Funding

Funding as a central element in policy implementation has proved to be a very fruitful litmus test that has revealed something of the dynamics that have operated within the Prevent agenda and its relationship with Community Cohesion. Thus, for example, the initial funding of the early Pathfinder programme within Prevent was a textbook example of the fecklessness of central government rolling out a policy driven by political expediency rather than via considered planning and collaboration with the local authorities. As one manager put it:

> 'The whole thing was a huge lash with proposals having to be in and, you know, pulling things together in a matter of days and weeks.'

Another manager said:

> 'The government suddenly issued some Pathfinder funding, which you probably are aware of. We had to respond very quickly and it created tension in both the authority and the community.'

The revulsion of the Muslim community organisations to the stigmatising politics of Prevent gave the personnel responsible for the implementation of the Pathfinder funding streams immediate problems in the unwillingness of Muslim organisations to come forward and bid for funding. One manager who had had over 150 applications for a previous funding call reported that after having put out the call for bids:

> 'After two weeks I'd not had one enquiry. I'd not had one person ring me up and ask for an application or anything. Well I didn't know what it was, so I rang up some of the organisations that I thought might apply, and the message I got very strongly was that the Muslim community were boycotting this programme.'

In fact, the Pathfinder experience was widely regarded as a central government shambles that had put the local authority personnel in a very difficult position. But Pathfinder, as with later Prevent funding, was a source of revenue, and funding had its own logics. Thus, although four of the authorities had refused to sign up to NI 35, and hence to fully embrace Prevent, they nonetheless accepted the Prevent funding. Similarly for the Muslim communities, the initial response was a widespread condemnation of Prevent and, as we have already seen, an extensive resistance to participate in Pathfinder-funded projects. But the political dynamics of the funding environment are far from simple and initial resistance to accepting Prevent funding changed over time. In the words of one Muslim staff member:

'At first the Muslim community was actually quite reserved about this and said, *oh no, this is targeting us.* But after a while the Muslim community felt that because the council had decided that it wanted to do one or two projects, the Muslim community then asked, *well, why are YOU doing that; why aren't you giving the money to us?* So there's a contradiction for me really when I'm looking at it. At first it was a threat to the Muslim community – they didn't want anything to do with it – but as soon as they found out there was some money coming forward they said, *why aren't we getting some of this?*'

Another Muslim respondent additionally discussed the competition for resources and prestige between local Muslim organisations, stating:

'I certainly think between organisations there's competition there…. So there is an element of competitiveness most definitely for the monies and for people pursuing what they feel is most appropriate and how they go about things within their localities as well.'

Thus one of the impacts of Prevent funding has been to provide a basis for expressing, and possibly enhancing, competition between different positions and interests within the Muslim communities, and crucially, between Muslim and non-Muslim organisations and communities. Clearly Muslim participation in the Prevent initiatives is essential to both their success and their perceived legitimacy. And it should be recognised that there are Muslim groups who wish to be seen as actively confronting the threat of terrorist radicalisation, and its terrible effects on their communities, who want "to do something positive in terms of tackling extremism or supporting vulnerable individuals" (Muslim fieldworker). However, one of the problems has been the government's attempt to distinguish between 'good Muslim organisations' and 'bad Muslim organisations' in terms of their location within Islam and their perceived connection to 'fundamentalist' ideologies. Thus there has been a very skewed access to Prevent, and other funding, as these ambiguous criteria have been applied on behalf of the protective state by local authorities (see *The 'usual suspects'*, below).

One respondent put this scenario into a larger context, by pointing out that:

'People are looking to the Prevent agenda as an alternative because a lot of people feel that there's more money now for Prevent than there is for community cohesion type activities so *we might as well go for that.* It's 'by any means necessary' – anything they need in order to survive. And some people have [done] some creative writing in terms of their application, in terms of how it will fit their own agenda, but also the Prevent agenda.'

Participation in Prevent–related activity by Muslim organisations has thus to be seen in the context of the changing funding environment for voluntary organisations and the competitive need to sustain their own distinctive viability within the wider Muslim community, both aspects being framed by the securitisation agenda that has permeated British civil society. As a senior member of staff with detailed knowledge of the funding regime said:

'Again, I would say although it's always about partnership working and so forth, organisations at the end of the day are worried about their own livelihoods, their own survival.'

A related concern that emerged within the interviews was directed at the perceived perversity of funders' inability to control the continuity of work on projects that had been funded through Prevent or Community Cohesion initiatives. Effort had been put into recruiting acceptable and competent partners to engage in new initiatives, on time-limited contracts. The problem arose when these initiatives were seen to have been successful. One concern was the familiar problem of time-limited funding, which was that there was no guarantee of further funding for continuing the project. This is a consequence of a limited funding stream and pressure to be seen to bring in new players and dispense the local authority largesse over as wide a field as possible. As one senior manager put it:

'I think that sometimes there's often a drive, particularly from central government, around this sort of innovation agenda, and innovations, great – we need some innovation. But I also think there's a real need for us to look at what works and how we can continue it and support it moving forward, and develop it and allow it to evolve.'

There is nothing new in this dilemma, but that does not render it inconsequential. A variant on this problem was given in one instance where a successful project that became regarded as a highly successful exemplar of good practice was funded for further development, but the funding was not given to the Muslim person who had developed it but instead given to a non-Muslim 'expert'. In the context of this project it was not possible to delve more deeply into the decision making around this case, but it was perceived as a case of bad faith on the part of the authority.

Funding as a process also provided valuable insights into the development of interagency activity which is at the heart of the Prevent/Community Cohesion nexus. If the initial round of activity under Pathfinder was frenetic and dysfunctional, across the interviews there is evidence of a steep learning curve as the new organisational structures, noted above, provide a vehicle for developing a local authority house style in managing these initiatives. A funding reality that has facilitated this process has been the fact that the post-Pathfinder three-year tranche of Prevent funding has not been 'ring-fenced' with highly prescriptive rules tying it explicitly to Muslim communities. This financial flexibility has clearly been entirely in step with the logics of these local authorities as they have sought to optimise the meshing of Prevent and Community Cohesion; some respondents clearly took some pride in their success in translating Prevent funding in what they regarded as more agreeable, and effective, Community Cohesion activities. This was particularly consistent with the oft-repeated concern to resist central government's fixation with Muslim communities and to widen the focus of initiatives and consequently to also spread the allocation of funding to a wider constituency of local citizens.

The interviews also reveal that there has been a rich diversity of funding streams that have been available over the last few years to address the issues of Community Cohesion and counter-terrorism coming through a range of government departmental sources and being managed by different local agencies. This could potentially have been a recipe for initiative anarchy, but there is a strong strand of evidence coming through which points to a serious attempt to impose some local order on this chaotic fiscal bounty. Working through their own management structures these authorities have sought to coordinate the impact of different funding streams. As one manager put it:

> 'We got the people who were working to these different
> agendas and strands together and tried to join them in

commissioning – it's very much a joint commissioning approach you see.'

Interestingly, one cautious voice did suggest that this relative largesse in the early years of Prevent, accompanied by the positive energies that had been poured into developing interagency collaboration, may have constituted a form of false dawn in which hard decisions had not yet been addressed. The argument is that in developing this working environment colleagues have found innovative ways of working that have not required them to defend too strongly their own professional areas of work and their own use of their core budgets. But the suggestion is that as hard times approach, a retreat to the professional and departmental identities of their particular communities of practice may create new competitive and defensive interdepartmental politics. Thus they conclude:

> 'So I think it's going to be an interesting time ahead when we don't have that bonhomie of all the money coming in, and we are going to sit as partners and face each other and really look at what we're doing, and set ourselves some real key priorities and work to those.'

And the expectation here is that:

> 'You sure have to make some tough decisions. And from my view around XXXXX, and probably many other authorities, those tough decisions are tough!'

It could usefully be said that tracking the flow of funds into the local authorities around these two agendas would be an unobtrusive measure of the lack of joined-up thinking at central government level and a means, in a complementary way, of making a substantive demonstration of the ways in which local autonomy very actively restructures the purpose and practice that was implicit in these different funding streams. The manipulation of the allocation of budgets is one of the concrete manifestations of the local pride and political vision that was identified above. In addition, its collaborative management through a variety of local organisational structures is a concrete expression of the interagency logics that are structured into these two programmes.

It is too early to make any truly informed interpretation of how the emerging policies of the new Conservative–Liberal Democrat coalition government will change the pattern of activity around these policies. But we can be certain that in the pursuit of reducing the British fiscal debt the radical cuts in public sector funding will have a dramatic effect on the terrain in which the future operation of these policies operate. The power of 'communities of practice' that have been recognised above as playing a significant positive role in making sense of the implementation of these policies at the local level, may, under these conditions, prove to be a potent force for inter- and intra-agency competition. As budgets are cut and staff become overwhelmed with maintaining the pretence that services have not been radically affected, professional and departmental identities can be anticipated to have a new and different relevance.

Within majority and minority communities we can also anticipate that the impact of the budget cuts into the life experiences of communities already routinely stressed by low incomes and limited resources will heighten those forces, noted in Chapter Four, that will create new levels of realistic intergroup threat. The pressure on traditional community work will become greater and more urgent, just as the resource base from which to address it will be extensively diminished. Competition for funding will increase as the total pool of funding from different sources contracts, and intergroup postures of conflict will be more likely, as a heightened sensitivity to the distribution of scarce resources produces an intense awareness of the slicing of the local authority cake.

The 'usual suspects'

Given what will be said below about the nature of the respondents' knowledge of local communities, it is surprising that when in the interviews we talked about the recruitment of people to bid for Prevent funding, or to participate in Community Cohesion initiatives, there was concern expressed about the routine visibility of the 'usual suspects'. This issue of the 'usual suspects' was raised by members of all of the categories of respondents in the study and was a cause of concern to them all. The 'usual suspects' refers to the availability, and the usage, of a narrow range of familiar players to participate in the various initiatives that have been rolled out in the name of Prevent or Community Cohesion. One variation on this, but very much a less frequently aired concern, relates to the various fora set up by central government as part of the consultation process in developing these programmes. As one person put it:

> 'The other thing is – people up in positions of power and responsible decision making do not really have the kind of understanding; and again it's the kind of forums that the government are creating, are usually in a sense the usual suspects as well, and nobody ever questions that.'

This was from a Muslim respondent who, among other things, was referring to the way in which the government has a need of people to 'speak on behalf of' the Muslim population, and consequently sanctions some voices and not others as responsible sources of opinion. Indeed, it is reasonable to assert that a key element in the Community Cohesion–Prevent synergy is the construing of 'capacity building' as the facilitation of the emergence of new 'acceptable' leadership within the Muslim communities of Britain. Later, a different variation on this concern with central government's ignorance of local sensitivities took a distinctively regional twist:

> 'It's the same guys they get sitting around the table and it's usually people from the South!'

More often the issue of the 'usual suspects' was raised in relation to the ways in which the local authority staff found themselves frequently dealing with the same individuals when they embarked on any new initiative. This was certainly expressed in relation to the people coming forward, and being funded, in the early phases of the Prevent programme, and continued to be raised as a generic challenge in relation to any attempt to engage with any client community. As one manager said in relation to engaging with Muslim communities:

> 'I think that the issue is we only ever scratch the surface of those communities. So we work with the usual suspects and the usual suspects will hold their hands up and say, *yep, we know we're the usual suspects*.'

This person is talking about a collusive mutual dependency on each other. The authority needs to be seen to be consulting, while specific community groups are in competition for legitimacy and funding. Crucially, some actors constitute 'a safe pair of hands' whereas others are an unknown quantity, or worse. With the political environment surrounding these two policies, where securitisation has come to permeate all local policy, there is every reason for local authority personnel to be risk-averse. We shall see below, when examining *Prevent as morally problematic,* how concerns with the risk of being accused of being in anyway associated with 'radical' Muslim groups has powerful implications for local authority staff's anxiety about who they should collaborate with. The potential costs of being perceived to have got it wrong, in an environment where not everyone feels fully in the loop of relevant information, makes a conservative policy of working with established contacts who have a proven track record of delivering the goods a personally and professionally rational option. One officer reported a personal sense of this dilemma:

> 'Having worked in the front line previously with communities, there's definitely ex-colleagues who feel that they are under pressure to deliver: they are watched more not only by the authority but by external audits as well. They feel, like I said, the ability to be innovative, which is key to me, to cohesion, to community relations, actually fundamental – it's about being innovative, trying things/making mistakes – absolutely fundamental – there's a reticence around that. And maybe I'll put my hand up; maybe I'm part of the problem with that.'

There is of course another side to this dilemma which is that even where the local authority personnel, through their local knowledge of their patch, know of potential actors they would like to bring into their sphere of operation, their approach may be turned down. As we have seen above, the initial phase of the Prevent agenda was marked by resistance on the part of many Muslim groups to be seen to be associated with such a politically noxious programme.

In fact, the whole issue of funding projects within the Muslim community has opened up an internal process of change and contention within these communities. From these interviews there is evidence of a changing relationship between the local authority as holder of funds and the Muslim community. Since at the initial stage of the Prevent agenda some Muslim actors did accept funding, it raised an issue of credibility and viability for other Muslim groups who at that stage had withheld their cooperation. Since groups within the Muslim community, as in any other community, exist in a friable arrangement of competition and cooperation with other groups, those who persist in a principled stance of non-cooperation are likely to suffer financially, even if their prestige remains high. There can at times be an uncomfortable trade-off in trying to balance these two commodities. Virtuously sinking into oblivion is not the ambition of any organisation facing financial starvation, and over time there has indeed been an increase in the number of actors from within the Muslim communities who have sought funding within the Prevent agenda. Others, however, have sustained their original position of non-participation. It could be of course that those who have continued to refuse to participate have by now been defined by the CTU as being unfit for funding through Prevent, since their principled actions have defined their deviant politics. What remains an issue is that the politics surrounding the definition and operation of the Prevent agenda has *de facto* contributed to a funding environment in which the attraction of the 'usual suspects' has remained a real element in the equation of finding partners in the communities.

It should also be noted that a small number of respondents equated the existence of the 'usual suspects' to the existence of 'an industry' around Prevent and Community Cohesion in which people and groups set themselves up as experts and consultants and build a network of contacts that become self-fuelling. As one councillor put it:

> 'A lot of people that are in the game, well I won't use the word "in the game", but probably in the network, in the loop, are probably people who have other agendas, ie, they might be consultants, or they might be community organisations with vested interests. There's a lot of funding at stake so, *we'll get in there, we'll create a little niche*, and they perpetuate the industry....'

It has to be said that a public interest enquiry into where central government funding has gone in feeding the machine of Prevent training and policy dissemination would be interesting reading. At the same time we should also recognise that the need of Prevent to demonstrate success has of itself produced a market for expertise in disseminating good practice, which again has a centripetal effect of turning back to the established players to proselytise the success of the programme. Examples of such processes are to be found in the interviews within this project. In this context, it is useful once again to make relevant the notion of social capital that, according to Bourdieu and Wacquant, can be defined as:

> ... the sum of resources, actual or virtual, that accrue to an individual or group by virtue of possessing a durable network of more or less institutionalised relationships

of mutual acquaintance and recognition. (Bourdieu and Wacquant, 1992: 119)

For Bourdieu, then, social and cultural capital were exploited as a means of maintaining personal and group advantage. Thus, while Community Cohesion is fixated with the problematic formation of social capital within Muslim communities from a perspective defined by Putnam, we might balance this with a useful reflection on the exploitation of social capital, in Bourdieu and Wacquant's terms, by those who compete for funds and prestige within the funding regimes of Community Cohesion and Prevent.

This issue of the recurrent featuring of the 'usual suspects' in these areas of policy implementation is troubling and probably not easily amenable to change. If we were a society of frenetic 'active citizens' then this process would be much easier. But then a large element of the Community Cohesion agenda would be simultaneously obsolete. The stigmatisation of Muslim communities within both the Community Cohesion and the Prevent agendas has itself done little to help to create an environment in which members of that community might feel enfranchised to join in any government initiative, and yet voices in this project have spoken passionately about the energy and locally grounded wisdom that is to be found in both Muslim and white working-class communities. Breaking the cycle of dependency on the 'usual suspects' emerges as a significant issue of deep concern within this data.

Prevent as morally problematic to local authority staff

Although the Prevent agenda is very largely driven through local authority action, it is intimately enmeshed in interagency collaboration; the police and the CTU have a clear primacy within this nexus. As one councillor put it:

> '... clearly the Prevent agenda is part of the overall cohesion agenda, but it is a narrower focus – a focus driven by MI5 and the police, with a lot of support it has to be said from the council's community safety people.'

The counter-terrorism agencies are the ones who ultimately define the nature and extent of the security threat. They are the ones who sit at the top of the pyramid of need-to-know where the assumed integrated 'big picture' is held. Where responsible councillors and senior managers may have no meaningful engagement with the information flows that pass through the 'bronze', 'silver' and 'gold' hierarchies of information exchange within CONTEST, and where personnel with immediate management responsibility for the implementation of Prevent may sit low on this food chain of information exchange, then knowledge is truly power.

Local authority managers and those responsible for the operational delivery of Prevent know that they sit within this web of knowledge and accountability where they will be required to act 'as if' they are in possession of all the knowledge that is held by those who will ultimately judge their performance. This is where the politics that permeates Prevent mutates into a new moral environment within which local staff must operate. A moral shift has occurred in the professional domain of those implementing the Prevent programme; they have become, in a novel and disturbing way, subject to a new order of moral exposure.

Prevent, in its operational delivery, is very dependent on the professional skills, personal networks and organisational infrastructures that are traditionally located in community development, youth work or equality departments. As such, the staff working in such departments know that if they get something wrong they will be called in by the departmental manager, 'have their knuckles rapped' and be told not to do it again. Now, with Prevent, the potential harm is not merely a modest failure in service delivery; it is potentially a contribution to facilitating a future terrorist outrage. That is a heavy responsibility and a new and often, heavy moral burden. And, given the ambiguity about what constitutes the processes of radicalisation and the inherent secrecy of the operation of a terrorist cell, local authority staff are ill equipped to identify which of their current professional actions may turn out to be problematic.

But they know that they will be judged if such a situation arises, judged not only by their immediate line manager, but through an invisible and potent chain leading back to the arbiters of security in the CTU. In the guaranteed confidentiality of this project, concrete instances of potentially fraught consequences have been given. People who have given bookings in council property to a Muslim organisation that it later transpires is on a CTU 'radicalised' list find themselves summarily summoned by senior management to account for themselves, and then are subsequently interviewed several times by the CTU. In another example, an individual who, having found themselves in a comparable situation, with a person later convicted of a terrorist offence, found this to be a grievous personal burden. As a fieldworker said:

> 'This agenda you know, we say people could make a mistake and it could be headline news and the impact of that could be on your whole service, the whole XXXXX gets burdened with it; and probably the whole council gets burdened with it.'

A practical example illuminated the issue further:

> 'I know some colleagues who have done some of the operational stuff and they were questioned ... because some of the funding went into some of the organisations where those people were linked in.'

The nature of terrorism is to pollute normal life with suspicion and fear and it appears to have penetrated into the professional environment of local authority personnel. It seems clear that for those engaged in the delivery of Prevent a new penumbra of moral anxiety has been introduced into their professional life. This issue did not have the salience and visibility across the whole sample that was apparent in the data on the political objections to Prevent, but the support for this to be registered as an issue certainly justifies it being taken seriously as an issue for the staff working with Prevent. It draws together issues about the implications of the interagency working and the consequent inherent 'unknowability' attached to where any information you provide may feed into a future action by the counter-terrorism service, with potentially grievous negative impacts on the local community. In relation to intelligence gathering, since the nature of 'relevant' information is so ambiguous, and the expertise to make use of the collated 'radicalisation' data seems always to lie beyond the domain of those who collect it and send it on into the counter-terrorism system, then there may be a realistic anxiety among staff about the consequences of their actions. And since the biographies of convicted terrorists tend to confirm their distressing 'normality', there is no guarantee that initiatives promoted as part of a Prevent or Community Cohesion project may not have succoured 'radicalised' proto-terrorists.

For the staff engaged in Prevent work, and perhaps also Community Cohesion, the clear separation of the two does not always seem obvious in organisational structure or practice. The intersection of the political problematic surrounding Prevent, and the always immanent moral implications of their work, produces real anxiety. Some, but by no means all, of the interviewees felt that these pressures place a particular burden on chains of communication within the organisation.

Particularly for some of the staff members at the operational delivery end of the process there was an expressed need for more open channels of communication.

From what has been argued above, the challenge of managing the new risks attached to delivering Prevent and Community Cohesion may reasonably be seen as a significant issue that merits managerial concern. It is the operational staff who have the closest interface with the communities who have a range of reasons for holding strong views about these policies and their implementation. It is they who particularly feel the direct stress of the new demands of Prevent as a challenge to their well honed, and valued, ways of professional practice. And yet it is they, who, in relation to the information flow within the interagency system that is Prevent/Community Cohesion, are farthest removed from full access to information. Consequently the nexus of communication and trust that holds together a coherent and confident service delivery has become particularly important. This is not to say that there is no evidence of management awareness of these new circumstances and the demands they place on managers. As the quote below, from a manager, indicates:

> 'It's recognising that some colleagues can handle working on this sort of thing, and almost thrive on it, and can see we are trying to get some quite positive things and so on. Others really struggle, and there are one or two colleagues you just wouldn't want to give this work to, or they'd feel personally accountable if they were managing a piece of work and that was then involved in some investigation or whatever.'

And there are examples that will easily identify the interviewees if used, of very strong managerial support for colleagues who have become professionally exposed through their Prevent-related work. However, it is appropriate to recognise that the 'need-to-know' logics of security do not translate comfortably into the operational activity of a local authority trying, in good conscience, to deliver a highly problematic policy. Staff at the lower levels of the knowledge food chain have expressed their need to be kept better informed, and to be given support in the difficult work that they are doing. The skills that they are employing may be those of their long acquired activity in community development or youth work. While the client population that they are dealing with may not have changed, there is a real sense that the political and professional context in which they are working has altered radically. There is consequently a need for a revisiting of the routine ways in which staff are built into a more open communication flow, and are provided with support. Trust between layers of the organisational system may have been stretched by the new stresses of the current experience of working in tandem with Community Cohesion and Prevent.

The specific experience of Muslim staff

> 'I think that this is probably the most challenging time that we as officers have ever experienced, or ever perhaps will experience; you know, given the delivery or implementation of Prevent.'

Within this policy and workplace environment, the position of Muslim staff emerged as having particular sensitivities. Issues raised by non-Muslim managers and by Muslim staff themselves, at different levels in their organisation, pointed to the particular stresses that they felt in working in an environment permeated by the presence of Prevent and its ubiquitous manifestations. At a basic level the widely perceived Islamophobic ideology built into the initial construction of Prevent meant that for some Muslim staff any involvement with this project carried with it a sense of personal ambivalence and exposure – *ambivalence* because this was an inherent part of their job description and they were expected to take on board their responsibility for implementing local authority policy, even though they had sound reason to find it objectionable; *exposure* because in taking on this role and acting as an agent of the local authority, and ultimately the government, in implementing the Prevent agenda they may be putting at risk their credibility and standing in their own communities. As one member of the fieldwork staff expressed it:

> 'What the Prevent agenda has done for us workers is that it has to an extent alienated us further; and so that battle for trust and confidence has been hard to achieve.'

These views were strongly supported within the interviews with Muslim personnel, many of whom felt concerned with protecting their standing in their own community, and this led some of them to put down very clear markers about the ways in which they would allow themselves to be used within this policy framework. The notion of 'being used' is employed here quite deliberately as within the Muslim workforce there was a clear evidence of their understanding of their distinctive competence in acting as a bridge between the local state and the Muslim communities, and consequently of their vulnerability to being used by their employers in certain contexts specifically because they were Muslim. This view was further supported in some instances by a strong assertion of the ignorance about the local Muslim communities within the local authority that resulted in a dependency on their Muslim colleagues to work with these communities. Some spoke quite explicitly of refusing 'to front' for the local authority in certain contexts where they felt that the implication for them was to be put in a position where they would be too closely allied to initiatives of which they and the community were deeply critical. Additionally because of the strong interagency control of the Prevent agenda there was the perceived added difficulty that dialogue with the communities was not a balanced two-way flow of information and opinion; the policy options within Prevent were already heavily over-determined by the top-down management structure of Prevent, raised above, in relation to communication and trust. As one Muslim worker said:

> 'But what we are trying to do is that people who are making policy and make decisions are actually depending on people that know their communities; and that particular communication is not as it should be. Because if I say to my Head of Service, *look this is what needs to be done here,* my Head of Service is going to say, *OK, I hear what you are saying – but – we're actually bound to do it this way.'*

The strength of feeling among the Muslim interviewees about their particular exposure as individuals and professionals when caught in the policy mix of Prevent and Community Cohesion was one of the strongest bodies of opinion coming out of this data. The range of examples provided below give some insight into the necessary complexity of the situation.

> 'As a Muslim myself, I would hope that I've been employed based on my skills and experience and so forth, rather than being a Muslim.... I've no doubt I've opened up many doors for the local authority. The local authority as well has been very supportive of some of the work that I've done and some of the pressure as well that I might be placed under: you know, being a Muslim ... the contacts I have and so

forth. They've been very very clear that they want to protect me; they don't want to compromise me.'

At the same time this same respondent talks about the nature of some of these stresses:

'When I took on this job there was some people who would say, *Oh, XXXXX's a police informer now....* Someone said, a very close family friend as well, *oh, you're the enemy within.*'

Which led this respondent to conclude that:

'There is going to be that level of suspicion, you know. Anyone who works with communities now, on Community Cohesion or whatever, it all comes back to Prevent.'

This example reveals the inevitable internal tensions that being a Muslim worker within Prevent is likely to present. Although very well supported, and believing that they were employed because of their professional competences, it still becomes clear that some part of the distinctive contribution of this person was through being able to 'open doors', and irrespective of their generic professional status they were still judged by members of the Muslim community in relation to their place within the community.

This link between knowledge of the Muslim communities and credibility within these communities is also pointed up by this respondent, who said:

'I've been here a long time and I've built up my reputation around the work that I do to support the Muslim community and other communities in XXXXX.... If I call a meeting they'll be there within the hour. Whereas if the police or the authority try to call them the chances are there might be a few. But again, it's because I've worked with the communities.'

This respondent talked at length about the importance of maintaining their personal reputation within the Muslim communities, and the importance of not being associated within any particular interest groups within the communities. Consequently the respondent spoke about a very strong line on determining what activities they would be involved in on behalf of the authority, and which tasks they would refuse.

> 'The thing about it is I've been very clear in terms of, you know, where I fit into it. If it means I will lose my reputation, then I will not get involved in it … and there have been a number of occasions where I have [said], *I'm not attending that meeting* … and I've been criticised by senior management.'

Another respondent spoke of their reasons for actively avoiding contact with the Prevent agenda to the best of their ability, saying:

> 'I think that there is a lot of pressure, and to be honest that's why I've shied away from being involved with it; because it's loaded. I can't go straight faced to my community and say, *I'm here to help you.* I know what they want me to do. It's like working as an informant, a spy, at the same time. It goes against my morals to do that.'

But as already noted above there is evidence of the sensitivity of management to the pressure that their staff are put under and the examples noted are echoed in this statement by one of the Muslim staff:

> 'It's a two-way thing because of us as well, and because sometimes people in the authority will also know that by asking me to do something they will then compromise my position in the community. They will say, *on this occasion we won't ask you to do it. We'll do it ourselves.*'

It should also, perhaps, be recognised that many of the stresses experienced by Muslim members of the council staff were also applicable to Muslim councillors who were expected to mediate between the local state and the Muslim communities. Their role was explicitly acknowledged by one non–Muslim manager, who said:

> 'It's not always easy for the council to disassociate itself from the state. It's kind of mediated by the role of the local councillors who are not really seen as organs of the state; they're seen as players or important figures in the community, and particularly if they're from the community – if they're Asian councillors. And that kind of helps too in some ways.

> I've been on the receiving end of some considerable abuse
> at times from local members from the Asian community.
> They have played quite a useful role I think.'

As *elected* members, therefore, they were doubly accountable to their community. More generally, the dynamics regarding the political and moral problematics of Prevent's permeation of local authority community interventions can be seen to take on an additional, and significant, nuance when these stresses are mediated through the experience of Muslim professionals. There is clear evidence in this data of this reality being acknowledged by management in a variety of ways, but even where this sensitivity is present the unique pressures on Muslim staff remain a reality.

This experience of the Muslim staff points to a continuing tension within any professional practice in a multi-ethnic context. Major professional bodies and institutions have over the last four decades invested considerable thought and some commitment to enabling their staff to work effectively with an ethnically diverse client population. This has typically involved some form of training in transcultural communication for the majority white staff. What frequently proves more contentious is when members of a profession seek to infuse their professional practice with a sensibility derived from their experience as a minority within the country (Husband, 2005a). Such a commitment carries at least two elements. One is a willingness to employ their experientially based cultural knowledge to facilitate their working with *their* ethnic community. Another element involves a political commitment to recognise the ways in which members of this community have been marginalised and discriminated against in society at large and through the routine practices of their profession.

The first position leaves such professionals vulnerable to being exploited as 'instant experts' who can relieve their majority colleagues of any responsibility to acquire the appropriate transcultural competences. As they rise up the managerial pyramid they are at risk of being rendered latter-day 'district commissioners' for the minority population, seeking to ameliorate the effects of a system that has not systemically addressed the challenge of serving a diverse population.

On the other hand, the second position leaves them at risk of being accused of having 'gone native', of being unprofessional in their identification with the community they serve. There is within professionalism a retreat from engaging with your complete humanity, of setting bounds to your responsibilities and affective attachment to those you serve. Professional codes of ethics typically set limits on your responsibilities, and circumscribe an open moral *being for the other* by a much narrower *ethical* set of expectations (Husband,1995; Husband and Alam, 2001). In the current context of risk aversion and securitisation, this second position, taken by a Muslim professional in the employ of a local authority, must place them in a permanent tension with the routine operational expectations of Prevent, and its clones in Community Cohesion.

Communities, identities, governance

One of the themes that emerges in a variety of modes of expression and in relation to a range of specific issues is the sense of pride and competence that the respondents feel in their local knowledge. As might be expected, given the views expressed above, some of this self-reflexive pride is honed in comparison with the 'outsiders' who define policies and comment on local performance. But just as powerfully, it is felt in relation to providing a quite specific competence to address the needs of the local communities. One obvious expression of such sentiments is from Muslim staff members who regard their own knowledge of the Muslim faith, and of the local communities' unique fusion of ethnic identity, Islam and history of migration, as providing a vital basis for mediating between the needs of these communities and the policy imperatives sent down from Westminster. They have a competence to work within the system and yet retain identification with, and a sensibility toward, the concerns of the Muslim communities who have been specifically targeted by these policies.

For these Muslim staff, and the non-Muslim staff, there is also a distinct awareness of the value of their knowledge of the local majority communities. In working to build community cohesion, an in-depth understanding of what constitutes the defining boundaries of local communities, socially and territorially, is a fundamental basis for any initiative. This 'thick' (Geertz, 1973) understanding of the terrain of local communities and their distinctive culture is also a vital ingredient in being able to anticipate and intervene in growing intergroup tensions. Understanding what symbolic or realistic threat may be being experienced by a particular community requires exactly this expertise and the interviews were rich in anecdotes that revealed exactly this sort of insight. Such tensions were just as likely between two established white communities as they were between a white community and a minority ethnic community. The quote below gives a feel of exactly this level of local historically embedded community identity (non-English names have been used to help ensure anonymity):

> 'Vantaa's quite disparate – nobody says I come from Vantaa – they come from Espoo, they come from Espoo [old established small townships that have been absorbed into the metropolitan authority]. We've got quite strong levels of social capital in these communities, but it's insular social capital. It's *very*: *I'm from Espoo, I don't like the people up the road; and I've been from Espoo for a hundred years.*
>
> 'About a hundred years ago miners moved from Vantaa into about three streets in one town – that area is still called "Little Vantaa".'

Anecdotes like this reveal an understanding of the very finite nature of local identities and their fit into quite specific territorial spaces. These spaces of identity and of people's imagined social boundaries were recognised as not sitting in a comfortably meaningful relationship with the political territory of the local authority. These large metropolitan authorities had an administrative terrain that encompassed many large townships that had their own history and strong identities that included strong local stereotypes about each other's residents. Thus it was recognised that given the option, many of these local citizens would prefer to revert to being within the administrative domain of their old town halls, rather than this alien imposition. Equally, as the anecdote above exemplifies, within townships there were very strong local identities associated with quite specific areas. Such imagined social territories have implications for the capacity of local staff to engage in meaningful 'community work'; the interviewees' sensitivity to these dynamics was central to their understanding of the basis for local expressions of symbolic and realistic threat. Seen from within such a perspective, such sentiments are not seen as offensive expressions of 'pathological' prejudices, but rather as social constructs that have a specific history and *reasonableness* that must be engaged with through empathetic understanding rather than with righteous political condemnation. It is questionable how many of the respondents were familiar with the social psychological literature sketched in Chapter Four earlier, but they showed sensitivity and understanding that certainly made it implicit in their work.

It is worth noting that metropolitan authorities are routinely monitoring ethnically and class-defined communities against a large number of benchmarks including variables around educational attainment, income, employment, health indicators et cetera. Thus, there is already an established and sophisticated demographic database that identifies 'vulnerable' groups in terms of socioeconomic indices and markers. In this sample there was clear evidence of staff having knowledge of such data collected by their authority. For the managers, for example, it was a significant tool in informing their decision making around priorities and the allocation of resources. A sophisticated and nuanced understanding of the socioeconomic determination of the life chances of people in specific minority ethnic and white communities appeared to be a routine element in the professional repertoire of many of the senior staff interviewed in this study.

We should not take this for granted, neither in terms of the availability of data, nor in the capacity of local personnel to deploy it meaningfully in relation to their own workplace priorities. We might want to pause to note that in many countries the collection of data by ethnic category is illegal, and in Britain there have been those from minority ethnic and liberal/left positions who have objected to this practice in the UK (some of the concerns around data collection and its illegitimate use are summarised in ECCAR, 2010). However, it seems unlikely that the forces of racist exclusion, whether institutional or personal, need this data to effectively continue their discriminatory practices, but it is clear that such data does help reveal the consequences of such actions. It is notable that both the European Roma Rights Centre (ERRC, 2004) and the European Network Against Racism (ENAR, 2007), which between them represent over 600 non-governmental organisations (NGOs) across Europe, have spoken out explicitly in support of the collection of disaggregated ethnic data as a tool in the fight against racism.

It is not patronising to pause to recognise the knowledge of such demographic data that was routinely drawn on by respondents when talking about their perception of the challenges they faced. They frequently made use of a nuanced combination of personal existential knowledge of their patch and the statistical data that was produced within their own authority. This very strong existentially based knowledge of their local patch, and the capacity to integrate this with the demographic data generated by their own research departments, was a striking feature of the competence of the managerial, and other, staff interviewed in this project.

Community perceptions

Across the interviews a wide range of voices spoke of their insight into the ways in which different communities had responded to the current policy agenda around Prevent and to their perceptions of the ways in which government policies had impacted on them. These dialogues of course represent these interviewees' own perceptions of what is going on in these communities and as such are second generation data. However, the consistent themes that emerge across these interviews deserve to be recorded. They often address quite directly the issue of intergroup threat discussed in the previous chapter, where the different communities experience themselves as objectively disadvantaged, and this perception provides a foundation for quite strong senses of symbolic and realistic threat. For Muslim communities with their quite distinct community experiences of migration and settlement, some long established (former) economic migrants, others quite recent refugees and asylum seekers, there are particular experiences of the processes of marginalisation and racism that are likely to have been part of their shared experience. Many will have a strong sense of their British identity and of the legitimacy of their British citizenship (Alam, 2006). For them, in seeking to live with an accommodation of their British status and their ethnic and religious heritage they have reason to regard the contemporary assaults on them in the name of the 'War on Terror' and counter-terrorism in the UK as illegitimate. We should therefore not be surprised if in the interviews we find evidence of these communities' sensitivity to their treatment within their own local authority and neighbourhood.

Equally in a country with a long history of 'race relations', and as we noted above with a new formation of xenophobic racism providing a contemporary variant on established British racisms, the majority 'white' population, and others, have a capacity to code intergroup tensions through the language of racism. This is particularly likely in the current climate of heightened sensitivity around citizenship and identity, with the attendant neo-nationalist promotions of conceptions of the 'real British'. We have already seen how immigration policy is integrally linked with community cohesion, both conceptually and practically. The different class-based experiences of this majority population mediates their experience of symbolic and realistic threat as their relationship with Muslim communities is shaped by the demographic profile of both populations (see Hewitt, 2005).

Muslim communities

Not surprisingly concerns about the intrusive nature of CONTEST, and the state's counter-terrorist incursions into their communities, figure strongly in some of the accounts. Within some of these authorities there have been arrests, and prosecutions, of individuals for terrorist offences. It was suggested that this may have produced a sense of shame and confusion within these communities, shame that 'one of their own' should have done such a thing and confusion that the response of the 'new protective state' should be so collective and indiscriminate. Because the Muslim communities have been explicitly targeted by the anti-terrorist policies of CONTEST and because these communities have *felt* the impact of these policies within their communities, there is a real anxiety about the nature of their contact with the state and its systems. As one senior manager with extensive community work experience in such an authority put it:

> 'It's created suspicion about what's your real agenda; and particularly among younger Muslim men … you know, expressing the view that they're worried their phones are being tapped, they're worried that they're being spied on. They worry about where they'd spy on them and they don't know whose going to be arrested next in their community. And there's a feeling that wider concerns about international events – disagreement with government policy in terms of Iraq and Afghanistan – are then perceived as a support for terrorism.'

This quote reveals something of the chilling effect of the securitisation of everyday life (Huysmans, 2009); the mundane activities of making a telephone call, or of expressing your views about the folly of British foreign policy – which the mainstream press does routinely with impunity – becomes a source of anxiety simply because you are Muslim.

A powerful issue within the interviews relating to the reported experience of the Muslim communities was the highly negative response to the police raids and arrests in Muslim communities. One Muslim community worker expressed it in these terms:

> 'There's a key thing – and that is the extensive number of people that have been arrested who have not been convicted. That has been absolutely tantamount to the loss of trust. I mean as communities – forget whether it's a Muslim or anybody – if people break the law and they're taken to court and convicted, the community or the neighbourhood can somewhere substantiate that particular process and say: *well, we have confidence in that process, and as a consequence we can understand or even support it.* We have a situation here where you know by far the greatest number

of people that have been arrested have actually not been convicted, and that has been a real issue.'

Another Muslim member of staff from a different authority repeated this reported concern and in doing so provided some insights into why the separation of 'hard' from 'soft' Prevent might prove to be difficult:

'The arrests in XXXXX had an impact most definitely.... You know, questions were asked in terms of, all people assume that we know everything that happens around Pursue and Protect, and that's not the case at all: obviously. But people make the assumption that local authority staff who work on Prevent will know exactly if them arrests come in, why they happened, who the individuals were and so forth; and seek answers from us. And all we can do is give back to them what we're fed through CTU in terms of *These are the key messages that need to go out*. But actually some of them are not very helpful and communities will not understand: *well if you've released them we want to know the full facts*. They won't understand some of the issues in terms of protecting sources of information and if there's an ongoing investigation.'

These Muslim communities, at various levels, were reported to have come to feel resentful of the way they had been isolated and stigmatised through government policies. Individuals were reported as feeling that their personal liberties had been put in jeopardy as the veil of counter-terrorism shrouded their every activity with suspicion. They were said to feel resentment at their collective punishment for the behaviour of a very small extreme minority, whose behaviour was regarded by the majority as 'un-Islamic'. The 'raids' into their communities – frequently *not* leading to prosecution, let alone conviction – were resented and seen as speculative exercises of excessive force by a hostile intelligence service. And, others, whether through Community Cohesion or Prevent, resented suddenly being the recipient of government attention and modest largesse, after what they saw as years of neglect. As one fieldworker said:

'I think as well, some Muslim organisations and Muslim individuals would be quite suspicious really of all these groups wanting to come in and work with them.... I think that one or two of them feel quite offended as well that all of a sudden, now it's around extremism and terrorism, that you want to work with us. But before we've never had no support from anyone, nobody's wanted to work with us before.'

And for some this resentment at this new urgency in state attention was linked to a dislike of the government's attempt to use Prevent and Community Cohesion as a vehicle for the external imposition of a model of 'acceptable Islam' that reduced it to a matter of personal faith and morality with minimal social relevance. As one Muslim interviewee put it:

> 'If you understand Islam you have to be interactive with the community; you do public service, you've got to be a social servant, you've got to do all good things – look after your neighbours, look after the community, get involved with all sorts of things. That's what Islam tells you. But what the Prevent agenda is saying is that *you don't want to be that type of Muslim; you want to be this type of Muslim where you can just keep Islam in your thoughts, be spiritual, don't worry about the policies we're implementing, don't worry about our foreign policy. This is the type of Muslim we would like.*'

The reported views of Muslim communities presented here provide a complementary insight into the resistance to Prevent reported above. The wish to have the legitimacy of their Muslim identity and faith respected and nurtured raises serious questions about the model of citizenship that underpins the community cohesion that is pressed on these communities. (Chapter Six addresses this issue in more detail.)

Non-Muslim communities

As we have noted above, and will discuss further in the final chapter, there has been a considerable concern with the experience of the white working class in terms of their relation to a variety of policies and specifically in relation to their sense of competition with urban minority ethnic communities. In the context of these interviews the respondents' awareness of this sense of competition, and resentment, felt by the white working-class communities in their area was made quite explicit. Consequently the material presented in this next section deals particularly with the reported concerns of the white working class. But we should keep in mind the large numbers of non-Muslims in Britain who do not fit into this category, and who will experience their own intergroup rivalries with both the white working class, the affluent white, Muslim communities and other, minority, populations.

There is a perverse effect of the policy focus on Muslim communities in that it upsets both the Muslim and the majority white community. As one manager expressed it:

> 'So within the Muslim community there's resentment that there's all this attention on the whole community. From the white community there's a resentment and a perception that resources and attention goes to the Muslim community at the expense of those white communities.'

The sense of realistic threat shared by white working-class communities was recurrently visible in the discussions with councillors, senior managers and staff. Often the reported evidence of tensions within the white community were strong and concrete, as these quotes indicate:

> 'Tension within white working-class communities around the perception that everything goes to the Muslim community – we're ignored – is extremely strong.'

> 'There is a perception out there in communities that the Muslim community's getting all the money now.'

And of course these perceptions are not entirely self-generated. As one councillor noted:

> 'I mean – the ward that I represent is predominantly white, so there's been some activity from the British National Party. It's a classic area with a very small Asian-British population, and you know they [the white constituents] hear about things and the BNP play on those sorts of fears. So you get quite a lot of the white British community who are uncomfortable with their perceptions of the Muslim community. You know – to think, *well ... is every Muslim a potential terrorist?*'

The same councillor spoke of how the different wards within the authority had quite different intergroup relations, some marred by overt racism and others having no major issues around racism and Islamophobia. They then discussed how this varying pattern was reflected in the different experience and priorities of the councillors, with the effect that it was not always possible to have a discussion in which a shared sensibility to the issues was grounded in individual councillors' experience. Certainly councillors in these interviews spoke of very different dynamics in their patch, and this was reflected in the views that they expressed.

The assumption that a strong sense of interethnic tension is routinely at the top of the agenda of white communities was not supported in these interviews, where again the specific demography of particular communities and their interface with minority ethnic communities was critical in determining the nature of community anxieties. One officer illustrated this quite graphically in describing the concerns of a relatively affluent white area within the authority, reporting their priorities as "almost to a person.... Oh, without a doubt intergenerational tensions".

A community worker from another authority underlined this mismatch of central government priorities and neighbourhood priorities. Again, asserting the relative unimportance of counter-terrorism to a white community they noted the contradiction when a community presented a very explicit statement of their priorities, and yet the local authority staff found themselves saying:

> 'We're being asked to focus on something else; but the residents are saying: *yes but the problem we've got is this.*'

Where local authorities are having to make hard decisions about the allocation of resources, the determination of priorities obviously becomes a fraught issue between meeting targets set by central government and addressing the priorities as seen by specific neighbourhoods. This dilemma is made all the more difficult if there are streams of funding which are linked to specific communities and specific activities.

The complexity of urban demography and the interethnic relations that are developed within them have received extensive attention. The dynamics of Muslim–non-Muslim interaction has had a special focus (for a recent relevant example, see Jayaweera and Choudhury, 2008). The evidence from this data points to the very considerable differences in demography, affluence and concerns between different areas in the same authority. Security has wide relevance in terms of the control of unruly youth, and provision of services and access to reasonable quality housing are concerns that many communities share as a reflection of their class position. Regrettably in the context of the current focus on Islam there has been a capacity for both white and Muslim communities to adopt perspectives that reflect their own experiences mediated through the salience of Islam. For both communities their need to be seen to be treated equitably has become a salient issue. However, they have become defined by contemporary political discourse as opposing interest groups in intergroup competition for scarce resources.

Despite this there are some strong voices of optimism among the interviewees. One senior officer, while recognising the great deprivation in their Muslim community and in white neighbourhoods within the authority, chose to point out that people living in those neighbourhoods often had very strong bonds towards them, that is, they had strong bonding capital. And instead of seeing that as a problem for social cohesion, it was seen as the platform on which positive intergroup relations could be built. They had a basis for engagement with the local authority, and they had a shared sense of their 'northern' identities. Another officer from a different authority was concerned to point to the dangers of defining 'community' in too narrow a way, particularly in terms of faith or ethnicity. They spoke of the importance of 'non-geographically based identities', such as age, gender or disability, that cut across other identities and provided a basis for developing a more complex model of service provision and local constituencies of interest. The ways in which government policies construct 'top-down' taken for granted identities, and construct unreflective definitions of community, was a challenge to the complexities that these respondents saw in their own locale.

Myth busting

An area of local practice that drew explicitly and successfully on this grounded local knowledge lay in the area of 'myth busting'. If there was one area where the respondents felt confident in talking about their ability to make a difference it was in relation to identifying developing local intergroup conflicts, isolating the specific perceived grievances that were feeding them, and then moving in to defuse this developing situation with concrete relevant information. This activity depended on the quality of their ability to monitor local tensions, one aspect of the community surveillance process where information was fed back from a variety of sources. Given the reasonable concerns about the intrusive nature of surveillance that has been normalised under Prevent, it is somewhat ironic that the extensive local mechanisms of tension monitoring have proven to be so critical in enabling the local authority to intervene and defuse developing intergroup tensions. However, it is exactly this sort of ambiguity about 'good' and 'bad' monitoring that permeates the local politics of this policy overlap.

Tension monitoring draws on a very wide range of inputs, but also depends crucially on having good contacts with opinion leaders and groups in these communities. This means having an established basis of routine contact and mutual trust which provides the basis for a direct exchange of information in both directions. (It should be noted that it was exactly this sort of relationship of trust that was threatened by the negative impact of some of the Prevent initiatives noted above.) Often the basis of the developing grievances could be traced back to a sense of realistic threat, where a neighbouring community was believed to be getting preferential treatment. This was not necessarily a conflict between established white working-class communities and new immigrant communities but could also be between established minority ethnic communities and newly arriving asylum seeker populations. The staff involved in interventions of this sort rightly took pride in their ability to work at the local level, with local knowledge and professional skills, in order to make a significant contribution to maintaining good working relationships between adjacent communities.

It is worth noting that while professional skills in community work may be readily transferable from place to place within Britain, the sensitive local knowledge and trust that makes this professionalism have any real value relies heavily on having a stable and committed workforce. One manager who spoke of the benefit of having a long established stable team with local knowledge at times of growing tension expressed this in these terms:

> 'Those groups became crucial in terms of providing some reassurance and contact with communities: in being able to pick up very quickly what some of the fears and concerns of the community were. And, where there were sort of rumours myths circulating or inaccuracies circulating, being able to very quickly say: *look this is what people are feeling: is this true or not?* We were able to get messages out, so in terms of two-way communication at times of tension – we're absolutely clear.'

In these interviews, as we have noted, there was clear evidence of very strong working relationships between immediate colleagues who saw themselves as a mutually supportive team of individuals who had respect for each other and had a shared ethos. The strength of the professional and personal bonds within such 'communities of practice' was also capable of providing a strong and shared disdain for some of the other players who were part of the interagency networking of service delivery. And, as we have seen above, within such groups there was a capacity for a shared rehearsal of their concerns about the ways in which the reshaping of practice under the influence of negotiating these two policy agendas placed new stresses on their relationship with the chain of command above them. Perhaps rightly, they see themselves as the people at the coalface, doing the 'real work', and for some this gives them a perceived legitimacy for being critical of the judgement and level of support offered by 'their betters'. These coalface workers most acutely experienced the impact of Prevent, and CONTEST, in its full repertoire, in undermining the trust and networks of cooperation that they had so carefully established, and tenaciously sought to defend.

In echoing some of the argument from the previous discussion it is worth noting the extent to which knowledge of the historically sedimented bases for quite specific territorially localised community identities were central to an empathetic understanding of how intergroup tensions were formed and elaborated. Without in any way wishing to be patronising, it is apparent that the staff employed in this activity of 'myth busting' were employing a range of skills and knowledge in order to carry out exactly the sort of context-specific analysis of intergroup dynamics advocated by Reicher (2004), and required by Halliday's grounding of anti-Muslimism in specific local circumstances. For example, in some instances an understanding of long established white working-class communities and their radical transformation through changes in the local labour market, along with the gender and age-related tensions woven into this collective biography, were brought to bear in contextualising current events. Additionally, the significance attached to local spatial and institutional sites was used to recognise their potential as 'trigger points' for contestation that might not have been apparent to an outsider. Through such sensitive insights a capacity to recognise how specific identities were being brought into focus aided an untangling of the elements of symbolic and realistic threat that were being fed into an emerging local situation. While the staff involved in myth busting may certainly not have expressed their competence and actions in the terms used here, nevertheless, it was such competencies that enabled them to identify the sources of emergent grievances with some sophistication and to address the participants in terms that made sense to them.

Interference from other government policies

In the data presented above we have seen considerable evidence of the contradictions experienced in the implementation of Community Cohesion and Prevent policies. However, within the interviews there were occasional references to other forms of contradiction between government policies. These deserve to be at least recognised, for we might remember the conclusion of the councillor above, who, when discussing the interaction of Community Cohesion and Prevent, declared that:

> '... contradictions between policies are much more common than that.'

As has become widely recognised in political analyses, the attempt by the Labour government to maintain the belief that their foreign policy had no impact on internal domestic ethnic relations cannot be sustained. As one manager put it.

> 'We are invited by the government to gloss over foreign policy, and these communities are very very concerned about people that they see as part of their community in a religious sense. And that has an impact: and you can't avoid it.'

A similar scenario of policy contradiction was presented in another city where a councillor for that authority explained, with some exasperation:

> 'ZXYT has been in the regeneration team's sights for quite some time and regeneration officers have been working very hard to stop things getting worse. What do housing do? Under government instructions they say: *we need emergency housing, we need emergency housing for asylum seekers, we need emergency housing for all sorts of people. Where will we get emergency housing cheapest?* Answer: *the most deprived areas you can you find!* So, cheek by jowl with regeneration officers trying to stop things getting worse, you've got housing officers complicit in putting in all sorts of people for a short period, with no long-term roots, and the effect of that is just to make things worse.'

These examples point to the almost inevitable consequences of different divisions within the same authority being driven by differing government departmental priorities, and being held accountable to meet performance indicators that, in their practical expression, produce contradictory outcomes. Behind these processes you can also discern the professional pride, the cohesive power of communities of practice, that have been invoked positively elsewhere in this analysis, but which here have dysfunctional consequences as local council divisions seek to pursue their goals. Because of such effects, in at least one local authority the myth busting prowess of the local staff was employed in diffusing building tensions between one established Muslim community and another recently arrived Muslim community as the pursuit of independent policies produced resentment between two communities of different ethnic background and different migratory experience.

Other interviews have produced a variety of instances of contradiction between the agendas of pursuing Community Cohesion and those of other government departments, leaving one officer to conclude that:

> 'So cohesion, unless we address those issues [of contradiction], and government works in a joined-up way – and actually works across its own departments – well what we are actually doing here is an ultimate contradiction, ultimate contradiction! And, it's leaving local authorities and partnerships like spinning plates.'

For the local state the policies that emerge in confident isolation from specific ministries cannot be kept operationally within the sphere of their pristine departmental origins. Governmental policies on migration and asylum seeking feed the racist and xenophobic sentiments that infect local intergroup resentments. The neglect in challenging the chronic levels of inequality within a wealthy state like Britain guarantees the reproduction of the conditions for the nurturing of strategic Islamophobia, and reproduces the closure of community boundaries as opportunities for mobility are restricted. And most certainly British foreign policy cannot be isolated from the negative effects it has on intergroup sentiments within Britain.

Community Cohesion, Prevent and inequality

As discussed in Chapter Two, the British translation of social cohesion into 'community cohesion' elegantly included a political evasion of the core issues of inequality in Britain in its focus on culture and contact. Equally, although Prevent included an acknowledgement of the impact of inequalities as a trigger for radicalisation, the reality has been a focus on the internal dynamics of Muslim communities and an attempt to manage a transition in personal identification with 'British' culture and the state. A meaningful attempt to address the systemic inequalities in British life that may dispose the white majority population to experiencing symbolic or realistic threat in relation to the Muslim minority, or which might contribute to the discontent that becomes a trigger for radicalisation among Muslim communities, has been markedly absent. We might wonder whether this has any significance for those given the remit to implement Prevent and Community Cohesion. The answer, not surprisingly, is that of course it does. Everything that has been said above about their knowledge, and identification, with their 'patch' would lead us to expect that they have an acute awareness of the significance of the material circumstances that shape the lives of their client populations. And this is apparent in their dialogue. Additionally for many (perhaps all) of them, their commitment to public service, whether as professional members of staff or as elected councillors, comes with a vision of making things better. This comes coded through a unique personal fusion of political commitment, professional values and biography, but it is evident in its variety of expression. At a time when public service professionals are going to become scapegoated as feather-bedded, over paid and scandalously over-pensioned drains on the public coffers, it may be necessary to assert the obvious evidence from these interviews, namely, that salary and conditions are not the reasons that these people hold the positions that they do. Consequently it would be naive to expect this cohort of people to comfortably, and unreflectively, embrace the politics inscribed into both of these policies. There is therefore in some of these interviews a clear expression of the painful recognition of the limited impact of the policies they are pursuing.

A senior officer laid out something of the dilemma:

> 'Whether it's someone who's going to tie himself to a tree that's being cut down, or whether they're going to become a so-called terrorist, I think that there is a felt unfairness and injustice in the first place. So what we'll have to do – and this is where we have to tie into the cohesion agenda – is provide another narrative that also tackles the underlying causes of the injustice ... we can't achieve this without attacking issues about equality. We can't do it. And what's been happening nationally – there's a separation of

these agendas, without a doubt. Cohesion now for the last five years has become the buzz word – used in turn by government ministers and civil servants who write speeches etc; and the links to poverty, discrimination, injustice have gone from it, absolutely gone … unless we address that, cohesion falls down at the first hurdle.'

Another interviewee, in talking about their specific Prevent work, said:

'And, really there is a whole other agenda that one doesn't really talk about – that's inequality we have in our society and what are the opportunities.'

Another manager reflected on the relative impact of Community Cohesion work in effecting change in these terms:

'And I think that without social justice and equality, cohesion will not work. But there's the challenge, and we ain't cracked that for quite a number of years. So I think, [the] absolute acknowledgement that work on tackling equality in all spheres is vital to underpin the cohesion agenda…. The kind of stuff my staff does is not going to solve the problem on its own; it's sticking plaster stuff to some extent. I think it's very important. I think that it's key, but it's only part of a bigger picture. So the decisions taken around Building Schools for the Future will have a much bigger impact on cohesion than any of the projects my staff are involved in.'

This is the opinion of a committed and experienced manager who takes very seriously the work of their staff but who nevertheless finds themselves reflecting on the relative impact of structural investment in equality in comparison to the impact of reactive community work. As this interviewee makes very plain, it is not a matter of either community work or a radical programme of assaulting the reproduction of inequalities; the issue lies in recognising the limited potential of Prevent and Community Cohesion work. If the high profile attention that is given to work in these areas is used as a smoke screen to obscure the political neglect of addressing inequality in a meaningful way, then at a moral level the commitment of these individuals is being abused. At a political level it has to be recognised as a cynical strategy that is part of a generic policy of refusing to engage with the redistribution of wealth and opportunity in a meaningful way.

Conclusion

The insights provided through the data presented above show a picture of local authorities engaged in the difficult role of mediating between central government politics and policy, and the priorities presented to them within their populations. From social scientists, who are routinely regarded as incorrigibly critical and possibly 'nasty', the account of the commitment and competencies of the local personnel may seem perversely positive. That is as it was seen. This is not a rose-tinted account of everything as being wonderfully coherent and endlessly flawless in its execution. But it is an account of the importance we might want to attach to the role of local authority personnel in mediating the worst impacts of flawed central government policy.

The data provides substantive support for the concerns that have been expressed elsewhere regarding the damaging impact of Prevent on Community Cohesion initiatives. It also shows something of the personal costs that are experienced in being caught in this policy cross-fire.

In the next, and final chapter, we explore further the implications of the findings discussed here.

Note

[1] As an element of the governmental monitoring of the implementation of policy at the local level, performance indictors have been developed against which local authority activity is judged. NI 35 was a performance indicator attached to Prevent that many felt was Islamophobic in nature. Four of the five local authorities refused to sign up to NI 35 as a statement of the strength of their feeling on the matter (see Audit Commission, 2010).

SIX

Conclusion

Introduction

This final chapter seeks to draw out some of the implications of the data presented in earlier chapters. Linking back to the context presented earlier, the argument developed here is presented in three sections. The first outlines some of the implications for our understanding of the operation of the local state in implementing central government policy. The consequences for local authority personnel, and for the communities they seek to serve, of the simultaneous operation of the Prevent and Community Cohesion policy programmes, is explored. Additionally this section of analysis reveals the practical challenges of managing policy at the local level, and the wider issue of the problematic nature of the governance of local communities.

The second section adopts a wider perspective to ask whether the Prevent and Community Cohesion policies can be credible in the absence of a robust assault on the reproduction of inequalities in Britain. This introduces a political critique of the assumptive framework that has sustained these policies. This analysis returns to some of the questions raised in Chapters Two and Three about the ideological, rather than practical, consequences of the massive political investment that has gone into developing and implementing these two policies. We suggest that it is unhelpful to assess these policies solely on the terms on which they were established. Rather, understanding their political significance requires that they be placed in relation to other political projects which are excluded from the governmental definition and operation of these policies.

The third and final section addresses the broader conceptual issues of how a democratic polity may be constructed which can promote both security and cohesion. It uses the critique of existing policy approaches to argue for a more positive dialogue about the political environment that will be necessary in order to sustain both equitable social cohesion and security for all citizens. Of necessity this can only be a brief invitation to take up a political dialogue that already has an extensive and contested history. But it is hoped that this section will further make explicit the questions that are not adequately present in the current formulation of counter-terrorism and Community Cohesion policies.

Implications of the data on the implementation of Community Cohesion and Prevent

Organisational context and response

The data on local government responses to the implementation of Community Cohesion and Prevent provided ample evidence of the intersection of these two policies at an organisational level. The close managerial linkages between these two policies and the extensive nature of the interagency working that was implicit in their delivery made for a routine synergy between them (although this was expressed in different ways at different levels within local authorities' management structures). Additionally, the absence of any party political tensions in defining how the elected councillors understood the demands on the local authority presented by these two policy agendas fed a practical consensus about how the authority would respond to and manage them. Not only did this apply at the level of the individual local authority, but there was also a strong sense of the, largely, shared political agenda that existed across all the five case study local authorities. This was nurtured through the network of joint committees and other fora through which a continuous dialogue was maintained about these, and other, policies. It is likely that this organisational network, and the shared regional sense of purpose, was conducive to the production of the self-confidence that marked respondents' willing ownership of their responsibilities for managing these policies.

The negative views expressed toward both central government competence and individual representatives of 'Whitehall' was a reflection of, and indeed likely to be a stimulant to, this sense of local competence. The recurrent irritation with elements of central government in relation to both the Prevent and Community Cohesion policies constitutes a form of intergroup comparison within which the personnel of the local state assert their greater local knowledge and closer alliance with the local population. This is not only a claim to personal professional competence, but is also an invocation of the greater political legitimacy felt by these individuals in pursuing their role in mediating between central government and policy implementation at the local level. For some this is linked to their perception of their role as ameliorating in practice what are regarded as the failings of central government. For local authority chief executives and others with *back channels* to 'Westminster', this may be linked to their role in dialoguing with ministers and others in order to better inform government thinking and consequently improve emergent policy. The willing exercise of local discretion in the face of the policy overload that came from central government's attempt to micro-manage policy was one concrete expression of this self-regard and confidence.

In the light of this evidence, if the current proposals from the Conservative and Liberal Democrat coalition government to devolve power from central government to the local state were to proceed, it seems unlikely that it would be met by horrified cries from timorous local authorities panicked by the prospect. However, whether Westminster could remain sanguine about the particularities that would be expressed in the formulation of policy at the local level is a quite different question.

The political impact of Prevent

The political impact of the Prevent policy can be seen as lying first with the construction of the policy itself and second with the extent to which the interpenetration of Community Cohesion with the practices of Prevent resulted in a permeation of Community Cohesion with the negative suspicions associated with Prevent. The specific targeting of the Muslim population within CONTEST, and hence Prevent, resulted in a strong response from Muslim communities within Britain who regarded themselves, with some reason, as having been subject to a form of collective punishment for the heinous offences of a very small minority. Our research participants indicated that sections of their local Muslim communities felt stigmatised by the narrow focus of the policy, and violated by the nature of its intrusive impact on their lives. As noted above, the staff reported the particular sensitivity of the Muslim communities that they served to the impact of police raids into their communities that resulted in the arrest of young men who were subsequently not prosecuted, or convicted. As we saw in Chapter Four there has been an extensive assault on the culture and beliefs of Muslims across Europe, the recent bans on the veil in Belgium and France being indicative of this process. Although in Britain in July 2010 the British immigration minister, Damian Green, suggested that such a ban in the UK would be 'un-British', this does not adequately counter the popular support there has been for a ban. Indeed, former Prime Minister Tony Blair was reported as saying that he regarded the wearing of a veil as 'a mark of separation' (*The Times*, October 2006). As was argued in Chapters Two and Three, the impact of these policies must be assessed in relation to the wider political context within which they operate.

Findings such as these demonstrate the difficulty of separating 'hard' and 'soft' versions of Prevent and Contest, as the communities make their own linkages between the elements of the counter-terrorist strategy. The interpretation of 'reasonable' action lies critically with those who are the recipients of counter-terrorism policy as much as with those who determine these policies. The flows of information among members of Muslim communities are likely to have very different characteristics compared with those that exist within and across non-Muslim communities. The latter, for example, are more likely to have a different sense of their being targets of these policies and will consequently bring a different sensibility to the mediated accounts of the rationale behind counter-terrorism. Members of Muslim communities are not only likely to have different perspectives, but are also, as noted above, likely to be embedded within a different media environment where the over-determined homogeneity that may be found in the mainstream media accounts of counter-terrorism is likely to be challenged by alternative analyses. The attempt of the state to manage the presentation of its counter-terrorism strategies through the media is likely to be more congenially achieved with a non-Muslim audience than it is with Muslim communities that have different experiences of the implementation of CONTEST, different media and personal networks of communication, and which rehearse shared 'Muslim' experience through the prism of their neighbourhood.

Many non-Muslims shared the concern about the definition and practice of Prevent, and for the local government personnel in this sample it became all too apparent that the negative impact of Prevent within Muslim communities had a direct secondary effect in polluting their relations with these Muslim communities, to the extent that some non-Prevent policies became problematic in practice. Where it is possible to claim, as noted above, that – "I could imagine that there is nothing that you can do in social cohesion that can't be perceived as a front for Prevent" (see Chapter Five) – it is possible to see why local authority personnel may feel that Prevent has seriously impacted on their ability to work with Muslim communities. This is a workforce that has specific professional values relating to trust and transparency, a workforce with an established workplace sensitivity to issues of equality.

The history of the mainstreaming of anti-discriminatory policies across local authority practice has had a significant impact on professional sensibilities. There may have been a retreat at the level of national politics from a commitment to plural multiculturalism, but within the professional cadres of local authority staff there exists within this sample a widely established acceptance of what would once have been called 'anti-discriminatory' principles forged through the practical successes of anti-racist and feminist politics, among others, over the last five decades in Britain. The long history of British anti-discriminatory policy and practice, that may indeed be under threat given the changing political environment around diversity, has had an impact on the normative value system within professional communities of practice that should not be lightly dismissed, nor neglected. The continuing critiques of the endemic racism within British institutions and British life accurately point to the awesome inertia in systems of exclusion and the power of established privilege to reproduce itself. But the sensibilities widely found among this sample deserve to be recognised as a relatively recent historical accomplishment of anti-discriminatory politics and a continuing critical element in the struggle to resist racism and discrimination in Britain. The clarity and strength of the resistance to some of the internal logics of Prevent point to a commitment to values of equality and respect at the local level that, as we have seen, is being eroded from national and international politics.

From the perspective of the security forces operating within the emergent 'protective state' the logics underlying the Prevent element of CONTEST were doubtless seen as a rational response to the perceived level of threat. To a central government that was responding to a new, and radical, escalation of their engagement with the 'War on Terror', Prevent represented an expression of due diligence on the part of a government that was already heavily involved in developing a 'flexible' understanding of the domestic implications of human rights principles. Indeed, for the government Prevent may have seemed a reasonable and specific variant on its existing commitment to promoting a communitarian sense of citizenship. For Muslim communities, and for those with a continuing commitment to pursuing multicultural equity within a framework of human rights, this policy smacked of 'Big Brother' and over-reaction. It would be reasonable to say that from a range of perspectives, the Prevent agenda, as it was delivered to local authorities from central government, was politically noxious.

Managing Community Cohesion and Prevent

The evidence that emerged around the significance of funding for shaping the relationship between the local authority and the communities that they worked with revealed how a number of strong factors interacted in determining the outcome of this relationship.

The very strong initial negative reaction of Muslim communities to funding coming from within Prevent put a strain on the local authorities' ability to deliver the expected outcomes of the Pathfinder initiative. Where there were few willing partners coming forward from the Muslim communities to engage with the local authority in developing Prevent initiatives, then the capacity of the authority to reach into these communities was severely limited. However, even as the situation on the ground changed over time, the generic concern about security, and the specific political and CTU concern about identifying and excluding Muslims regarded as a risk to public safety, resulted in a rational anxiety within the local authority staff about who were 'safe' and 'unsafe' partners. The moral risk of issuing contracts and facilitating partnerships with particular individuals and organisations had clearly changed the terms under which the local authority staff operated. In such circumstances being risk-averse in decision making was a logical and safe option. Consequently the concern about working with the 'usual suspects' reflected an awareness about the limited reach of the local authority in tapping into a wide and representative range of communities across both Muslim and non-Muslim organisations. In relation to the specific aims of Prevent in challenging the radicalisation of members of the Muslim communities, this scenario of risk-averse engagement with the 'usual suspects' must be self-defeating, for it suggests that it is precisely those individuals and organisations that are regarded by the security forces as problematic whom they are least likely to engage with. Consequently the sense of marginality of such groups is increased by exactly the policy which aspires to consolidate their connection to the wider society. Post CONTEST II, and in the environment that may exist in a future replacement of Prevent by some other process, the shift to 'soft' variants on Prevent are highly dependent on working with Muslim communities and on maintaining their trust. Where groups within the community are regarded as a 'risk' by security services and local authority personnel, then their selective exclusion from engagement in community initiatives leaves as available only 'hard' options for intervention.

The dynamics of funding also revealed the ways in which state resources channelled through the local authority necessarily impacted on the dynamics within the Muslim communities. As we found, the initial widespread resistance to accepting any funding linked to Prevent weakened over time as the competition between Muslim community organisations made a continued principled refusal to accept this funding problematic. At some future time it may be possible to find some evidence of the nature of the compromises that have had to be entered into by some Muslim organisations in order to participate in this largesse. But we can be relatively certain that external funding is seldom a neutral process. The analysis of Anthias and Yuval-Davis (1993) of the impact of state funding on the construction of social spaces, defined by the intersection of identities and politics, remains as relevant today as when it was written. They observed that:

> The funding process has also played a major role in the categorization or naming of groups, and the criteria for designing groups in terms of race, colour, oppression, deprived, not only are imposed from the outside, but are both opportunistic and contradictory.... This then leads to ghettoization of 'needs groups'. It is in this way that the minorities indirectly become defined and constructed by the state and their 'empowerment' can be of a very limited and specific nature. (Anthias and Yuval-Davis, 1993: 182)

The application of Prevent funding has, for Muslim organisations in general, necessarily confirmed their Muslim status over other potentially relevant social categories. It has reasserted the primacy of Islamic faith over other social characteristics in singling them out for funding. In the context of Prevent it has inherently linked this identity to their definition as a security risk, the foundational basis for the allocation of these monies. Consequently a willingness to participate in Prevent funding may itself have become a criterion for distinguishing between 'good' and 'bad' Muslim organisations, thus becoming a self-fuelling cycle. In such circumstances what may have been a principled political critique of Prevent by a Muslim organisation, similar to those aired by non-Muslim senior staff in the previous chapter, becomes potentially recoded as a marker of Islamic radicalism.

As noted above, those Muslim groups that retain a principled objection to accepting Prevent funding may enhance their prestige within segments of their community, but they will nonetheless suffer financially. Thus, in the context of the voices that are being facilitated within the community as a consequence of Prevent funding rationales, their distinctiveness vis-à-vis other groups is being sharpened while simultaneously their resource base may be suffering a relative decline. If it could be assumed that such groups are by definition part of a dangerous radicalising tendency, then this outcome may be regarded as positive in counter-terrorism terms. But regrettably there is no available simple calculus that would allow such a conclusion to be routinely drawn. Serious, devout and politically intelligent groups that have a critical perspective on the British state's relation to Islam, nationally and internationally, may be marginalised. If such is the case, the translation of a neutered political discourse, defined by a middle way, from national Labour Party politics to the construction of an 'acceptable' discourse of British Islam, is a great disservice to a meaningful and diverse public sphere (Keane, 1991; Husband and Moring, 2009). If the space for reasoned and principled criticism is artificially narrowed in the name of counter-terrorism, then segments of these Muslim communities must of necessity be forced into other modes of political expression.

In the context of the continuing potency of anti-Muslimism within British popular and elite discourse, an erosion of the communicative space within the public sphere where people feel enabled to engage with the real challenges of intergroup tensions in an open and robust way is lamentable. Where a pre-emptive censoring of Muslim voices in the name of security constructs an artificially narrow repertoire of opinion, then necessarily the development of an inclusive and well grounded understanding of current dialogues *within* Muslim communities is muted. The focus on the cultural dimension of Muslim experience, to the relative neglect of their material circumstances, exacerbates this situation by providing a policy focus on faith and culture within Muslim communities. A fetishist pursuit of facilitating 'good' Muslim leadership further skews the nature of the majority society's engagement with this population. If the aim is to counter radicalisation and to promote harmonious community relations, then the state must allow its citizens access to a flow of information that will provide insights into reality that have not been filtered through a security process, an approach that regards the public as having the ability to make their own judgements on the basis of a wide range of information. We saw in Chapter Four the regrettably biased and partial coverage of Islam and Muslim communities that is offered in the British press. We have also noted the great diversity of expressions of faith, and of ethnic identity, within Muslim communities. There is consequently a need to promote an understanding of the complexity of contemporary experience and perspectives within Muslim communities, a process that counters the simplicities of essentialist accounts of Muslim identities that all too frequently dominate British political debate.

The evolving practice of Prevent funding necessarily has attached to it a spiral of post hoc justification as the funding system seeks to make coherent what, in many instances, has been a series of pragmatic decisions made in local contexts within a limited range of options. This applies to the funders, those who have been in receipt of funds, those who applied and were refused and those who chose not to apply for funding.

The stories that need to be told about the success of funding are a critical element in this conversation. The research reported here did not have a remit to follow up on the success or otherwise of funded projects, but respondents were keen to mention initiatives that they felt had been successful. Success is of course defined within the remit of the Prevent agenda itself, and consequently this evidence of the impact of these initiatives has a limited critical capacity because it excludes consideration of how the same funds and effort may have been employed within a different political and funding framework. As it is, we had evidence of one of the recurrent difficulties of limited term funding, namely, the guaranteed continuity of the projects that were successful.

With the transition to CONTEST II there was a shift in the discretionary capacity of the local authority in the allocation of funding that was accompanied by an attempt to widen the definition of radicalism to take it beyond the narrow focus on Muslim communities. This was itself linked with a move to employ Prevent funds for funding more of the 'soft' end of Prevent work that brought it into closer proximity to extant Community Cohesion work. Thus, with the extensive interagency working noted above, we have seen a complex web of funding reaching out into both Muslim and non-Muslim communities. With the cut-backs in state funding currently being seen in British public spending (circa October 2010), and the reality of its consequences to be increasingly apparent over the next two to three years, the concerns expressed about interagency and intercommunity competition for funding are likely to become acute. The local competition for resources will echo the situation sketched by Anthias and Yuval–Davis (1993) above, as specific interest groups seek to fit their collective identity to the demands of the emerging funding regimes. Group identities are likely to become highly salient as competition creates quite specific local intergroup rivalries. As we saw in Chapter Four, perceived intergroup threat is grounded in an objective reality, and competition for resources may be built into the provision of local authority funding such that realistic threat becomes exacerbated through the machinations of local media and political discourse. We should remind ourselves that realistic threat is not hermetically sealed from symbolic threat, and in the context of current British sentiments toward Islam, it is entirely probable that the politics of realistic threat, in Muslim–Non-Muslim intergroup dynamics, will be nurtured and legitimated by complementary creative discourses that invoke the fundamental nature of the symbolic threat in order to further legitimate the reasonableness of the outrage felt at the realist threat.

The universalist, assimilationist values of Community Cohesion will be challenged by the particularistic circumstances and priorities of specific communities of interest. If the ambiguous and aspirational politics of the current government's heavily sold message of promoting the 'Big Society', where voluntary organisation and activities of the third sector at the local level will manage a radical transition of power from the central state to the local, become a reality, we may reasonably expect strong local identities to be co-opted and energised in the pursuit of local legitimacy. In such a context, established tensions related to identity politics at the level of the city and neighbourhood may be expected to find new currency. The communitarian aspiration of Community Cohesion will find the ideological appeal to 'one nation' citizenship is seriously compromised by the harsh realities of intergroup rivalries as the frayed supportive web of the welfare state creates new experiences of realistic competition among groups of British citizens, defined among other things by class, region, gender, ethnicity, faith and age.

The experience of local authority personnel

The local authority personnel engaged in managing and delivering Community Cohesion and Prevent operate within the constraints and contradictions already noted above. The response of Muslim communities, and of their colleagues, to the politically problematic nature of Prevent and its ambiguous interpenetration of Community Cohesion has introduced new and very real stresses into their routine practice. The reality of interagency working has made the ring-fencing of their own work within a defined professional network difficult to guarantee, and the values that brought many of them into public service, and which sustain them there, do not always sit comfortably with the new realities of the securitisation of public service practice. The inherent unknowability of where information gathered in one context may end and the uses to which it may be put, make certainty in relation to an individual's moral accountability to a community they work with problematic. Some of the quotes in the previous chapter point to exactly the sort of professional anguish that may be felt when the core values of traditional community work, involving trust, transparency, confidentiality and accountability, are challenged by the intelligence-gathering priorities of the new regime. For professionals socialised into working with and for the communities *they serve*, the shift to becoming ambivalent agents of 'the new preventive state' is potentially distressing. The long-term professional commitment to one authority and its own particular populations, which was a feature of many of the staff, and a basis of their unique competence, is contributory to the building of a partisan commitment to the local which goes beyond a detached professional responsibility. There is often a local emotional engagement and commitment which fuels some of the resistance, and it has to be said resentment, at what is seen as inept central government intervention on their patch. The permeation of community work by the new policies of Prevent was widely regarded as having had a seriously negative impact on their established relationships with some local communities.

The new moral agenda of potential culpability for the unintentional nurturing of real or suspected terrorist activists was a further troubling innovation into the working environment of local authority staff. As we saw above, those who define the nature and the extent of security threats sit high in the hierarchy of the Contest/Prevent communication chain, well beyond the reach of most of those personnel engaged in delivering Prevent and Community Cohesion. And yet the latter are required to act 'as if' they were in possession of the relevant information to inform their practice. They are simultaneously held accountable, and kept in the dark. For some of the councillors and staff interviewed this was a paradox that came with the job and was therefore accepted. For others this was an unnerving situation to be in, and one which placed clear demands on the flow of information and support within the organisation. In particular it produced in personnel lower in the hierarchy a need to be able to feel that they would have the support of their line managers and others should an issue arise. It has to be said that within the interview data there was clear evidence of councillors and managers who were completely prepared to stand and 'take the flak' should such situations arise. But we should be careful that we do not let the potentially robust integrity of a local authority system mask the reality of the continuing disparity of power and knowledge that characterises the protective state as it operates through the routine practices of a local authority. Prevent is presented as a community-focused element of counter-terrorism with a natural affinity to extant community work, yet its logics and ultimate control are those of the intelligence community. This is a reality that should not be masked behind the willing professional acceptance of managerial responsibilities by those who have found themselves responsible for this policy. The possible replacement of Prevent with some other regime by the new coalition government will not remove the processes of information collection that are inherent in the counter-terrorism world. The concerns expressed above, therefore, will continue to be a present issue for local authority personnel and staff.

The question of accountability was made concretely sensitive when we explored the specific experience of Muslim staff members. It was here that the focus on the Muslim communities that had been defined into both Community Cohesion and Prevent became pointedly challenging. Both policies require the local authority to be able to employ sensitivity to the basic tenets of Islam, and to possess knowledge of the local Muslim communities specifically in order to engage with their Muslim communities. In such a context Muslim staff members, and Muslim councillors, represent unique resources. However, Muslim staff members were explicit in seeking to protect their standing in their own community. There are multiple risks for such individuals. They are sensitive to the many different factions and identities within what Prevent might generically regard as Muslim communities. Consequently they do not wish to become identified as the spokespeople for any particular community or element within it. Nor do they necessarily wish to be presented as the acceptable face of the local authority in order to facilitate the introduction of highly unpopular Prevent initiatives into Muslim communities.

Additionally, as noted above, Muslim staff members may be comfortable with a nuanced fusion of their ethno-religious identity and their professional identity. As such they will wish to infuse their practice with a Muslim sensibility which leads them to seek to mediate between any generic policy and its expression in relation to Muslim communities. Where this policy is Prevent or Community Cohesion it is to be expected that this may introduce a necessary critique of the policy itself. The question will always be whether the local authority management can positively engage with such a position, or whether it will result in the professionalism of the staff member being challenged. A personal moral stance informed by an Islamic faith will, within the contemporary local state, sit uncomfortably with the penumbra of Islamophobia that has pervaded the new protective state. Yet, if mutual comprehension is at the core of both Prevent and Community Cohesion, it is exactly such voices that need to be present within the dialogue between the state and its Muslim citizens.

Communities, identities and governance

The data directly cited from the interviews relating to the perceptions of specific communities is, as has been noted, secondary data, the reported opinion of the interviewees about the views of the communities they deal with. But these views are consistent with other data reflecting the views of different ethnic communities in Britain (see, for example, Ameli et al, 2004; Blick et al, 2006; Dench et al, 2006; Collins, 2004). Through the data presented we have a cumulative picture of the territorially defined and historically embedded context in which specific communities exist within the five local authority areas studied in this research. Each has its own ethnic, class and gender mix and each has come to have a sense of its own history and its 'natural' competitors. In every instance this rich shared social construction of identity, neighbourhood and defining characteristics points out the dangers of speaking of communities as if they existed only as electoral wards or demographic entities. Neighbouring towns have stereotypical views of each other, and within townships particular areas have their own sedimented views of their unique distinctiveness. This is exactly the sort of dynamics that Elias and Scotson (1965) sought to reveal in their groundbreaking study of the 'established' and the 'outsiders'; more recently the micro politics of ethnic identity and territory have been revealed in their nuanced complexity by academics such as Eade (1997), Back (1996), Alexander (2000), Keith (2005) and Alam (2006). No entirely homogeneous communities are to be found in the populations of the five local authority localities we have focused on although specific identities do emerge as powerful constructions, among others, that shape people's relationship to their street, neighbourhood and town. We have seen how the governmental structures of 'metropolitan authorities' may have little resonance for people who still occupy the imagined boundaries of the prior township, and these old affiliations may frame the more local views of a diverse range of people within these townships. Alam (2006), for example, showed how young Muslim men in Bradford had clear affiliations to Bradford that included stereotypical views of occupants of neighbouring towns (and neighbourhoods within Bradford) which were extended to both their 'white' and South Asian' populations. And while we may make distinctions in our analysis between Muslim and non-Muslim communities, we should bear in mind the realities of Back's (1996) 'neighbourhood nationalisms', where differences of gender, ethnicity and faith may, at the local level, be merged within a super-ordinate local shared identity. When politicians speak of transferring power downward, we have sound reason to be concerned about just what democratic mechanisms might be employed to enable the diversity of the 'local' to be reflected in policy and practice.

Questions of voice, legitimacy and power haunt the evidence presented which relates to how different interest groups experience their life in specific urban settings and how they seek to make sense of this.[1] As individuals switch the group identity through which they filter this experience, then so too their perception of the priorities and constraints of their world are likely to shift. A sense of relative deprivation and the specifics of the intergroup threat that they experience is directly shaped by which identity is salient at any specific time. As we have seen, the state has made faith identities, and specifically Islamic identities, highly salient through the formulation of its policies of Community Cohesion and Prevent. If, as we argued in Chapter Four, Islamophobia is a complex phenomenon, it is nevertheless reasonable to view its consequences as concrete; one consequence has been to construct adherence to the Islamic faith as the major category of self-definition for many people who would previously have seen themselves through the lens of ethnicity and national heritage. Muslim communities thus do exist as social and political entities and the state has established a range of quite specific policies in which the Muslim population of Britain is the designated target, Community Cohesion and Prevent being obvious instances.

It is important to reflect on the construction of these policics, as outlined in Chapters Two and Three, where the linkage of Muslim identity and urban community becomes quite concrete. These policies are not merely about an engagement with Muslims as individuals, they are also very much about the shaping and regulation of Muslim communities. Much of Prevent and Community Cohesion is about the construction of leadership and 'acceptable' political coherence within extant Muslim communities in contemporary Britain. Thus curricula development in *madrassas* to inculcate shared values and a proper understanding of citizenship are just one element in a network of interventions that seek to shape the political imagination of Britain's Muslim citizens. However, in the post-9/11 world distorted by the rhetoric and policies of the 'War on Terror', and its fusion of faith with terrorism, Islam as a faith has become *in itself* problematised by the logics of security. Thus, part of Western states' political intervention in the name of counter-terrorism has included an attempt to remould Islam in the image of European patterns of faith in practice. In the British case this has included dubious attempts to distinguish categorically between safe and dangerous branches of Islam, and to facilitate new patterns of leadership within Muslim communities. While politically there is a reasoned rationality for this, there remains a fundamental question of whether this is capable of being instituted while maintaining a reflexive respect for Islam as a faith. There is a pervasive sense that when it comes to Islam in contemporary Britain, being devout is in itself a suspicious act. Contemporary attempts to 'privatise' Islam as a personal faith detached from any political relevance seem to reflect this distorted reading of Islam. The current traumas of the Church of England, as it seeks to negotiate between its own fundamentalists and the politics of difference, expressed in terms of feminism and gay rights, demonstrate the naivety of such attempts. The attempt to narrow the range of 'legitimate' voices that may enter into the public dialogue around diversity, faith and security represents a significant concern. If the voices from within these communities cannot be allowed to express themselves then the citizenship which the state is seeking to promote has a hollow ring to it. Nowhere would this be more apparent than in the ways in which British foreign policy intersects with domestic sensibilities.

When we recognise the global significance of the *Ummah* for members of Britain's Muslim population then the reality of unity and diversity within this population becomes apparent where individuals of quite different ethnic and national background identify strongly with fellow Muslims in other countries. As we have seen it is not possible to isolate British foreign policy from the internal policies of Community Cohesion and Prevent. In the contemporary world where migration and settlement have produced a rich mosaic of communities, each with their own history of reasons for migration, their own experience of settlement and their own distinct pattern of continuing connections to their country of initial migration, we are used to the idea of diasporic identities. While not without its ambiguities (Dufoix, 2008), this concept encourages us to be aware of the historicised understandings people may have of their current identities and their current experience. They may be British citizens and have a strong sense of their regional and local identity and yet at the same time have a biographic and continuing emotional tie to their shared ancestral homeland. Additionally, they have a 'transnational sensibility' (Vertovec, 2009) which reflects the multiple ties and interactions, and their associated institutions, which people may sustain across the borders of different nation states. Thus, the Muslim communities in Britain are internally fragmented by ethnic and national affiliations that continue to tie them into the history of their migration and settlement in Britain. Pakistani communities which developed from the 1960s onwards, and that were fuelled by a process of economic migration shaped by rapidly changing British border policies, are now living in cities where they may be living adjacent to newly emergent communities of Iraqi refugees. They may have Islam in common but they will have very different ethnic identities and very different experiences of migration and settlement. Furthermore, they may not even share a common identity within Islam. Thus the current transnational sensibilities of the Muslim communities dwelling in these five authorities are likely to differ widely. But there is ample evidence that for many of these individuals, events in overseas countries that impact on distant kith and kin in Afghanistan, Iraq, Somalia or Pakistan have real salience for them here in Britain. And events elsewhere in the world that impact on their fellow co-religionists are likely to be perceived as part of their legitimate repertoire of concerns.

Thus, events in Palestine, Afghanistan and Iraq are relevant to both fermenting proto-terrorist sentiments, and more generally, are seen as germane to the circumstances and concerns of Muslim communities in inner-city Britain. Government policy that seeks to sustain an arbitrary *cordon sanitaire* between foreign policy and the internal policies of counter-terrorism can only be kindly described as naive wishful thinking. In January 2009 former Prime Minister Gordon Brown's security and counter-terrorism minister, Lord West of Spithead, offered up an insight into the previous regime's view on this matter. He is reported in *The Guardian* (Booth, 2009) as saying:

> We never used to accept that our foreign policy ever had any effect on terrorism....Well, that was clearly bollocks.... They [the Blair administration] were very unwilling to have any debate about how our foreign policy impacted on radicalisation.

A privatised Islam of personal faith, which seems to be part of the wish list of elements of the new protective state, would be incapable of articulating the legitimate concerns that members of Britain's Muslim population feel about aspects of British foreign policy. Citizenship should not be about inculcating habits of complacency, acquiescence and an avoidance of conflict. Realistic threat is frequently based on an objective basis of a conflict of interest between different groups, and a denial of such realities does not provide a basis for meaningful democratic participation. The British government has itself been exercised to promote active citizenship; how ironic then if such laudable examples of the fusion of bridging capital and political engagement as can be found in the diasporic consciousness of Muslim communities should be damned because it exposes the contradictory and compromised policies of a current British government.

There is an uncomfortable juxtaposition of a government vigorously trying to promote new 'responsible' leadership within Britain's Muslim communities and to identify new voices in enabling the 'resilience' of young Muslims to the temptations of radicalisation, while simultaneously demonstrating a startling willingness to disregard the Muslim experience of life in Britain in pursuing the securitised priorities of the new protective state. It suggests a form of institutional anti-Muslimism, a routinised organisational incapacity to recognise, let alone valorise, the diversity of voices within the British Muslim population. The consequences of this are then amplified by the narrow, and strangely ahistorical, focus employed in defining the challenge of Islam in Britain in cultural terms, which makes peripheral the material conditions that continue to build intergroup tensions despite the rhetoric of more recent government statements.

The priorities of Muslim communities in Britain are likely to have much in common with those of any other community. Safe and quiet neighbourhoods, good local facilities, good educational provision and an absence of intergenerational tension are issues that transcend faith or ethnicity (see Alam, forthcoming). At the same time the very marked differences between Muslim communities in their ethnic and class profiles constitute a further source of diversity, while the significant differences in class profiles within specific Muslim communities renders any attempt to generate a one-size-fits-all Muslim policy doomed from the outset. Governance is inevitably a fraught attempt to match universal democratic principles and institutional mechanisms to the particularistic needs and concerns of specific interest groups. In the British context the continuity of concerns and wishes across faith and ethnic groups provides a basis for this universalist ambition. At the same time, active citizenship cannot be an invitation from the state for a wide range of interest groups to participate in endorsing policies handed down from on high. Active citizenship must be an invitation to participate in formulating policy, as well as in implementing it in your own community. This requires a willingness to engage with diversity and with the initial conflict that is often inherent in this process. Community Cohesion must be based on establishing a viable capacity for sustaining uncomfortable dialogue, not through manufacturing a specious consensus through a variety of forms of coercion. The risk-averse core of the current policy environment, however, is ill-suited to promoting such a mode of practice.

Symptoms and causes: the marginalisation of inequality

In the previous chapter we saw that among some of the local authority personnel there was an explicit concern that their application of the interventions that flowed from current policies on Community Cohesion and Prevent failed to address the fundamental underlying problem of the reproduction of class inequality in Britain. Consequently it was possible to see these policies as a reactive treatment for some of the consequences of inequality rather than as a robust assault on the fundamental causes of radicalisation or intergroup tension and political disinterest. This issue is taken up here more fully as a means of both better understanding the potentially inherent limitations of Community Cohesion and Prevent in their own terms and in order to reveal the political obfuscation that arises from taking these policies at face value.

The impact of the disturbances of 2001 has left a long-lasting eddy within local political and authority consciousness. There is a sensitivity to community tensions that is part of a professional responsibility to manage community cohesion, and indeed tension monitoring has become a routine and sophisticated process of local governance (see CLG, 2008). In this political context the excluded experience of *the affluent boom of others* that has characterised many working-class communities' experience of the *middle way* courtship of the middle class in the 13 years of the Labour governments has laid down the basis for a generic sense of discontentment. Additionally their experience of material decline, the frustrations of the housing market and of crime and anti-social behaviour, that has often been accompanied by a loss of the local link between modes of employment and a shared culture, added to the sense of dislocation and grievance. And importantly, it has been a discontent that has not had the traditional party political means of expression; the evacuation of class from British political discourse through the retreat to the middle has left party politics devoid of a language and will to address systemic disadvantage. The 'evilisation' of political language feeds a MUD (see Chapter Two) discourse in which moral failure and personal fecklessness are capable of being invoked as credible explanations for continued inequalities. In such a political environment the concerns of stressed working-class communities are likely to find expressive modes of release which may include xenophobia and Islamophobia.

As we saw in Chapter Two the Labour government was sensitive to the concerns of the white working class in relation to the perceived privileged attention and resources being given to minority ethnic communities. The *Strength in diversity* (2004) Home Office consultation paper and the 2005 *Improving opportunity, strengthening society* government strategy to increase 'race' equality and community cohesion both gave explicit attention to the role of structural inequalities and discrimination in promoting extremism; *Improving opportunity* in particular showed significant concern with the perception that some groups rather than others were being given preferential treatment. But the emphasis within that strategy on strengthening the capacity of local government and Muslim leaders as a means to marginalise extremism leaves the foundational causes of inequality sidelined. The government, in recognising the concerns of the white working class in these policy documents, was reflecting, and consolidating, an explicit concern with the invisibility of the voice of white working-class communities. This was something of an emergent vogue political agenda with academics (for example, Dench et al, 2006), giving a voice to the perceived symbolic and realistic threat experienced by white working-class communities. At the same time, populist commentators pressed the case of the white working class, arguing that they had been left behind by a ('politically correct') fixation on the disadvantage of minority ethnic groups.

It is a matter of interest and political significance that a concern to defend the 'legitimate' sense of relative deprivation of the white working class has become a recurrent element within the UK discourse around diversity and community cohesion. This sits uncomfortably with the contrasting, simultaneous and meticulously maintained unwillingness in governmental and wider political debate to explicitly address the challenge of the very evident reproduction of class inequalities in the UK. It seems that invoking the marginalised working class as a discursive foil when engaging with the challenge of the particularistic needs and demands of minority ethnic groups is not only acceptable, it is packaged as reasonable and obvious. It is a discourse wherein the sense of symbolic and realistic threat of the majority working class vis-à-vis minority ethnic communities can be made both explicit and concrete. In terms of providing a grounded and reflexive understanding of contemporary intergroup relations, this is a fruitful contribution. But what is disturbing is that this opening up of the realities of perceived intergroup threat is framed by an overarching British 'race relations' paradigm, ring-fenced from any Old Labour (socialist) concern with the larger context of the reproduction of generic class inequalities. In other words, it is acceptable to introduce class as a basis for a horizontal comparison of people occupying comparable degrees of economic and social marginalisation but it is not acceptable to introduce class for the purpose of a vertical comparison that reveals the moribund state of social mobility in Britain, and the endemic reproduction of class inequalities. It is not that there is *no* debate on the reproduction of class inequalities in Britain; rather, there is a wealth of research literature. See, for example, Dorling et al (2007, 2008), Dorling and Pritchard (2010) and Dorling (2010). There are reports on health inequalities that are shocking (Marmot, 2010), and there are NGOs that campaign on these issues. Nevertheless, the point remains that class was effectively evacuated from the conceptual lexicon of New Labour and its continued absence has been nurtured by the right wing media (see Sveinsson, 2009).

It is necessary to indicate just how real the impact of class in contemporary Britain is. In a country with the absolute levels of wealth that are to be found in Britain it should be a source of national shame that: 'Levels of income inequality ... within Britain have now returned to their Victorian highs despite increases in overall material wealth' (Dorling and Pritchard, 2010: 94). Or that, 'Almost a quarter of children in the UK live below the family income poverty level' (Dorling and Pritchard, 2010: 101). It is therefore perhaps not surprising, but no less disturbing, that the same paper cites the Innocenti report (Adamson, 2007) as demonstrating that in an international comparison of children's subjective perception of wellbeing, the UK came bottom of a list of 20 nations (Dorling and Pritchard, 2010: 96). The general context is further illuminated in Dorling et al's (2008) study *Changing UK: The way we live now*, which provides a comparative look at how different areas within Britain have prospered in recent decades. The report concludes that:

> The evidence presented suggests that British society has been moving towards demographic segregation and economic polarisation, social fragmentation and political disengagement since at least the late 1960s.... Britain has also seen increasing levels of economic polarisation over the last three decades: areas that were already wealthy have tended to become disproportionately wealthier and areas that experienced high levels of relative poverty saw these levels increase. (Dorling et al, 2008: 35)

This report points to the significance not only of individual poverty and marginalisation, but also to the cumulative effects when these economic and social disparities are scaled up to the level of townships and local communities. Poverty and marginalisation when shared in this way affect the ability/inability of communities to attract resources to service them, whether it be good schools, employment, good health provision or an infrastructure for entertainment.

The recent *Marmot Review: Strategic review of health inequalities in England post-2010* (Marmot, 2010) provides a distressing analysis of the secondary consequences of class inequalities, in this case in relation to health. The report makes the general point that:

> Inequalities in health arise because of inequalities in society – in the conditions in which people are born, grow, live work, and age. So close is the link between particular social and economic features of society and the distribution of health among the population, that the magnitude of health inequalities is a good marker of progress towards creating a fairer society. (Marmot, 2010: 10)

One potent example of class-related health inequalities is given in relation to death rates. The report records that:

> In England, people living in the poorest neighbourhoods, will on average, die seven years earlier than people living in the richest neighbourhoods.... Even more disturbing, the average difference in disability-free life expectancy is 17 years.... So, people in poorer areas not only die sooner, but they will also spend more of their shorter lives with disability. (Marmot, 2010: 10)

Class and ethnicity have an important interaction in determining individuals' life experiences, and it is certainly the case that some minority ethnic communities have very high levels of economic marginalisation; it would be a mistake to simplistically equate minority ethnic status with economic deprivation. As Dorling et al (2008: 35) point out in the report cited above:'Although Britain has been dividing and segregating in every way measured by the data presented in this report.... Britain is less segregated by race and ethnicity than it was in 1991'. Similarly Finney and Simpson (2009) report on the growing *class* differentiation within the British Muslim population. Where economic deprivation and minority ethnic status overlap then we may expect particularly harsh levels of exclusion from social support to exist and there will be a continuing need to address the particular demands of minority ethnic marginalisation in Britain. But equally we may anticipate a growing minority ethnic affluence to provide the basis for emerging new class alliances that cut across 'ethnic' interests.

While a concern with the reproduction of class inequalities expressed here may smack of socialist sentiments that may be regarded as misguided, old-hat or plain anathema to many, there remains an urgent need to recognise the political consequences of class inequalities. The government, for example, in the text of Parliamentary Committee reports, can be frequently seen to express cogent and nuanced concerns about the implications of economic inequalities in Britain. And yet, what remains problematically absent is a political will to carry through this insight into political action and robust policy. The centre right middle ground that has come to define and maintain a British party political consensus has made such linkages uncomfortable at best, unattainable at worst.

The retreat from the painfully obvious implications of class inequalities has multiple implications. Among these is the facilitation of the reproduction of those structural features of inequality that feed racisms and political extremisms. There is the suppression of a perspective on diverse Britain that would reveal that class interests cut across ethnicity and faith and gender. Class does not obliterate these differences, but it does provide one form of linkage across ethnicity and faith. The comfortable juxtaposing of the interests of the white working class against those of minority ethnic communities allows affluent members of the majority society to rehearse their liberal credentials without having to expose the privileged context from which they make their intervention. It also contributes to framing the situation of the white working class in terms of an intergroup opposition to those of minority ethnic groups. It feeds the sense of intergroup threat and builds exactly that sense of interethnic conflict which Community Cohesion is then invoked to address.

In political terms it is about how to salami slice the limited urban renewal budget, or the social welfare budget; it is not about confronting the routine reproduction of the gross class inequalities that should shame a society that claims to be so concerned with a communitarian engagement with citizenship. It is as if the distinction between formal and substantive citizenship (Marshall and Bottomore, 1992) had never been made. Formal citizenship resides in the legal and political framework that defines a person as a full member of a nation state. However, the legal status of citizen is not of itself a guarantee that all individuals can equally realise their rights in practice. *Substantive* citizenship therefore refers to the network of civil, political and social resources that enable a person to equitably enjoy the rights that they notionally own through their formal citizenship. Seeking through Community Cohesion to persuade people to engage with a democratic process that is so palpably inequitable in both its operation and practice is an act of supreme hubris. It requires a degree of cynical political dishonesty in government, and the rule of the self-interested *culture of contentment* among a large proportion of the population.

In the emerging contraction of the relative affluence of the middle class that can be anticipated in the next four years, the sense of embattled self-interest among this narrow cohort of the electorate that has been so carefully nurtured by New Labour cannot be expected to decline. The white working class, whose growing disdain for the electoral process has been an indication of their sense of estrangement from the political process in the UK, face a period of severe strain as they in particular face the impact in the cut-backs in public sector spending. Class-based responses to the competition for resources continue to be very real, while any attempt to develop an honest and explicit engagement with a class-based analysis of inequality in Britain remains likely to be dismissed as an unwelcome eruption of 'loony left' thinking. At the same time this is a context where Muslim communities find their class concerns addressed by a government that sees them preponderantly through a religious and cultural lens; the same framing routines additionally and repeatedly signal their marginality from mainstream British life. The reliance on variations of the *contact hypothesis* as the theoretical underpinning of so much work in Community Cohesion is consistent with this focus on cultural difference rather than substantive inequalities. Focusing on the dynamics between adjacent ethnic communities helps divert attention from the much greater, and more effective, segregation of the affluent from the poor.

In Chapter Five we saw evidence of the capacity of local authority staff to empathise with the history and current circumstances of specific communities and to use this in identifying intergroup tensions. There were also indications of the frustrations that some felt in their inability to address the fundamental inequalities experienced by these same communities. In this context, tension monitoring and myth busting amounts to treating symptoms and ignoring underlying real and systemic issues. We can discern quite distinct consequences of this avoidance of engaging with the continuing class inequalities in Britain. At the most obvious level it contributes to the reproduction of these dramatic inequalities, and asks fundamental questions about the nature of a liberal democracy that can deliver the widening of the gap in social and economic wealth, and the extension of the gap in lifespan between those who live longest and those who do not.

What exactly is the nature of the social contract that is being offered at the heart of a communitarian-informed conception of citizenship where the nurturing of the life experiences of citizens can differ so widely? If the balance of obligations and benefits that is at the heart of the Community Cohesion message may be so wide, then surely the democratic deficit that can currently be seen within the British electoral system is not some Putnamesque falling from grace but is rather a logical expression of the *de facto* disenfranchisement of sections of society from meaningful participation within the system.

Consequently the politics of Community Cohesion are in large part a major effort of hegemonic artifice. It is an attempt to win the support of individuals for a social contract, that depending on their class location, is manifestly unprepared to address their circumstances and needs. Thus the attempt to weave a newly constructed form of nationalism into the formulation of the bundle of values and beliefs that frame citizenship is consistent with an attempt to invoke the affective in-group sentiments of 'the nation'. It is an attempt to sell a sense of affective unity that belies the great disparity of treatment that you might expect as a citizen. The ideological work that is done by the concept of Community Cohesion, raised in Chapter Two, can now be seen as an inherent element of a larger political agenda.

Additionally, because inequalities in British life are shared by both non-Muslim and Muslim members of society, a sense of alienation from the mainstream of British life may be experienced by significant segments of both populations. As we have seen in Chapter Four, the government itself recognises that such inequalities contribute to the capacity for the growth of extremist sentiments of whatever variety, including the burgeoning white far right, epitomised by the BNP and the English Defence League. The invasive processes of CONTEST that aim to counter terrorism therefore sit alongside a calculated nurturing of the conditions that can contribute to radicalisation. The contemporary interplay of class interest and party ideology that shape the British party political environment routinely produce internally inconsistent policies and aspirations. We saw in Chapter Five how foreign policy may be entirely inconsistent with the aspiration to win the hearts and minds of Britain's Muslim populations. So too an unwillingness to address the remarkable inequalities within the social structure of British life is inconsistent with an aspiration to reduce intergroup tensions, and a sense of alienation from the body politic in British life, among large segments of British society.

Perceived intergroup threat is not a random expression of individual psychological pathology. It is the outcome of an attempt by individuals to make sense of their experience of life in a specific context. And, as we have seen, the ways in which people come to construe their understanding of the salience of particular identities, and the ways in which these identities are framed in narratives of historical and current opposition, are critical to the type of intergroup dynamics that develop. The fusion of securitisation, with immigration, with ethnic relations, with counter-terrorism and with Community Cohesion in the British context, has produced a backdrop against which anti-Muslimism has become an all too easy option. The role of government, through the statements and actions of its ministers and party spokespeople, in courting the xenophobic and racist sentiments in the electorate, has done much to racialise individuals' understanding of their world. The explicit targeting of Muslim communities that we have seen throughout the narrative has also contributed to the heightened salience that Islam has for many citizens who previously encountered their identity as being more heavily framed by their ethnicity or skin colour. Thus, when individuals consider their circumstances in the contemporary context they are likely to frame this in terms of their group identity, consequently engaging in intergroup comparisons informed by these identity politics. The government's aspiration to promote harmonious civic sentiments, therefore, sits in opposition to their simultaneous failure to address those inequities that are experienced through the lens of heightened ethno-religious sensitivity.

Making explicit a theoretical framework for Community Cohesion and counter-terrorism

In this final part of our conclusion it is necessary to step back from the immediacy of the Prevent and Community Cohesion policies in order to consider what might be the framework of political values and perspectives that might appropriately nurture equitable policies for a multi-ethnic Britain. We have suggested that there are sound reasons for questioning the ideological purposes of the language of social cohesion that has been deployed in constructing the particular British policy of Community Cohesion. Additionally we have argued that, in order to understand the impact of Prevent, it is necessary to place it within the wider context of the securitisation of everyday life and the erosion of support for human rights principles. Consequently, in order to go beyond critique, and in order to provide a positive basis for developing social policy in a multi-ethnic Britain, in this section we provide a brief account of elements of a political framework that must be in place in order to promote equity, security and substantive citizenship in Britain. This necessarily will deal with issues on which there is an enormous extant literature, and very pointed disagreements, in a heavily simplified form.

In trying to conceive of a political framework that will provide a binding structure within which the diversity of identities can been recognised and nurtured there are a number of critical elements that must be carefully assembled. First there must be an explicit agreement on the manner in which diversity is recognised. There has been a considerable debate within political philosophy regarding the nature of diversity and its proper recognition (Young, 2000; Benhabib, 2002; Fraser and Honneth, 2003).

A prior condition to any policy response to ethnic diversity is a recognition of difference, and the terms within which that difference is constructed are crucial to the inter- and intragroup dynamics that develop. Thus, at the heart of any policy on the management of ethnic diversity lies the system of beliefs that frame the understanding of the relationship between people marked by difference. Powerful ideologies of, for example, gender, age, 'race' and religion, have provided apparently coherent accounts of the inherent nature of these differences and of the relative worth of individuals demarcated by their location in one category or another. Equally, we have seen the growth of identity politics based on forms of collective resistance to the status implications of these attributed identities. For example, Black Power and Feminism have provided political movements which have sought to contest the inferiorisation that has been implicit in the construction of the identities of individuals defined by 'race' categories or by gender.

Here, our concern focuses on how the management of the relation between different categories of homo sapiens defined in ethnic, religious and national terms is normalised and legitimated. Clearly, 'race' theory and racist practice manages these relations coherently through an ordering of the world into hierarchies of superiority: 'us' superior and 'them' inferior. Such notions, however, do not sit comfortably with the universalist inclusion that is implicit in the contemporary language of citizenship; rather, there is an inevitable fracturing of the unity of the citizenry by imposing arbitrary criteria of inclusion and exclusion from full membership. At the same time, the linkage of nation and citizenship is always inherently about boundaries of membership and the exclusion of the 'other'. At an extreme the language of *citizenship* forms the basis for a system of Apartheid with legally defined separate rights for different categories of people. In a less extreme form it provides for the normative construction of partial access to the rights of citizenship that marginalises sections of the population and results in intergroup conflict and hostility.

Citizenship is a political construct that binds the individual to the state and in a complementary manner provides the legitimacy for excluding others from the privileges of membership of the national collective body. Quite clearly the language of citizenship has emerged as a central element in the neo-nationalism that has been central to the formation of the 'crisis of multiculturalism' (Titley, forthcoming), and to shaping the political reframing of the new national settlement between citizens and the state. As Fekete (2009) and others have argued, the last decade has seen across Europe a new xeno-racism that has attempted to tie acceptance into the family of the citizen to a narrow nationalist conceptualisation of identity, defined in terms of shared values and common beliefs. This contemporary political development operates in denial of the multi-ethnic reality of contemporary states. While 'politically' it is possible to seek to impose an assimilationist nationalism on a diverse national population, what is not possible is the denial of the *de facto* multi-ethnic nature of contemporary European national populations. Thus political models of managing diversity seeking to ignore this reality, by their nature, construct an ideology of homogeneity that is ahistorical and does a violence to lived biographies.

To better understand the fundamental nature of this violence it is helpful to reflect on contemporary insights into the nature of political recognition. There is a common, deep-seated sentiment that links many Western European social democracies and it is their commitment to liberalism and what Charles Taylor (1992) has called the 'politics of recognition'. He argues that:

> The importance of recognition is now universally acknowledged in one form or another; on an intimate plane, we are all aware of how identity can be formed or malformed through the course of our contact with significant others. On the social plane, we have a continuing politics of equal recognition. (Taylor, 1992: 36)

In social psychology we have an extensive literature which has opened up our understanding of the profound significance of the individual's management of their identity, of the essentially social nature of viable identities (Burkitt, 2008). We therefore have no excuse for underestimating the potent consequences, both individually and socially, that may arise from the denial of an individual's identity claims. Taylor (1992) is, at a political level, acknowledging this reality and we can note that at the heart of this politics of *equal recognition* there lies an assumed common humanity in which we share common universal needs; in essence, you respect me and I respect you, and we treat each other equally. This foundational universalism has been central to many national multicultural policies, in which showing respect for others has essentially meant treating all people the same, a practice which is not the same as being treated equally. While recognition of one's existence and identity claims may be a necessary starting point for equality within the state, it does not provide a sufficient basis for guaranteeing their realisation. Recognising a common humanity may of itself lead to an insidious denial of significant and important human *differences*. Indeed the denial of human diversity that is at the core of assimilationist notions of integration constitute the basis for a routine perversion of the essence of recognition, for it asserts that: *we know who you are*, without asking *tell us who you are, and what are your priorities and needs*. This was the arrogance of patriarchy operating within liberal democratic systems, and this is the arrogance of an integration policy that asserts a universalist commonality of identity for all citizens.

We are now familiar with the reality that, in the context of universalist provision for diverse populations, it is the interests and the priorities of the majority, and/or the hegemonically powerful, that define the normative needs and cultural practices that should be addressed through equal provision (Young, 1989; Kymlicka, 1995; Phillips, 2007). Resistance to this paternalist and discriminatory politics of equal provision has from the 1960s onwards led to a series of powerful social movements that have contested this version of the politics of recognition. For example, Black Power and the Civil Rights movement in the US, Feminism and Gay Pride. These movements articulated the oppression inherent in unthinking universalist citizenship, and presented a new assertive politics of aspiring to equality through recognising diversity and its necessary particularistic demands. Among other things the critique of universalist rights has produced a sustained argument between those who believe that individual rights are capable of addressing the needs of diverse identities (Barry, 2001) and those who believe that we need to employ a legal recognition of collective rights in order to guarantee the particular needs of distinct communities (Kymlicka, 1995, 2001). As will be apparent below, we support a complementary counter-balancing of both.

Over the last three decades, then, an alternative conception of structuring a response to managing diversity has been developed through what Taylor (1992) has called the *politics of difference*. He has argued that:

... the development of the modern notion of identity, has given rise to a politics of difference. There is of course a universalist basis to this as well, making for the overlap and confusion between the two. Everyone should be recognised for his or her unique identity. But recognition here means something else. With the politics of equal dignity, what is established is meant to be universally the same, an identical basket of rights and immunities; with the politics of difference, what we are asked to recognise is the unique identity of this individual or group, their distinctiveness from everyone else. The idea is that it is precisely this distinctness that has been ignored, glossed over, assimilated to a dominant or majority identity. (Taylor, 1992: 38)

As Taylor makes eloquently clear, the flaw in the universalist politics of recognition lies precisely in the assumption, indeed insistence, that people be treated, quite literally, equally. This pre-empts any meaningful acknowledgement of individuals' and communities' quite different needs and priorities. Instead of reducing equality to identical resources and provision, the politics of difference retains the fundamental acknowledgement of individual worth, while tenaciously retaining an awareness of unique individual needs. In other words, the politics of difference in effect insists on the following idea: *if you want to treat me equally, you may have to treat me differently*. In order to live up to this expectation, a raft of equal *rights* have to be expressed in an *appropriate range* of particularistic responses. First and foremost, this requires a sensibility that is comfortable with diversity. It requires the commitment to an ideology of multiculturalism, as demonstrated by Verkuyten (2006) in Chapter Four, that facilitates acceptance of diversity and resists the lazy logics of prejudice. If we have common rights, then they must allow for the possibility of the exercise of those rights in the pursuit of (group) particularistic needs. We must develop a creative *differentiated citizenship* that allows for the expression of universal rights in particularistic ways.

The well rehearsed decencies of the liberal politics of recognition have very adequately served a state policy pivoted around a benign universalism. This has provided a reassuring articulation with the humanistic principles of equivalence built into a wide range of theisms, with political paradigms including liberalism and socialism. It has been a political philosophy and practice that has simultaneously nurtured the self-regard of the privileged and powerful, and the dependence and compliance of the powerless. The fundamental challenge of the politics of difference has radically destabilised this hegemonic package.

This has not only resulted from the inherent arguments of the politics of difference, but also because the emergence of this paradigm was also parallelled by a powerful mobilisation of identity politics *per se* within different nation states. Across different continents nation states have witnessed a powerful surge of identity politics expressed within, and outside, established political structures. Often with strong international dynamics, these movements have been a political adjunct to the radical transformation of communication and the extensive construction of transnational identities that have been products of the process of globalisation, and its attendant flows of migration. Frequently, contemporary manifestations of the politics of difference have an inherent transnational consciousness, and power base, that makes them spontaneously alert to the inhibiting constraints of nationalisms.

The politics of difference, as articulated through the particularistic demands by minorities *to be recognised in their difference*, is a genie that will not go back into the bottle. We may be seeing the retrenchment of nation state nationalisms as governments seek to manage the substantive cultural changes within their populations that have followed from the concrete demographic changes of the last five decades, but the sense of a right to that difference is spread over too wide a constituency. It is not just once migrant, or recent refugee communities, it is also gendered identities, disability, age, sexual orientation and faith – the hyphenated identities of the *majority* ethnic populations – who are invested in asserting their collective needs and rights. Invoking an *ersatz* national identity as a common glue will not address the needs of promoting cohesion.

We know that the idea of the nation is profoundly interwoven with an homogenising logic of sameness (Anderson, 1983; Bauman, 1990; Goldberg, 2002), and hence invoking 'the nation' as a crucible within which to forge a united citizenry seems a perverse logic. If the nation is to be a viable collective enterprise then its definition must be a collective enterprise. Where, as in Britain, the great majority of our minority ethnic communities *are* citizens, then their enfranchisement should include participation in framing 'the nation'. The debates surrounding the viability of *constitutional patriotism* as a political construction that could accommodate this dynamic tension between universal procedural rules of citizenship and particularistic interests tells us that this is not a conundrum with easy solutions waiting to be riveted on (see, for example, Lacroix, 2002; Cronin, 2003; Baumeister, 2007).

Minority ethnic communities who have learnt to reject the homogenising logics of majority liberal universalism have very frequently sought to reject assimilation into the national cultural norm. In the language of social identity theory, they have defined the existing status differentials between themselves and the majority population as illegitimate and unstable, and many have moved toward a conflict model of intergroup relations. From a rights perspective, citizenship requires of them loyalty to the state, not uncritical investment in a national identity and culture which assigns them a marginal and/or inferior status. Explicitly discernible in the dynamics of diasporic communities, and equally apparent in the identity politics of ethno-religious groupings, the politics of difference argues for the essential compatibility of a common obligation to participate in civil society as equals, and a commitment to autonomy in defining the policy implications of their particularistic needs. There is of course no simple formulaic means of implementing this aspiration. It is a task that must be worked through appropriate political systems, and will not be without its ambiguities.

The clarity and assertiveness with which the logics of the politics of difference are often expressed by minority ethnic politics easily create a reaction in which the majority constituencies within society feel that the *reasonableness* of their privileged status is challenged and threatened. In truth it is being challenged: the legitimacy of the majorities' established privileges and the legitimacy of their supportive ideology is frequently contested. One only needs to look to the history of resistance to feminist critiques of patriarchy as an example of the backlash that may be generated by such challenges to established privilege. For the convinced xenophobe and racist nationalist this challenge is experienced as an outrageous expression of minority ethnic arrogance and rapacious greed. The challenge to the taken for granted world view that sustains their privileged status is experienced as a symbolic threat, while the challenge to their illegitimate privileges are experienced as a realistic threat. Equally, progressive liberals within the majority ethnic populations may feel confused and angry when what they see as their tolerant niceness is reflected back as tokenistic, paternalistic and self-interested. Sometimes, referred to as 'the victimisation of the majority' (Wodak and Matouscheck, 1993), this defensive response leads to renewed attempts to reassert the 'limits of tolerance' as natural and reasonable, and necessary for the continued cohesion of the nation state. For all members of a diverse society the politics of difference represent a challenge as the negotiation of the practical limits of the recognition of difference are worked out. The challenges between the secular state and faith communities, and between freedom of speech and hate speech, between cultural practice and gender equality, are just some of the more obvious examples. Kymlicka (2001, 2007), among others, is under no delusions about the difficulties that may be experienced in seeking to implement a model of differentiated citizenship.

However, the pursuit of Community Cohesion that does not simultaneously engage in an exposure of the reproduction of inequalities inevitably facilitates this form of 'majority outrage'. For in selling cohesion as a communitarian collective virtue *with no cost* it is founded on a lie. An educational programme in civic values of commonality that goes hand in hand with the reproduction of inequality is an oppressive hegemonic strategy. Building bridging social capital is not merely a matter of adopting a new perspective on out-groups. As Bourdieu (1985; and see also Field, 2003: 13-20) initially conceived it, social capital is a self-interested expression of relative power and hence changing social capital requires a complementary change in power relations. The implicit rhetorical conflation of community cohesion with the removal of conflict is at best a political aspiration and at worst a calculated and cynical ideological ploy. If community cohesion is to be an attainable goal, or at least a serious aspiration, then it will require a capacity for interaction on the basis of equivalence as citizens. Yet in the current situation the disparities between formal and substantive citizenship, for members of many communities, is considerable. A national polity galvanised as an active citizenry is unlikely to be characterised by collective bonhomie, but there will be a contestation of positions operating within an equitable legal and political framework. Managed creative contestation will be the order of the day.

An acceptance of ethnic pluralism is not a position that can be taken for granted in the governmental or popular politics of our time. It has been a perspective that has observably had a visibility and salience across a wide range of states over the last five decades. However, it remains a value position and a political practice that is far from consensual; as we have seen, it has been extensively challenged and disavowed by European countries in the last decade. It means that there is no off-the-peg normative package of theory and practice that can be invoked to inform our quest for a model for the management of multi-ethnic societies.

In the British context a recognition of the limits of universalist principles of rights has already been established in practice through legislation which, for example, allows Sikhs to be excluded from the requirement to wear crash helmets, the funding for Welsh language media and special provisions based on gender distinctions. If Community Cohesion is to be grounded in 'active citizenship' then there must be an honest and necessarily protracted debate about the political construction of citizenship that underpins it. This must embrace the realities of the politics of difference and must struggle with making transparent the awkward tensions between universal rights and particularistic needs. A necessary adjunct to this process must be the interrogation of the ways in which the idea of 'the nation' has been employed in government rhetoric. Parekh (2000) offered us the language of a 'community of communities' as the basis for the imaginative bond that would facilitate a shared patriotism while allowing for diversity. Something of the optimism and conceptual fluidity that might be necessary is suggested in Cronin's (2003: 16) invitation to 'reject chauvinistic interpretations of national identity while preserving a distinctive national character'. We must *define our collective identity through the way we live with difference, rather than by the desperate assertion of sameness.*

Substantive citizenship is not realised through the collective commitment to common values and a modicum of cultural commonality. These may be necessary foundational elements for a basic civility among fellow citizens, but they most certainly are not sufficient to guarantee meaningful substantive citizenship. Substantive citizenship requires an equitable capacity to access your citizenship rights and to possess the means to express them in addressing the shared human aspirations of self-fulfilment. It is only through substantive citizenship in action that individuals can be meaningfully empowered to fulfil their obligations to their family, neighbours and fellow citizens. This requires a political commitment to a foundational basket of rights which will frame the political settlement that sets the conditions for establishing the balance between rights and obligations that themselves constitute the social contract that renders citizenship meaningful and viable. Active citizenship cannot be realised by a rhetorical assertion of formal citizenship rights but must be underpinned by a commitment to a body of rights that in practice enables the realisation of substantive citizenship in the real world.

For these reason a liberal assertion of the tolerant credentials of British social values and a political nurturing of tolerance as the basis for managing diversity is simply inadequate. The act of tolerance always requires that there is something to be tolerated. In political terms the act of tolerance requires the exercise of discretionary power by the powerful toward those who are relatively powerless. As we have argued previously:

> For tolerance to be necessary, there must be a prior belief that the person to be tolerated has an intrinsically undesirable characteristic, or that they are not fundamentally entitled to the benefits which are to be allowed them. Those to be tolerated, by definition, possess some such social stigma.... Tolerance is the exercise of largesse by the powerful, ultimately on behalf of the powerful. It is the generous extension of forbearance toward someone who is intrinsically objectionable or not deserving of the privilege being allowed. (Husband, 1994: 65)

Where tolerance is the basis for managing diversity, then those being tolerated are expected to be grateful for the privilege that has been extended to them[2] (Husband, 2005a). The recipients of tolerance are thus stripped of their rights, and of their status as equals. It is for this reason that promoting a common citizenship through a politics of Community Cohesion that is framed by an ideology of xeno-nationalism is fundamentally flawed. The nationalist agenda is always asking who are *the real* citizens, a process that inevitably feeds intergroup comparisons and perceived intergroup threat. As argued above the meaningful recognition of diversity requires an explicit rights-based political framework, an explicit commitment to the recognition of collective rights, *protecting* minorities from the invidious consequences of universalism. This then must itself be complemented by a robust recognition of individual rights, *protecting* individuals from the potential constraints imposed by their community (see Downing and Husband, 2005: Chapter 9). This model of balancing *collective* and *individual* rights in order to realistically address the challenges of managing diversity does not provide a political formula that can be painlessly adopted to meet the specific needs of the British case. But it does provide for a political imagination, framed in a system of rights, that allows for a difficult and contested political process that has viable foundations.

As we saw in Chapter Three, there is at present a disturbing erosion of support for fundamental human rights. The balancing of Community Cohesion, security and individual autonomy cannot be aspired to in a world where rights can be relativised as an act of political expediency. One consequence of the contemporary realities of the politics of difference, as they are routinely expressed in popular action, is that members of specific identity-based interest groups do not plead to be tolerated; rather, they assert their rights. At the time of writing, the current dialogue within the Church of England in relation to women and gay priests is an example of this reality. If the state chooses to deny the fundamental legitimacy of human rights claims then it erodes the perceived legitimacy of the political system itself. The social contract between the state and the citizen requires a certainty about the terms of that contract and about its credible delivery. Where a political commitment to securitisation has *de facto* resulted in the erosion of citizen rights, then the social contract has been violated. Too much of the political rhetoric around cohesion has been a rehearsal of the definition and virtues of formal citizenship; too little has been done to guarantee the achievement of substantive citizenship for all.

Notes

[1] As we have seen above the political focus on the securitisation of urban life provides a generic framing of the urban environment as uniquely problematic, which then frames the specific 'challenge' of managing Muslim communities.

[2] See Brown (2006) for an invaluable analysis of the political uses of tolerance discourses.

Bibliography

Abbass, T. (ed) (2005) *Muslims in Britain: Communities in Britain*, London: Zed Books.

Abrams, D. and Hogg, M.A. (eds) (1999) *Social identity and social cognition*, Oxford: Blackwell.

Adamson, P. (2007) *Child poverty in perspective: An overview of child well being in rich countries*, Innocenti Report, Card 7, UNICEF, Florence: Innocenti Research Centre.

Afshar, H. (1994) 'Muslim women in West Yorkshire: growing up with real and imaginary values amidst conflicting views of self and society', in H. Afshar and M. Maynard (eds) *The dynamics of 'race' and gender: Some feminist interventions*, London: Taylor and Francis, pp 127-50.

Akhtar, S. (1989) *Be careful with Muhammad!*, London: Bellew Publishing.

Alam, M.Y. (2006) *Made in Bradford*, Pontefract: Route Publishing.

Alam, M.Y. (forthcoming) *The invisible village: Small world, big society* [title to be confirmed], Pontefract: Route Publishing.

Alam, M.Y. and Husband, C. (2006) *British-Pakistani men from Bradford: Linking narratives to policy*, York: Joseph Rowntree Foundation.

Aldridge, S., Halpern, D. and Fitzpatrick, S. (2002) *Social capital: A discussion paper*, London: Her Majesty's Government Performance and Innovation Unit.

Alexander, C. (2000) *The Asian gang: Ethnicity, identity, masculinity*, Oxford: Berg.

Allen, C. (2007) 'Islamophobia and its consequences', in S. Amghar, A. Boubekeur and M. Emerson (eds) *European Islam: Challenges for public policy and society*, Brussels: Centre for European Policy Studies, pp 144-68.

Allievi, S. (2005) 'How the immigrant has become Muslim', *Revue Européenne des Migrations Internationales*, vol 21, no 2, pp 135-63.

Ameli, S.R., Elahi, M. and Merali, A. (2004) *British Muslims' expectations of the government: Social discrimination: Across the Muslim divide*, London: Islamic Human Rights Commission.

Amghar, S., Boubekeur, A. and Emerson, M. (eds) (2007) *European Islam: Challenges for public policy and society*, Brussels: Centre for European Policy Studies.

Amiraux, V. (2007) 'The headscarf question: what is really the issue', in S. Amghar, A. Boubekeur and M. Emerson (eds) *European Islam: Challenges for public policy and society*, Brussels: Centre for European Policy Studies, pp 124-43.

Anderson, B. (1983) *Imagined communities: Reflections on the origins and spread of nationalism*, London: Verso.

Anthias, F. and Yuval-Davis, N. (1993) *Racialized boundaries*, London: Routledge.

Appignanesi, L. and Maitland, S. (1989) *The Rushdie file*, London: Fourth Estate.

Archer, L. (2001) 'Muslim brothers, black lads, traditional Asians: British Muslim young men's constructions of race, religion and masculinity', *Feminism and Psychology*, vol 11, no 1, pp 79-105.

Arneil, B. (2007) 'The meaning and utility of "social" in social capital', in R. Edwards, J. Franklin and J. Holland (eds) *Assessing social capital: Concept, policy and practice*, Newcastle: Cambridge Scholars Press, pp 29-53.

Atkinson, R. and Helms, G. (2007) *Securing an urban renaissance: Crime, community and British urban policy*, Bristol: The Policy Press.

Audit Commission (2010) NI 35 Building resilience to violent extremism', 15/06/2010, www.audit-commission.gov.uk/localgov/audit/nis/Pages/NI035Buildingresiliencetoviolentextremism.aspx

Back, L. (1996) *New ethnicities and urban culture*, London: UCL Press.

Back, L. and Solomos, J. (1992) 'Black politics and social change in Birmingham, UK: an analysis of recent trends', *Ethnic and Racial Studies*, vol 15, no 3, pp 327-51.

Back, L., Keith, M., Khan, A., Shukra, K. and Solomos, J. (2002a) 'New Labour's white heart: politics, multiculturalism and the return of assimilation', *Political Quarterly*, vol 73, no 4, pp 445-54.

Back, L., Keith, M., Khan, A., Shukra, K. and Solomos, J. (2002b) 'The return of assimilationism: race, multiculturalism and New Labour', *Sociological Research OnLine*, vol 7, no 2 (http://socresonline.org.uk/7/2/back.html).

Bagguley, P. and Hussain, Y. (2008) *Riotous citizens: Ethnic conflict in multicultural Britain*, Aldershot: Ashgate.

Bailey, O.G., Georgiou, M. and Harindranath, R. (eds) (2007) *Transnational lives: Re-imagining diaspora*, Houndmills, Basingstoke: Palgrave Macmillan.

Ballard, R. (ed) (1994) *Desh Pardesh: The South Asian presence in Britain*, London: Hurst.

Banting, K. and Kymlicka, W. (eds) (2006) *Multiculturalism and the welfare state*, Oxford: Oxford University Press.

Barker, M. (1981) *The new racism*, London: Junction Books.

Barnett, B. and Reynolds, A. (2009) *Terrorism and the press: An uneasy relationship*, New York: Peter Lang.

Barry, B. (2001) *Culture and equality*, Cambridge: Polity Press.

Bauman, Z. (1990) 'Modernity and ambivalence', in M. Featherstone (ed) *Global culture: Nationalism, globalization and modernity*, London: Sage Publications.

Baumeister, A. (2007) 'Diversity and unity: the problem with "constitutional patriotism"', *European Journal of Political Theory*, vol 6, no 4, pp 483-503.

Beck, U. (1992) *Risk society*, London: Sage Publications.

Beck, U. (2002) 'The terrorist threat: world risk society revisited', *Theory, Culture and Society*, vol 19, no 4, pp 39-55.

Beck, U. (2006) *The cosmopolitan vision*, Cambridge: Polity Press.

Beckford, M. and Pitcher, G. (2009) 'Archbishop of Canterbury: "Labour treats us like oddballs"', 11 December, *Telegraph* (www.telegraph.co.uk/news/newstopics/religion/6792088/Archbishop-of-Canterbury-Labour-treats-us-like-oddballs.html).

Benhabib, S. (2002) *The claims of culture: Equality and diversity in the global era*, Princeton, NJ: Princeton University Press.

Benyon, J. and Solomos, J. (eds) (1987) *The roots of urban unrest*, Oxford: Pergamon Press.

Berger, P.L. and Luckman, T. (1966) *The social construction of reality*, Garden City, NY: Anchor Books.

Berry, J.W. (2006) 'Mutual attitudes among immigrants and ethnocultural groups in Canada', *International Journal of Intercultural Relations*, vol 30, pp 719-34.

Billig, M. (1978) *Fascists: A social psychological view of the National Front*, London: Harcourt Brace Jovanovich.

Billig, M. (2002) 'Henri Tajfel's "Cognitive aspects of prejudice" and the psychology of bigotry', *British Journal of Social Psychology*, vol 41, pp 171-88.

Bizman, A. and Yinon, Y. (2001) 'Intergroup and interpersonal threats as determinants of prejudice: the moderating role of in-group identification', *Basic and Applied Social Psychology*, vol 23, pp 191-6.

Blick, A., Choudhury, T. and Weir, S. (2006) *The rules of the game: Terrorism, community and human rights*, York: Joseph Rowntree Foundation.

Blommaert, J. and Verschueren, J. (1998) *Debating diversity: Analysing the discourse of tolerance*, London: Routledge.

Bonney, R. (2004) *Jihad: From Qur'an to bin Laden*, Houndmills, Basingstoke: Palgrave Macmillan.

Bonney, R. (2008) *False prophets: The 'clash of civilizations' and the global war on terror*, Oxford: Peter Lang.

Booth, R. (2009) 'Minister for terror: Gaza will fuel UK extremism', 28 January, *The Guardian* (www.guardian.co.uk/politics/2009/jan/28/terrorism-uk-gaza).

Bourdieu, P. (1985) 'The forms of capital, in J.G. Richardson (ed) *Handbook of theory and research for the sociology of education*, New York: Greenwood Press, pp 241-58.

Bourdieu, P. and Wacquant, L. (1992) *An invitation to reflexive sociology*, Chicago, IL: Chicago University Press.

Bowling, B. and Phillips, C. (2007) 'Disproportionate and discriminatory: reviewing the evidence on police stop and search', *The Modern Law Review*, vol 70, no 6, pp 936-61.

Bradford Commission (1996) *The report of an inquiry into the wider implications of the public disorders in Bradford which occurred on 9, 10 and 11 June 1995*, London: The Stationery Office.

Brewer, M.B. and Hewstone, R. (eds) (2004) *Self and social identity*, Oxford: Blackwell.

Bridges, L. (1999) 'The Lawrence Inquiry – incompetence, corruption, and institutional racism', *Journal of Law and Society*, vol 15, no 3, pp 298-322.

Brown, R. (1995) *Prejudice: Its social psychology*, Oxford: Blackwell [Chapter 6].

Brown, W. (2006) *Regulating aversion: Tolerance in the age of identity and Empire*, Princeton, NJ: Princeton University Press.

Burkitt, I. (2008) *Social selves: Theories of self and society*, London: Sage Publications.

Burkitt, I., Husband, C., MacKenzie, J. and Torn, A. (2001*) Nurse education and communities of practice*, London: English National Board of Nursing.

Burlet, S. and Reid, H. (1998) 'A gendered uprising: political representation and minority ethnic communities', *Ethnic and Racial Studies*, vol 21, no 2, pp 270-87.

Burnett, J. and Whyte, D. (2005) 'Embedded expertise and the new terrorism', *Journal of Crime, Conflict and the Media*, vol 1, no 4, pp 1-18.

Burnley Task Force (2001) *Report of the Burnley Task Force*, Burnley: Burnley Task Force.

Campbell, B. (1993) *Goliath: Britain's dangerous places*, London: Methuen.

Campion, M.J. (2005) *Look who's talking. Cultural diversity, public service broadcasting and the national conversation*, Oxford: Nuffield College, University of Oxford.

Cannadine, D. (2002) *Ornamentalism: How the British saw their empire*, London: Penguin Books.

Cantle, T. (2008) *Community cohesion: A new framework for race and diversity*, Houndmills, Basingstoke: Palgrave Macmillan.

Cantor, D. (2009) *The faces of terrorism: Multidisciplinary perspectives*, Chichester: Wiley-Blackwell.

Capozza, D. and Brown, R. (eds) (2000) *Social identity processes*, London: Sage Publications.

Casciani, D. (2004) 'Islamophobia pervades UK – report', BBC News Online, 2 June (http://news.bbc.co.uk/1/hi/uk/3768327.stm).

CCCS (Centre for Contemporary Cultural Studies) (1982) *The Empire strikes back*, London: Hutchinson.

Cesari, J. (2004) *When Islam and democracy meet: Muslims in Europe and in the United States*, Houndmills, Basingstoke: Palgrave Macmillan.

Cheong, P. H., Edwards, R., Goulbourne, H. and Solomos, J. (2007) 'Immigration, social cohesion and social capital: a critical review', *Critical Social Policy*, vol 27, no 1, pp 24-49.

Choudhury, T. (2007) 'Muslims and discrimination', in S. Amghar, A. Boubekeur and M. Emerson (eds) *European Islam: Challenges for public policy and society*, Brussels: Centre for European Policy Studies, pp 77-106.

CLG (Department for Communities and Local Government) (2008) *Guidance for local authorities on Community Cohesion contingency planning and tension monitoring*, London: CLG.

CLGC (Communities and Local Government Committee) of the House of Commons (2010) *Sixth report of session 2009-10, Preventing violent extremism*, HC 65, London: The Stationery Office.

Cohen, P. and Bains, H.S. (1988) *Multi-racist Britain*, Houndmills: Macmillan.

Cohen, S. (1972) *Folk devils and moral panics*, St Albans: Paladin.

Cole, D. and Lobel, J. (2007) *Less safe less free*, New York: The New Press.

Coleman, R. (2004) *Reclaiming the streets: Surveillance, social control and the city*, Cullompton: Willan Publishing.

Coleman, R., Tombs, S. and Whyte, D. (2005) 'Capital, crime and statecraft in the entrepreneurial city', *Urban Studies*, vol 42, no 13, pp 2511-30.

Collins, M. (2004) *The likes of us: A biography of the white working class*, London: Granta Books.

Commission on Integration and Cohesion (2007) *Our shared future*, London: Commission on Integration and Cohesion.

Community Cohesion Independent Review Team (2001) *Community cohesion: A report of the Independent Review Team, Chaired by Ted Cantle*, (The Cantle Report), London: Home Office.

Critcher, C. (2006) *Critical readings. Moral panics and the media*, Milton Keynes: Open University Press.

Cronin, C. (2003) 'Democracy and collective identity: in defence of constitutional patriotism', *European Journal of Philosophy*, vol 11, no 1, pp 1-28.

Curtis, P. (2009) 'Universities must reveal data on dropout rates and teaching time', *The Observer*, 1 November. (http://0-infoweb. newsbank.com.brum.beds.ac.uk/iw-search/we/InfoWeb).

Davies, C. (2010) 'Terror policy has caused stigma, Muslim police warn: MPs told that government's Prevent strategy has increased Islamophobia to "a level that defies all logic"', *The Guardian*, 21 January (www.guardian.co.uk/uk/2010/jan/21/muslim–police–terrorism–policy–islamophobia).

Deakin, N. (1970) *Colour citizenship and British society*, London: Panther.

Dench, G., Gavron, K. and Young, M. (2006) *The new East End: Kinship, race and conflict*, London: Profile Books.

Denham, J. (2002) Building Cohesive Communities: A Report of the Ministerial Group on Public Order and Community Cohesion, London: Home Office.

Denney, D. (ed) (2009) *Living in dangerous times: Fear, insecurity, risk and social policy*, Chichester: Wiley-Blackwell.

Denscombe, M. (2003) *The good research guide for small-scale social research projects* (2nd edn), Buckingham: Open University Press

DETR (Department of the Environment, Transport and the Regions) (2000) *Our towns and cities – The future: Delivering an urban renaissance*, London: The Stationery Office.

Dorling, D. (2009) 'From housing to health – to whom are the white working class losing out? Frequently asked questions', in K.P. Sveinsson (ed) *Who cares about the white working class? Runnymede perspectives*, London: Runnymede Trust, pp 59-65.

Dorling, D. (2010) *Injustice: Why social inequality persists*, Bristol: The Policy Press.

Dorling, D. and Pritchard, J. (2010) 'The geography of poverty, inequality and wealth in the UK and abroad: because enough is never enough', *Applied Spatial Analysis*, no 3, pp 81-106.

Dorling, D. and Thomas, B. (2004) *People and places: A 2001 Census atlas of the UK*, Bristol: The Policy Press.

Dorling, D., Vickers, D., Thomas, B., Pritchard, J. and Ballas, D. (2008) *Changing UK: The way we live now*, Report commissioned by BBC Regions and Nations, Sheffield: Social and Spatial Inequalities, University of Sheffield (www.sasi.group.shef.ac.uk/publications/index.html).

Dorling, D., Rigby, J., Ballas, D., Thomas, B., Fahmy, E., Gordon, D. and Lupton, R. (2007) *Poverty, wealth and place in Britain*, Bristol: The Policy Press.

Doughty, S. (2010) 'Islam divides us, say the majority of Britons', *The Daily Mail*, 11 January (www.dailymail.co.uk/news/article-1242048/Almost-half-Britons-oppose-mosque-built-area-finds-study.html).

Douglas, T. (1995) *Scapegoats*, London: Routledge.

Dovidio, J.F., Glick, P. and Rudman, L.A. (2005) *On the nature of prejudice: Fifty years after Allport*, Oxford: Blackwell.

Downing, J. and Husband, C. (2005) *Representing 'race': Racisms, ethnicities and the media*, London: Sage Publications.

Dufoix, S. (2008) *Diasporas*, Berkeley, CA: University of California Press.

Eade, J. (ed) (1997) *Living the global city: Globalization as local process*, London: Routledge.

ECCAR (European Coalition of Cities Against Racism) (2010) *European Coalition of Cities Against Racism/UNESCO study on the challenges in the development of local indicators – A human rights centred model* (www.unesco.org).

Edwards, D. and Potter, J. (2001) 'Discursive psychology', in A.L. McHoul and M. Rapley (eds) *How to analyse talk in institutional settings*, London: Continuum International, pp 12-24.

Edwards, R., Franklin, J. and Holland, J. (eds) (2007) *Assessing social capital: Concept, policy and practice*, Newcastle: Cambridge Scholars Publishing.

Eickelman, D. F. and Anderson, J.W. (eds) (1999) *New media in the Muslim world*, Bloomington, IN: Indiana University Press.

Elias, N. and Scotson, J. L. (1965) *The established and outsiders*, London: Frank Cass.

Ellemers, N., Spears, R. and Doosje, B. (1999) *Social identity: Context, commitment, content*, Oxford: Blackwell.

Elliott, A. and Lemert, C. (2006) *The new individualism*, London: Routledge.

Ellison, N. and Pierson, C. (eds) (2003) *Developments in British social policy*, Houndmills, Basingstoke: Palgrave Macmillan.

ENAR (European Network Against Racism) (2007) 'ENAR urges OSCE participating states to make real their commitment to combat discrimination', Press release, June (http://cms.horus.be/files/99935/MediaArchive/pdfpress/2007-06-07%20conference%20on%20combating%20discrimination.pdf).

ERRC (European Roma Rights Centre) (2004) *Ethnic statistics*, 2/2004 (www.errc.org/cikk.php?cikk=1998&archiv=1).

Esposito, J. L. (2002) *Unholy war: Terror in the name of Islam*, New York: Oxford University Press.

EUFRA (European Union Agency for Fundamental Rights) (2009) *EU-MIDIS data in Focus Report: Muslims*, Vienna: FRA.

EUMC on Racism and Xenophobia (European Union Monitoring Centre) (2006a) *Muslims in the European Union – Discrimination and Islamophobia*,Vienna: EUMC.

EUMC (2006b) *Perceptions of discrimination and Islamophobia: Voices from members of Muslim communities in the European Union*, Vienna: EUMC.

European Parliament (2007) *Islam in the European Union: What's at stake in the future*, IP/B/CULT/ST/2006-061, 14 May, Brussels: Directorate General, Internal Policies of the Union.

Evans, M. and Cerny, P. (2003) 'Globalisation and social policy', in N. Ellison and C. Pierson (eds) *Developments in British social policy*, Houndmills, Basingstoke: Palgrave Macmillan, pp 19-40.

Ewing, K. D. and Gearty, C. A. (1990) *Freedom under Thatcher: Civil liberties in modern Britain*, Oxford: Oxford University Press.

Fairclough, N. and Wodak, R. (1997) 'Critical discourse analysis', in T.A. van Dijk (ed) *Discourses as social interaction (vol 2)*, London: Sage Publications.

Fanshawe, S. and Sriskandarajah, D. (2010) *You can't put me in a box: Super diversity and the end of identity politics in Britain*, London: Institute for Public Policy Research.

Fekete, L. (2009) *A suitable enemy*, London: Pluto Press.

Fetzer, J.S. and Soper, J.C. (2005) *Muslims and the state in Britain, France and Germany*, Cambridge: Cambridge University Press.

Field, D. (2007) 'Islamophobia in contemporary Britain: the evidence of the opinion polls, 1988-2006', *Islam and Christian-Muslim relations*, vol 18, no 4, pp 447–77.

Field, J. (2003) *Social capital*, London: Routledge.

Finney, N. and Simpson, L. (2009) *'Sleepwalking to segregation'? Challenging myths about race and migration*, Bristol: The Policy Press.

Firmstone, J., Georgiou, M., Husband, C., Marinkova, M. and Steibel, F. (2009) 'Final report of study of press representation of ethnic minorities to fundamental rights agency'.Vienna: Unpublished.

Flint, J. (2009) 'Migrant information packs and the colonisation of civility in the UK', *Space and Polity*, vol 13, no 2, pp 127-40.

Flint, J. and Robinson, D. (2008) *Community cohesion in crisis? New dimensions of diversity and difference*, Bristol: The Policy Press.

Flint, J. and Smithson, H. (2007) 'New governance of youth disorder: a study of local initiatives', in R. Atkinson and G. Helms (eds) *Securing an urban renaissance: Crime, community and British urban policy*, Bristol: The Policy Press, pp 165-82.

Foot, P. (1965) *Immigration and race in British politics*, London: Penguin.

Frachon, C. and Sassoon,V. (2008) *Medias et diversité: De la visibilité aux contenus*, Paris: Panos Institute.

Frachon, F. (2009) *Media and cultural diversity in Europe and North America*, Paris: Panos Institute and Edition Karthala.

Fraser, N. and Honneth, A. (2003) *Redistribution or recognition?*, London: Verso.

Frost, D. (2008) 'Islamophobia: examining causal links between the media and "race hate" from "below"', *International Journal of Sociology and Social Policy*, vol 28, no 11/12, pp 564-78.

Furedi, F. (2009) 'Fear and security: a vulnerability-led policy response', in D. Denney (ed) *Living in dangerous times: Fear, insecurity, risk and social policy*, Chichester: Wiley-Blackwell, pp 86-102.

Galbraith, J. K. (1992) *The culture of contentment*, London: Sinclair-Stevenson.

Gardner, K. and Shukar, A. (1994) 'I'm Bengali, I'm Asian and I'm living here', in R. Ballard (ed) *Desh Pardesh: The South Asian presence in Britain*, London: Hurst, pp 142-63.

Garner, S. (2009) 'Home truths: the white working class and the racialization of social housing', in K.P. Sveinsson (ed) *Who cares about the white working class? Runnymede perspectives*, London: Runnymede Trust, pp 45-50.

Gearty, C. (2007) 'Terrorism and human rights', *Government and Opposition*, vol 42, no 3, pp 340-62.

Geertz, C. (1973) 'Thick description: toward an interpretive theory of culture', in C. Geertz (ed) *The interpretation of cultures: Selected essays*, New York: Basic Books, pp 3-30.

Georgiou, M. (2006) *Diaspora and the media*, Creskill, NJ: Hampton Press.

Georgiou, M. (2010) 'Media representations of diversity: the power of the mediated image', in A. Bloch and J. Solomos (eds) *Race and ethnicity in the 21st century*, Houndmills: Palgrave Macmillan, pp 166-85.

Giddens, A. (1998) *The third way*, Cambridge: Polity Press.

Gillan, A. (2006) 'Britons put work and fun before babies: ICM poll reveals changing attitudes behind UK's low birthrate', *The Guardian*, 2 May (http://society.guardian.co.uk/children/story/0,,1765568,00.html).

Gillborn, D. (2009) 'Education: the numbers game and the construction of white racial victimhood', in K.P. Sveinsson (ed) *Who cares about the white working class? Runnymede perspectives*, London: Runnymede Trust, pp 15-21.

Gilroy, P. (1987) *There ain't no black in the Union Jack*, London: Hutchinson.

Githens-Mazer, J. and Lambert, R. (2010) *Islamophobia and anti-Muslim hate crime: A London case study*, Exeter: European Muslim Research Centre (http://centres.exeter.ac.uk/emrc/publications/Islamophobia_and_Anti-Muslim_Hate_Crime.pdf).

Goldberg, D. (2002) *The racial state*, Malden, MA: Blackwell Publishing

Gonzalez, K.V., Verkuyten, M., Weesie, J. and Poppe, E. (2008) 'Prejudice towards Muslims in the Netherlands: testing integrated threat theory', *British Journal of Social Psychology*, vol 47, pp 667-85.

Gordon, P. (1983) *White law: Racism in the police, courts, and prisons*, London: Pluto Press.

Gordon, P. and Klug, F. (1986) *New right new racism*, Nottingham: Searchlight Publications.

Grant, P. R. and Brown, R. (1995) 'From ethnocentrism to collective protest: responses to relative deprivation and threats to social identity', *Social Psychology Quarterly*, vol 8, no 3, pp 195-211.

Grewal, I. (1996) *Home and harem: Nation, gender, Empire and the cultures of travel*, London: Leicester University Press.

Grewcock, M. (2003) 'Irregular migration, identity and the state – the challenge for criminology', *Current Issues in Criminal Justice*, vol 15, no 2, pp 114-35.

Hall, S. (2003) 'New Labour's double-shuffle', *Soundings 24*, Autumn, pp 10-24.

Hall, S., Critcher, C., Jefferson, T., Clarke, J. and Roberts, B. (1978) *Policing the crisis: Mugging, the state and law and order*, London: Hutchinson.

Halliday, F. (1996) *Islam and the myth of confrontation*, London: I.B. Tauris.

Halpern, D., Bates, D., Mulgan, G., Aldridge, S., Beales, G. and Heathfield, A. (2004) *Personal responsibility and changing behaviour: The state of knowledge and its implications for public policy*, London: Cabinet Office.

Hancock, L. (2007) 'Is urban regeneration criminogenic?', in R. Atkinson and G. Helms (eds) *Securing an urban renaissance: Crime, community and British urban policy*, Bristol: The Policy Press, pp 57-70.

Harris, T. (1990) *London crowds in the reign of Charles II: Propaganda and politics from the Restoration until the exclusion crisis*, Cambridge: Cambridge University Press.

Hartmann, P. and Husband, C. (1974) *Racism and the mass media*, London: Davis-Poynter.

Hennessy, P. (ed) (2007a) *The new protective state: Government, intelligence and terrorism*, London: Continuum.

Hennessy, P. (2007b) 'From secret state to protective state', in P. Hennessy (ed) *The new protective state: Government, intelligence and terrorism*, London: Continuum, pp 1-41.

Hewitt, R. (2005) *White backlash and the politics of multiculturalism*, Cambridge: Cambridge University Press.

Hicks, N. (2005) 'The impact of counter terror on the promotion and protection of human rights: a global perspective', in R. A. Wilson (ed) *Human rights in the 'War on Terror'*, Cambridge: Cambridge University Press, pp 209-24.

Hills, J., Brewer, M., Jenkins, S., Lister, R., Lupton, R., Machin, S., Mills, C., Modood, T., Rees, T. and Riddell, S. (2010) *An anatomy of economic inequality in the UK: Report of the National Equality Panel*, London: Centre for Analysis of Social Exclusion, London School of Economics and Political Science.

Hillyard, P. (2006) 'The "War on Terror": lessons from Ireland', in T. Bunyan (ed) *The war on freedom and democracy: Essays on civil liberties in Europe*, Nottingham: Spokesman Books, pp 5-10.

Hillyard, P. and Percy-Smith, J. (1988) *The coercive state: The decline of democracy in Britain*, Glasgow: Fontana/Collins.

HM (Her Majesty's) Government (2001) *Anti-terrorism, Crime and Security Act*, London: The Stationery Office.

HM Government (2002) *The strategic defence review: A new chapter*, July, Cm 5566, London: The Stationery Office.

HM Government (2003) *Delivering security in a changing world*, White Paper, Cm 6041-I, London: The Stationery Office.

HM Government (2004) *The Civil Contingencies Act*, London: The Stationery Office.

HM Government (2006) *Countering international terrorism: The United Kingdom's strategy*, Cm 6888, London: The Stationery Office.

HM Government (2008) *The Prevent strategy: A guide to local partners in England*, London: The Stationery Office.

HM Government (2009) *Pursue, prevent, protect, prepare: The United Kingdom's strategy for countering international terrorism*, Cm 7547, London: The Stationery Office.

Hobson, J. M. (2004) *The eastern origins of western civilisation*, Cambridge: Cambridge University Press.

Hoffman, B. (2006) *Inside terrorism*, New York: Columbia University Press.

Home Office (2004) *Strength in diversity: Towards a Community Cohesion strategy and Race Equality strategy*, London: Home Office.

Home Office (2005) *Improving opportunity, strengthening society: The government's strategy to increase race equality and community cohesion*, London: Home Office.

House of Commons, Home Affairs Committee (2005) *Terrorism and community relations, Sixth Report of Session 2004-05, Volume 1* [Report, together with formal minutes and appendix], HC 165-I, London: The Stationery Office.

House of Lords, Constitution Committee (2009) *Surveillance: citizens and the state*, HL Paper 18–I, London: The Stationery Office.

House of Lords/House of Commons JCHR (Joint Committee on Human Rights) (2010) *Counter-terrorism policy and human rights (Sixteenth report); Bringing human rights back in (Seventeenth report)*, HL 86/HC 111, London: The Stationery Office.

Hubel, T. (1996) *Whose India? The independence struggle in British and Indian fiction and history*, London: Leicester University Press.

Hughes, G. (2009) 'Governing the social and the problem of the "stranger"', in P. Noxolo and J. Huysmans (eds) *Community, citizenship and the 'War on Terror': Security and insecurity*, Houndmills, Basingstoke: Palgrave Macmillan, pp 13–31.

Huntington, S.P. (1996) *The clash of civilizations and the remaking of world order*, New York: Simon & Schuster.

Husband, C. (1991) '"Race", conflictual politics, and anti–racist social work: lessons from the past for action in the '90s', in CCETSW (Central Council for Education and Training in Social Work), *Setting the context for change*, London: CCETSW.

Husband, C. (1994) *'Race' and nation: The British experience*, Perth, Australia: Paradigm.

Husband, C. (1995) 'The morally active practitioner and the ethics of anti–racist practice', in R. Hugman and D. Smith (eds) *Ethical issues in social work*, London: Routledge.

Husband, C. (2000) 'The media and the public sphere in multiethnic societies', in S. Cottle (ed) *Ethnic minorities and the media*, Buckingham: Open University Press, pp 199-214.

Husband, C. (2003) 'Una buena practica sigilosa, aungue flirteando con el racismo', *Migraciones*, vol 14, no 203, pp 145-80.

Husband, C. (2005a) 'Doing good by stealth, whilst flirting with racism. Some contradictory dynamics of British multiculturalism', in W. Bosswick and C. Husband (eds) *Comparative European research in migration, diversity and identities*, Bilbao: University of Deusto, pp 191-206.

Husband, C. (2005b) 'Minority ethnic media as communities of practice: professionalism and identity politics in interaction', *Journal of Ethnic and Migration Studies*, vol 31, no 3, May, pp 461-80.

Husband, C. and Alam, M.Y. (2001) 'Beyond the rhetoric of codes of practice: ethnicity and media monitoring reviewed', *Nord-Sud Aktuell*, vol 15, no 4, pp 680-91.

Husband, C. and Moring, T. (2009) 'Public spheres and multiculturalism in contemporary Europe', in I. Salovaara-Moring (ed) *Manufacturing Europe: Spaces of democracy, diversity and communication*, Goteborg: Nordicom, pp 131-52.

Hussain, Y. and Bagguley, P. (2005) 'Citizenship, ethnicity and identity: British Pakistanis after the 2001 "riots"', *Sociology*, vol 39, no 3, pp 407-25.

Huysmans, J. (2006) *The politics of insecurity: Fear, migration and asylum in the EU*, London: Routledge.

Huysmans, J. (2009) 'Conclusion: insecurity and the everyday', in P. Noxolo and J. Huysmans (eds) *Community, citizenship and the 'War on Terror': Security and insecurity*, Houndmills, Basingstoke: Palgrave Macmillan, pp 196-207.

Hyam, R. (1991) *Empire and sexuality*, Manchester: Manchester University Press.

Inden, R. (1992) *Imagining India*, Oxford: Blackwell.

Islamophobia Watch: Documenting anti-Muslim bigotry (www.islamophobia-watch.com).

Jackson, R. (2007) 'Constructing enemies: "Islamic terrorism" in political and academic discourse', *Government and Opposition*, vol 42, no 3, pp 394-426.

Jacobs, D. and Tillie, J. (2004) 'Integration: social capital and political integration of migrants', *Journal of Ethnic and Migration Studies*, vol 30, no 3, pp 419-27.

Jayaweera, H. and Choudhury, T. (2008) *Immigration, faith and cohesion: Evidence from local areas with significant Muslim populations*, York: Joseph Rowntree Trust.

Jenkins, R. (1991) *A life at the centre*, London: Macmillan.

Jessop, B., Bonnet, K., Bromley, S. and Ling, T. (1988) *Thatcherism*, Oxford: Polity Press.

Johnston, B. and Shearing, C. (2003) *The governance of security*, London: Routledge.

Joppke, C. (2004) 'The retreat of multiculturalism in the liberal state: theory and policy', *British Journal of Sociology*, vol 55, no 2, pp 241-50.

Jordan, W.D. (1986) *White over black: American attitudes toward the Negro, 1550-1812*, Chapel Hill, NC: University of North Carolina Press.

Joshua, H., Wallace, T. with Booth, H. (1983) *To ride the storm: The 1980 Bristol 'riot' and the state*, London: Heinemann.

Kabbani, R. (1994) *Imperial fictions: Europe's myths of Orient*, London: Pandora.

Kalra, V.S. and Kapoor, N. (2008) *Interrogating segregation, integration and the Community Cohesion agenda*, Working Paper 2008-16, Liverpool: Cathy Marsh Centre for Census and Survey Research, University of Liverpool.

Kamin, L.J. (1977) *The science and politics of IQ*, Harmondsworth: Penguin Books.

Karim, K.H. (2000) *Islamic peril: Media and global violence*, Montreal: Black Rose Books.

Kastoryano, R. (2006) 'French secularism and Islam: France's headscarf affair', in T. Modood, A. Triandafyllidou and R. Zapata-Barrero (2006) *Multiculturalism, Muslims and citizenship*, London: Routledge, pp 57-69.

Kavoori, A.P. and Fraley, T. (eds) (2006) *Media, terrorism and theory*, Lanham, MD: Rowman and Littlefield.

Keane, J. (1991) *The media and democracy*, Cambridge: Polity Press.

Kearns, A. and Forrest, R. (2000) 'Social cohesion and multilevel urban governance', *Urban Studies*, vol 37, no 5/6, pp 995-1017.

Keith, M. (2005) *After the cosmopolitan? Multicultural cities and the future of racism*, London: Routledge.

Kettle, M. and Hodges, L. (1982) *Uprising: The police, the people and the riots in Britain's cities*, London: Pan.

Kiernan, V.G. (1969) *The lords of human kind*, London: Weidenfeld and Nicholson.

Kundnani, A. (2001) 'In a foreign land: the new popular racism' *Race and Class*, vol 43, no 2, pp 41-60.

Kundnani, A. (2002) 'An unholy alliance? Racism, religion and communalism', *Race and Class*, vol 22, no 2, pp 71-80.

Kundnani, A. (2007a) 'Integrationism: the politics of anti-Muslim racism', *Race and Class*, vol 48, no 4, pp 24-44.

Kundnani, A. (2007b) *The end of tolerance*, London: Pluto Press.

Kundnani, A. (2009a) *Spooked! How not to prevent violent extremism*, London: Institute of Race Relations.

Kundnani, A. (2009b) *The secret state: Domestic surveillance and control in Britain*, London: Institute of Race Relations.

Kymlicka, W. (1995) *Multicultural citizenship*, Oxford: Clarendon Press.

Kymlicka, W. (2001) *Politics in the vernacular*, Oxford: Oxford University Press.

Kymlicka, W. (2007) *Multicultural odysseys: Navigating the new international politics of diversity*, Oxford: Oxford University Press.

Lacroix, J. (2002) 'For a European constitutional patriotism', *Political Studies*, vol 50, pp 944-58.

Lambert, R. (2008) 'Empowering Salafis and Islamists against Al-Qaeda: a London counter-terrorism case study', *Political Science and Politics*, vol 41, no 1, pp 31-5.

Lave, J. and Wenger, E. (1991) *Situated learning*, Cambridge: Cambridge University Press.

Law, I. (2000) *Race in the news*, Houndmills, Basingstoke: Palgrave Macmillan.

Lawrence, E. (1982) 'In the abundance of water the fool is thirsty: sociology and black pathology', in CCCS (Centre for Contemporary Cultural Studies), *The Empire strikes back*, London: Hutchinson, pp 95-142.

Layton-Henry, Z. (1992) *The politics of immigration*, Oxford: Blackwell.

Lea, J. (2000) 'The Macpherson Report and the question of institutional racism', *The Howard Journal of Criminal Justice*, vol 39, no 3, pp 219-33.

Letherby, G. (2003) *Feminist research in theory and practice*, Buckingham: Open University Press.

Letki, N. (2005) *Does diversity erode social cohesion? Social capital and race in British neighbourhoods*, Nuffield College Working Paper, 2005-W10, Oxford: Nuffield College, University of Oxford.

Levitas, R. (2005) *The inclusive society? Social exclusion and New Labour*, Houndmills, Basingstoke: Palgrave Macmillan.

LGA (Local Government Association), ODPM (Office of the Deputy Prime Minister), Home Office and CRE (Commission for Racial Equality) (2002) *Guidance on community cohesion*, London: LGA.

Loury, G. C., Modood, T. and Teles, S. M. (2005) *Ethnicity, social mobility and public policy*, Cambridge: Cambridge University Press.

MacDonald, R. (ed) (1997) *Youth, the 'underclass' and social exclusion*, London: Routledge.

Macpherson of Cluny, Sir William (1999) *The Stephen Lawrence Inquiry: Report of an Inquiry by Sir William Macpherson of Cluny*, London: The Stationery Office.

McClenaghan, P. (2000) 'Social capital: exploring the theoretical foundations of community development education', *British Educational Research Journal*, vol 26, no 5, pp 565-82.

McDonald, H. (2009) 'Sinn Féin blames Real IRA for Belfast violence', *The Guardian*, 14 July (www.guardian.co.uk/uk/2009/jul/14/belfast-riots-real-ira-blame).

McGhee, D. (2003) 'Moving to "our" common ground – a critical examination of community cohesion discourse in twenty-first century Britain', *The Sociological Review*, vol 51, no 3, pp 376-404.

McGhee, D. (2005) 'Patriots of the future? A critical examination of community cohesion strategies in contemporary Britain', *Sociological Research Online*, vol 10, no 3 (www.socresonline.org.uk/10/3/mcghee.html).

McGhee, D. (2008) *The end of multiculturalism: Terrorism, integration and human rights*, Maidenhead: Open University Press.

McQuail, D. (2005) *Mass communication theory*, London: Sage Publications.

Mail Online (2007) 'Muslim majority schools "pose security threat and should be closed"', 22 January (www.dailymail.co.uk/news/article-430470/Muslim-majority-schools-pose-security-threat-closed.html).

Malik, K. (1996) *The meaning of race*, Houndmills, Basingstoke: Palgrave Macmillan.

Malik, K. (2009) *From Fatwa to Jihad: the Rushdie affair and its legacy*, London: Atlantic.

Malik, M. (ed) (2010) *Anti-Muslim prejudice in the West, past and present*, London: Routledge.

Malik, S. (2002) *Representing black Britain: Black and Asian images on television*, London: Sage Publications.

Marchand, S. L. (2008) *German orientalism in the age of Empire*, Cambridge: Cambridge University Press.

Marmot, M. (2010) *The Marmot Review (Executive Summary). Fair society, healthy lives. Strategic review of health inequalities in England post-2010* (www.marmotreview.org).

Marshall, T.H. and Bottomore, T. (1992) *Citizenship and social class*, London: Pluto Press.

Maussen, M. (2007) *The governance of Islam in Western Europe: A state of the art report*, IMISCOE Working Paper, No 16, June, Amsterdam: IMISCOE.

Miles, H. (2005) *Al-Jazeera: How Arab TV news challenged the world*, London: Abacus.

Miles, R. and Phizacklea, A. (1984) *White man's country: Racism in British politics*, London: Pluto Press.

Milne, S. (2004) *The enemy within: The secret war against the miners* (3rd edn), London: Verso.

Modood, T. (1990) 'British Asian Muslims and the Rushdie Affair', *Political Quarterly*, vol 61, no 2, pp 143-60.

Modood, T. (1998) 'Anti-essentialism, multiculturalism and "the recognition of religious groups"', *Journal of Political Philosophy*, vol 6, no 4, pp 378-99.

Modood, T. (2005) *Multicultural politics: Racism, ethnicity and Muslims in Britain*, Edinburgh: University of Minnesota and University of Edinburgh Press.

Modood, T. (2006) 'British Muslims and the politics of multiculturalism', in T. Modood, A. Triandafyllidou and R. Zapata-Barrero (eds) *Multiculturalism, Muslims and citizenship*, London: Routledge, pp 37-56.

Modood, T., Triandafyllidou, A. and Zapata-Barrero, R. (2006) *Multiculturalism, Muslims and citizenship*, London: Routledge.

Modood, T., Berthoud, R., Lakey, J., Nazroo, J., Smith, P., Virdee, S. and Beishon, S. (1997) *Ethnic minorities in Britain: Diversity and disadvantage*, London: Policy Studies Institute.

Monar, J. (2007) 'Common threat and common response? The European Union's counter-terrorism strategy and problems', *Government and Opposition*, vol 42, no 3, pp 292-313.

Moore, K., Mason, P. and Lewis, J. (2008) *Images of Islam in the UK: The representation of British Muslims in the national print news media 2000-2008*, Cardiff: School of Journalism, Media and Cultural Studies, Cardiff University (http://cardiff.ac.uk/jomec/resorces/08channel14-dispatches.pdf).

Mottram, R. (2006) *Protecting the citizen in the 21st century: Issues and challenges*, London: Queen Mary College.

Mottram, R. (2007) 'Protecting the citizen in the 21st century: issues and challenges', in P. Hennessy, *The new protective state: Government, intelligence and terrorism*, London: Continuum, pp 42-65.

Mouffe, C. (2005) *On the political*, London: Routledge.

Muntaner, C., Lynch, J. and Smith, G.D. (2000) 'Social capital and the third way in public health', *Critical Public Health*, vol 10, no 2, pp 107-24.

Nacos, B.L. (2007) *Mass-mediated terrorism: The central role of the media in terrorism and counterterrorism*, Lanham, MD: Rowman and Littlefield.

National Archives, The (nd) 'Demobilisation in Britain, 1918-20' (http://nationalarchives.gov.uk/pathways/firstworldwar/spotlights/demobilisation.htm).

Nayak, A. (2009) 'Beyond the pale: chavs, youth and social class', in K.P. Sveinsson (ed) *Who cares about the white working class? Runnymede perspectives*, London: Runnymede Trust, pp 28-35.

Norris, P., Kern, M. and Just, M. (eds) (2003) *Framing terrorism*, New York: Routledge.

Noxolo, P. and Huysmans, J. (eds) (2009a) *Community, citizenship and the 'War on Terror': Security and insecurity*, Houndmills, Basingstoke: Palgrave Macmillan.

Noxolo, P. and Huysmans, J. (2009b) 'Introduction: community, citizenship, and the "War on Terror": security and insecurity', in P. Noxolo and J. Huysmans (eds) (2009) *Community, citizenship and the 'War on Terror': Security and insecurity*, Houndmills, Basingstoke: Palgrave Macmillan, pp 1-10.

Oakes, P. (1996) 'The categorization process: cognition and the group in the social psychology of stereotyping', in W.P. Robinson (ed) *Social groups and identities*, Oxford: Butterworth-Heinemann, pp 95-120.

ODPM (Office of the Deputy Prime Minister) (2003) *Sustainable communities: Building for the future*, London: The Stationery Office.

ODPM (2005) *Sustainable communities: People, places and prosperity*, London: The Stationery Office.

Oldham Independent Panel Review (2001) *One Oldham, one future*, Oldham: Oldham Metropolitan Borough Council.

Omi, M. and Winant, H. (1986) *Racial formation in the United States*, New York: Routledge.

ONS (Office for National Statistics) www.statistics.gov.uk/
Bradford: www.statistics.gov.uk/census2001/profiles/00cx.asp
Calderdale: www.statistics.gov.uk/census2001/profiles/00cy.asp
Kirklees: www.statistics.gov.uk/census2001/profiles/00cz.asp
Leeds: www.statistics.gov.uk/census2001/profiles/00da.asp
Wakefield: www.statistics.gov.uk/census2001/profiles/00db.asp

Opotow, S. (1990) 'Moral exclusion and injustice: an introduction', *Journal of Social Issues*, vol 46, no 1, pp 1-20.

Ormand, D. (2003) 'The secret state revisited: Part II', *The RUSI Journal*, vol 148, no 4, August, pp 24-6.

Ormand, D. (2005) 'Reflections on secret intelligence', Lecture given at Gresham College, London, 20 October (www.gresham.ac.uk/event.asp?PageId=45&EventId=368).

Orr, D. (1999) 'The Lawrence Report: "The police officers behaved towards us like white masters during slavery"', *The Independent*, 25 February (www.independent.co.uk/news/the-lawrence-report-the-police-officers-behaved-towards-us-like-white-masters-during-slavery-1073001.html).

Ouseley, Sir Herman (2001) *Community pride – not prejudice: Making diversity work in Bradford (The Ouseley Report)*, Bradford: Bradford Vision, July.

Parekh, B. (2000) *The future of multiethnic Britain: The Parekh Report*, London: The Runnymede Trust.

Pettigrew, T. and Tropp, L.R. (2005) 'Allport's intergroup contact hypothesis: its history and influence', in J.F. Dovidio, P. Glick and L.A. Rudman (2005) *On the nature of prejudice: Fifty years after Allport*, Oxford: Blackwell, pp 262-77.

Phillips, A. (2007) *Multiculturalism without culture*, Princeton, NJ: Princeton University Press.

Phillips, D. (2006) 'Parallel lives? Challenging discourses of British Muslim segregation', *Environment and Planning D: Society and Space*, vol 24, no 1, pp 25-40.

Phillips, M. (2006) *Londonistan*, London: Gibson Square.

Phillips, R. (ed) (2009) *Muslim spaces of hope: Geographies of possibility in Britain and the West*, London: Zed Books.

Phillips, T. (2005) 'After 7/7: sleepwalking to segregation', Speech given by Commission for Racial Equality Chair Trevor Phillips at the Manchester Council for Community Relations (www.humanities.manchester.ac.uk/socialchange/research/social-change/summer-workshops/documents/sleepwalking.pdf).

Pilkington, A. (2003) *Racial disadvantage and ethnic diversity in contemporary Britain*, Houndmills, Basingstoke: Palgrave Macmillan.

Pollard, N., Latorre, M. and Sriskandarajah, D. (2008) *Floodgates or turnstiles? Post-EU enlargement migration flows to (and from) the UK*, London: Institute for Public Policy Research.

Poole, E. (2002) *Reporting Islam: Media representations of British Muslims*, London: I.B. Tauris.

Poole, E. and Richardson, J. (2005) *Muslims and the news media*, London: I.B. Tauris.

Poole, E. and Richardson, J. (eds) (2006) *Muslims and the news rhetoric of British broadsheet newspapers*, Amsterdam: John Benjamins.

Punch, K.F. (1998) *Introduction to social research: Quantitative and qualitative approaches*, London: Sage Publications.

Putnam, R. D. (2000) *Bowling alone*, New York: Simon & Schuster.

Raab, D. (2009) *The assault on liberty*, London: Fourth Estate.

Reese, S., Gandy, O. and Grant, A. (2001) *Framing public life: Perspectives on media and our understanding of the social world*, Mahwah, NJ: Lawrence Erlbaum.

Reicher, S. (2004) 'The context of social identity: domination, resistance and change', *Political Psychology*, vol 25, pp 921-45.

Respect Task Force (2006) *Respect Action Plan*, http://webarchive.nationalarchives.gov.uk/20080108014528/http://respect.gov.uk/uploadedFiles/Members_site/Articles/About_Respect/respect_action_plan.pdf

Richardson, J.E. (2001) 'British Muslims in the broadsheet press: a challenge to cultural hegemony', *Journalism Studies*, vol 2, no 2, pp 221-42.

Richardson, K. and Spears, D. (1972) *Race, culture and intelligence*, Harmondsworth: Penguin Books.

Rigoni, I. (2005) 'Challenging notions and practices: the Muslim media in Britain and France', *Journal of Ethnic and Migration Studies*, vol 31, no 3, pp 563-80.

Robinson, D. (2008) 'Community cohesion and the politics of communitarianism', in J. Flint and D. Robinson, *Community cohesion in crisis? New dimensions of diversity and difference*, Bristol: The Policy Press, pp 15-33.

Rumford, C. (2009) 'Social policy beyond fear: the globalization of strangeness, the "War on Terror" and "spaces of wonder"', in D. Denney (ed) *Living in dangerous times: Fear, insecurity, risk and social policy*, Chichester: Wiley-Blackwell, pp 71-86.

Runciman, W. G. (1966) *Relative deprivation and social justice*, Berkeley, CA: University of California Press.

Runnymede Trust (1997) *Islamophobia: A challenge for us all*, London: Runnymede Trust.

Ruthven, M. (1991) *A satanic affair*, London: Hogarth Press.

Saeed, A. (2007) 'Media, racism and Islamophobia: the representation of Islam and Muslims in the media', *Sociology Compass*, vol 1, no 2, pp 443-62.

Said, E. W. (1978) *Orientalism*, London: Routledge and Kegan Paul.

Samad, Y. (1992) 'Book burning and race relations: political mobilisation of Bradford Muslims', *New Community*, vol 18, no 4, pp 507-19.

Samad, Y. (1998) 'Media and Muslim identity: intersections of generation and gender', *Innovation: The European Journal of Social Sciences*, vol 11, no 4, pp 425-38.

Sardar, Z. (2009) 'Spaces of hope: interventions', in R. Phillips (ed) *Muslim spaces of hope: Geographies of possibility in Britain and the West*, London: Zed Books, pp 13-27.

Savage, M., Li, Y. and Tampubolon, G. (2007) 'Rethinking the politics of social capital: challenging Tocquevillian perspectives', in R. Edwards, J. Franklin and J. Holland (eds) *Assessing social capital: Concept, policy and practice*, Newcastle: Cambridge Scholars Publishing, pp 70-94.

Sayyid, S. and Vakil, A. (eds) (2010) *Thinking through Islam*, London: Hurst.

Scarman, Lord (1981) *The Brixton Disorders 10-12 April 1981. Report of an Inquiry by the Rt Hon Lord Scarman OBE (The Scarman Report)*, London: HMSO.

Scheufele, D. A. and Tewksbury, D. (2007) 'Framing, agenda setting, and priming: the evolution of three media effects models', *Journal of Communication*, vol 57, no 1, pp 9-20.

Schuster, L. and Solomos, J. (2004) 'Race, immigration and asylum: New Labour's agenda and its consequences', *Ethnicities*, vol 4, no 2, pp 267-86.

Scraton, P. (2002) 'Defying power and changing "knowledge": critical analysis of resistance in the UK', in K. Carrington and R. Hogg (eds) *Critical criminology: Issues, debates and challenges*, Cullompton: Willan Publishing.

Seidel, G. (1986) 'Culture, nation and "race" in the British and French New Right', in R. Levitas (ed) *The ideology of the New Right*, Oxford: Polity Press.

Sennett, R. (1998) *The corrosion of character*, New York: W.W. Norton.

Sennett, R. (2003) *Respect*, London: Alan Lane.

Sennett, R. and Cobb, J. (1972) *The hidden injuries of class*, New York: Vintage Books.

Shaw, A. (1994) 'The Pakistani community in Oxford', in R. Ballard (ed) *Desh Pardesh: The South Asian presence in Britain*, London: Hurst, pp 35-57.

Sherif, M. (1967) *Group conflict and cooperation*, London: Routledge and Kegan Paul.

Silverstone, R. and Georgiou, M. (2005) 'Editorial introduction: media and minorities in multicultural Europe', *Journal of Ethnic and Migration Studies (Special Issue)*, vol 31, no 3, pp 433-41.

Simpson, L. (2004) 'Statistics of racial segregation: measures, evidence and policy', *Urban Studies*, vol 41, no 3, pp 661-81.

Simpson, L. (2007) 'Ghettos of the mind: the empirical behaviour indices of segregation and diversity', *Journal of the Royal Statistical Society: Series A (Statistics in Society)*, vol 170, no 2, pp 405-24.

Simpson, L., Husband, C. and Alam, M. Y. (2009) 'Recognizing complexity, challenging pessimism: the case of Bradford's urban dynamics', *Urban Studies*, vol 46, no 9, pp 1995-2001.

Skellington, R. and Morris, P. (1992) *'Race' in Britain today,* London: Sage Publications/Open University Press.

Smith, G.J.D. (2007) 'The night-time economy: exploring tensions between agents of control', in R. Atkinson and G. Helms (eds) *Securing an urban renaissance: Crime, community and British urban policy*, Bristol: The Policy Press, pp 183-202.

Smith, L., Sajid, A., Stone, R., Muir, H. and Richardson, R. (2004) *Islamophobia: Issues, challenges and Action: A Report by the Commission on British Muslims and Islamophobia Research*, Stoke on Trent: Trentham Books.

Sniderman, P.M., Hagendoorn, L. and Prior, M. (2004) 'Predisposing factors and situational triggers: exclusionary reactions to immigrant minorities', *American Political Science Review*, vol 98, pp 35-49.

Solomos, J. (1986) *Riots, urban protest and social policy: The interplay of reform and social control*, Policy Papers in Ethnic Relations, 7, Coventry: University of Warwick.

Solomos, J. (2003) *Race and racism in Britain* (3rd edn), Houndmills, Basingstoke: Palgrave Macmillan.

Solomos, J. and Back, L. (1995) *Race, politics and social change*, London: Routledge.

Spalek, B. and Imtoul, A. (2007) 'Muslim communities and counter-terror responses: "hard" approaches to community engagement in the UK and Australia', *Journal of Muslim Minority Affairs*, vol 27, no 2, pp 185-202.

Spalek, B. and Lambert, R. (2008) 'Muslim communities, counter-terrorism and counter-radicalisation: a critical reflective approach to engagement', *International Journal of Law, Crime and Justice*, vol 36, pp 257-70.

Steet, L. (2000) *Veils and daggers*, Philadelphia, PA: Temple University Press.

Stenson, K. (2007) 'Framing the governance of urban space', in R. Atkinson and G. Helms (eds) *Securing an urban renaissance: Crime, community and British urban policy*, Bristol: The Policy Press, pp 23-38.

Stephan, W.G. and Stephan, C.W. (1996) 'Predicting prejudice', *International Journal of Intercultural Relations*, vol 20, no 3/4, pp 409-26.

Stephan, W.G., Ybarra, O. and Bachmann, G. (1999) 'Prejudice towards immigrants', *International Journal of Intercultural Relations*, vol 29, pp 2221-37.

Stephan, W.G., Renfro, C.L., Esses, V.M., Stephan, C.W. and Martin, T. (2005) 'The effects of feeling threatened on attitudes to immigrants.' *International Journal of Intercultural Relations,* vol 29, pp 1-19.

Sveinsson, K.P. (ed) (2009) *Who cares about the white working class? Runnymede perspectives*, London: Runnymede Trust.

Tajfel, H. (1981) *Human groups and social categories*, Cambridge: Cambridge University Press.

Tajfel, H. and Turner, J.C. (1979) 'An integrative theory of intergroup conflict' in W.G. Austin and S. Worchel (eds) *The social psychology of intergroup relations*, Monterey, CA: Brooks/Cole, pp 33-47.

Taylor, C. (1992) *Multiculturalism and 'the politics of recognition'*, Princeton, NJ: Princeton University Press.

Taylor, C. (2004) *Modern social imaginaries*, Durham, NC: Duke University Press.

Tebbit, N. (2007) 'Countering international terrorism: joining up the dots', in P. Hennessy (ed) *The new protective state: Government, intelligence and terrorism*, London: Continuum, pp 74-96.

Tileaga, C. (2007) 'Ideologies of moral exclusion: a critical discursive reframing of depersonalization, delegitimization and dehumanization', *British Journal of Social Psychology*, vol 46, pp 717-37.

Titley, G. (forthcoming) 'Mediated minarets, intolerable subjects: the crisis of "multiculturalism" in Europe'.

Tropp, L.A. and Wright, S. C. (1999) 'Ingroup identification and relative deprivation: an examination across multiple social comparisons', *European Journal of Social Psychology*, vol 29, pp 707-24.

Troyna, B. (1981) *Public awareness and the media*, London: Commission for Racial Equality.

Turner, J.C. (1987) *Rediscovering the social group*, Oxford: Basil Blackwell.

Turner, J.C. (1999) 'Some current issues in research on social identity and self-categorization theories', in N. Ellermers, R. Spears and B. Doosje (eds) *Social identity: Context, commitment, content*, Oxford: Blackwell, pp 6-34.

van Dijk, T. (1991) *Racism and the press*, London: Routledge.

van Dijk, T. (1993) *Elite discourse and racism*, Newbury Park, CA: Sage Publications.

Verkuyten, M. (2005) 'Ethnic group identification and group evaluation among minority and majority groups: testing the multicultural hypothesis', *Journal of Personality and Social Psychology*, vol 88, pp 121-38.

Verkuyten, M. (2006) 'Multicultural recognition and ethnic minority rights: a social identity perspective', in W. Stroebe and M. Hewstone (eds) *European review of social psychology*, vol 17, London: Psychology Press, pp 148-84.

Verkuyten, M. and Reijerse, A. (2008) 'Intergroup structure and identity management among ethnic minority and majority groups: the interactive effects of perceived stability, legitimacy and permeability.' *European Journal of Social Psychology*, vol 38, no 1, pp 106-27.

Vertovec, S. (2009) *Transnationalism*, London: Routledge.

Wacquant, L. (2008) *Urban outcasts*, Cambridge: Polity Press.

Walker, I. and Pettigrew, T.F. (1984) 'Relative deprivation theory: an overview and conceptual critique', *British Journal of Social Psychology*, vol 23, no 4, pp 301-10.

Walvin, J. (1971) *The black presence*, London: Orbach and Chambers.

Wenger, J. (2007) *Communities of practice*, Cambridge: Cambridge University Press.

Werbner, P. (2002) *Imagined diasporas among Manchester Muslims*, Oxford: James Currey.

Werbner, P. (2005) 'Islamophobia: incitement to religious hatred – legislating for a new fear', *Anthropology Today*, vol 21, no 1, pp 5-9.

Wetherell, M. (2003) 'Racism and the analysis of cultural resources in interviews', in H. van den Berg, H. Houtkoop-Steenstra and M. Wetherell (eds) *Analyzing race talk*, Cambridge: Cambridge University Press, pp 11-30.

Wilson, R.A. (ed) (2005) *Human rights in the 'War on Terror'*, Cambridge: Cambridge University Press.

Wodak, R. and Matouscheck, B. (1993) '"We are dealing with people whose origins one can clearly tell just by looking": critical discourse analysis and the study of neo-racism in contemporary Austria', *Discourse and Society*, vol 4, no 2, pp 225-48.

Wolsko, C., Park, B., Judd, C.M. and Wittenbrink, B. (2006) 'Considering the tower of Babel: correlates of assimilation and multiculturalism among ethnic minority and majority groups in the United States', *Social Justice Research*, vol 19, pp 277-306.

Young, I. M. (1989) 'Polity and group difference: a critique of the idea of universal citizenship', *Ethics*, vol 99, no 2, pp 250-74.

Young, I.M. (2000) *Inclusion and democracy*, Oxford: Oxford University Press.

Young, M. and Willmott, P. (1957) *Family and kinship in East London*, London: Institute of Community Studies.

Young, M. and Willmott, P. (1960) *Family and class in a London suburb*, London: Institute of Community Studies.

Young, R.J.C. (1995) *Colonial desire*, London: Routledge.

Zedner, J. (2006) 'Unveiling sentiments: gendered Islamophobia and experiences of veiling among Muslim girls in a Canadian Islamic school', *Equity and Excellence in Education*, vol 39, pp 239-52.

Index of subjects

S

Sacranie, I. 99–100
Satanic verses, The (Rushdie) 29
  see also Rushdie Affair
Scarman Report 23–5, 26, 36
securitisation 77, 87–91, 124, 152–3,
  157, 177, 225
self-segregation 45–8, 50, 51–2, 55
'shared futures' campaign 55
shared values 48, 73
SID (social integrationist discourse)
  38–9, 48
'slave' folk devil 114–15, 118, 119
social capital 20, 42–5, 163–4, 222
social cohesion 19, 20, 37–8, 39, 151
social contract 214, 223, 225
social deprivation 24, 25–6, 68, 69,
  122–3, 209
social exclusion 24, 38–9, 41, 44–5, 53,
  110
  by delegitimisation 123–4
social identity theory 119–20, 121–4
social integrationist discourse (SID)
  38–9, 48
social movements 218
social spaces, construction of 197
South Asian citizens 30, 45, 111–12, 121
spying accusation against Prevent 74–6
Stephen Lawrence Inquiry (Macpherson)
  18, 34, 36
stereotyping 120, 124
stigmatisation 71, 74, 164, 178, 193
stop and search policies 34, 35, 36, 86
stranger 109–11
Strategic defence review: A new chapter, The
  (HM Government) 65–6
Straw, J. 35, 98
Strength in diversity (Home Office) 209
substantive citizenship 212–13, 223
surveillance 86, 93, 145, 182–3
  of Muslim communities 4, 63–4, 74–6,
  86, 100, 113
symbolic threat 120, 122, 176, 209

T

tabloid press 80, 115
  see also media
Taylor, Sir Cyril 54
tension monitoring 182–3, 208
terrorism 63, 166
  and the media 80–1, 83–5
Terrorism Act (2006) 67
Terrorism and community relations
  (House of Common, Home Affairs
  Committee) 53
terrorist attacks
  7/7 bombings 51, 52–3, 84, 100, 106
  9/11: 2, 33, 51, 65, 84, 100, 105
  Birmingham, IRA bombing 64–5
  Glasgow 52

London bombings 51, 52–3, 84,
  100–1, 106
Thatcher government, response to the
  Scarman Report 25–6
Thatcherism 27–8, 39, 43, 106, 110
threat 85–6, 107–9
  realistic 120, 122–3, 176, 199–200,
  206, 209
  symbolic 120, 122, 176, 209
TIDOs (Terrorism International
  Defence and Overseas) 67
Times, The 32
tolerance 223–4
torture 93
transnational linkages 51, 70, 205–6

U

Ummah 70–1, 84, 205
unease 88, 91
unemployment 39
*United Kingdom's strategy for countering
  international Terrorism, The* (HM
  Government) 71
universalism 218, 219–20, 221
urban behaviour, criminalisation of 90
urban planning 89
urban social environment 90–1

V

veil, issue of 31, 103, 193
victimisation of the majority 221

W

Wakefield 7
'War on Terror' 51, 77, 93, 113, 195
West of Spithead, Lord 69–70
white working-class communities
  179–82, 184, 208–9, 212, 213
  and anti-Muslimism 115, 118
'witch' folk devil 114, 116
working-class communities 208–9

X

xenophobia 33, 101, 110, 111

Y

young people, criminalisation of 90
youth work 152

Index of authors

T

Tajfel, H. 119, 120, 121
Taylor, C. 49, 87, 103, 217, 218, 219
Tebbit, N. 62, 65, 66
Tewksbury, D. 21, 79
Thomas, B. 50
Tileaga, C. 123, 124
Tilley, J. 42
Titley, G. 217
Tropp, L.A. 123
Tropp, L.R. 56
Troyna, B. 79
Turner, J.C. 112, 119, 120

V

Vakil, A. 101
van Dijk, T. 80, 82
Verkuyten, M. 121, 124, 219
Verschueren, J. 124
Vertovec, S. 205

W

Wacquant, L. 35, 37, 48, 115, 163–4
Walker, I. 123
Walvin, J. 22
Wenger, E. 136
Werbner, P. 71, 112, 114, 116–17
Wetherell, M. 123
Whyte, D. 123
Willmott, P. 42
Wilson, R.A. 93
Winant, H. 20
Wodak, R. 123, 221
Wolsko, C. 124
Wright, S.C. 123

Y

Yinon, Y. 122
Young, I.M. 216, 218
Young, M. 42
Young, R.J.C. 104
Yuval-Davis, N. 197, 199

Z

Zedner, J. 123